Branding in Action

Branding in Action

Cases and strategies for profitable brand management

*Graham Hankinson and
Philippa Cowking*

McGraw-Hill Book Company

London • New York • St Louis • San Francisco • Auckland
Bogotá • Caracas • Lisbon • Madrid • Mexico • Milan • Montreal
New Delhi • Panama • Paris • San Juan • São Paulo • Singapore
Sydney • Tokyo • Toronto

Published by
McGRAW-HILL Book Company Europe
Shoppenhangers Road, Maidenhead, Berkshire, SL6 2QL, England
Telephone: 0628 23432
Fax: 0628 770224

British Library Cataloguing in Publication Data
Hankinson, Graham
    Branding in Action: Cases and Strategies
    for Profitable Brand Management. –
    (McGraw-Hill Marketing for Professionals
    Series)
    I. Title II. Cowking, Philippa
    III. Series
    658.827

    ISBN 0 07 707812 8

Library of Congress Cataloging-in-Publication Data
Hankinson, Graham
    Branding in action : cases and strategies for profitable brand
    management / Graham Hankinson and Philippa Cowking.
      p. cm. -- (The McGraw-Hill marketing for professionals)
    Includes bibliographical references and index.
    ISBN 0 07 707812 8
    1. Brand name products--Marketing--Management. 2. Brand name
    products--Marketing--Management--Case studies. 3. Corporate image--
    Case studies. I. Cowking, Philippa. II. Title. III. Series.
    HF5415.13.H348 1993   93-26441
    658.8'343--dc20   CIP

12345 CUP 96543

Typeset by Goodfellow & Egan Phototypesetting Ltd, Cambridge
and printed and bound at the University Press, Cambridge.

This book is dedicated to our offspring both great and small,
Jeremy, Frannie and Daniel, Julian and Marilyn

Contents

About the authors

Graham Hankinson is the Wimpey Professor of Management Studies at Thames Valley University. He has a wide range of experience in a variety of marketing positions, both as an academic and in the commercial world. He has worked with such organizations as the Electricity Council, the advertising agency Ted Bates, and Sterling Winthrop. This has given him first-hand experience of working with such brands as DHL, Panadol, and Solpadiene.

Philippa Cowking   After completing her MA in Psychology, Philippa Cowking trained as a Market Researcher and has worked both as a practitioner and as an academic in this field. Following a period as Research Director at PHD Research, she became Director of Research and Planning with Clarke Hooper Consulting Limited where her clients included Sony, United Distillers, Royal Mail, and the NatWest Bank. She now works as an independent consultant and lectures in marketing at Kingston and Thames Valley Universities.

THE MARKETING SOCIETY

The Marketing Society is the professional UK body for senior practising marketing people. It was founded in 1959 and currently has 2300 members.

The aim of the Society is to provide a forum for senior marketers through which the exchange of experience and opinion will advance marketing as the core of successful business growth. To this end it mounts a large and varied programme of events, and provides an increasing range of member services.

Preface

This book is intended for practitioners and students of branding. It is based upon extensive interviews with marketing directors and managers, product managers and managers in advertising, sales promotion and market research agencies about their perceptions of brands and brand building. It also draws upon the academic literature and the marketing press in a search for useful concepts, research findings and examples of good and bad practice. It has to be said that there is a certain confusion in the use of terminology and concepts related to branding and we have therefore developed our own definitions which provide a systematic approach to branding as we have observed it. There will inevitably be those who will disagree with our definitions and with our view of the branding process and we accept that perfectly valid alternatives can be postulated. However, our objective has been to establish a set of working definitions in order to avoid ambiguity and to set a framework for a systematic examination of branding and its associated issues.

We are extremely grateful to all those who have contributed to the compilation of this book, but in particular to those who have either contributed material for the chapters or provided the accompanying case studies and case histories. It has been our intention to write relatively short and hopefully concise chapters covering the relevant issues of each aspect of branding and to illustrate and provoke further thought on each chapter through these cases. We have not attempted to present the cases in a common style that might be found in other texts. Thus, some of the cases, particularly those written by practitioners themselves, are in the form of a case history, following the development from problem to successful solution. Others are written in the style of the case study used for teaching purposes, focusing more on the problem than on the solution.

The cases are therefore not necessarily all illustrative of best practice and there may be alternative approaches to the problems discussed in each. Thus, for practitioners, we hope the cases will provide insight into branding applications in other organizations. For students and teachers of branding we have tried to present the material in such a

way as to promote discussion. Some, but not all, of the cases have
already been tested in the classroom.

It is our view that branding of products, services and of organizations
is now so central to marketing in any industry or sector of the
economy that it should be given a higher priority not only in
marketing courses offered by institutions of learning but also by
organizations grappling with the job of balancing short-term financial
objectives with a coherent long-term strategy for survival. As
customers become more affluent and discerning, as the cost of product
launches continues to escalate and as the fight for a sustainable
competitive advantage in the marketplace becomes more intense, the
need to consider and plan the benefits and values which provide
continuity and cohesion to the product and service offering becomes
ever more important. This book aims to focus minds on this central
problem of marketing.

Graham Hankinson
Philippa Cowking

Acknowledgements

The authors would particularly like to thank the people and organizations who helped with the preparation and writing of the case studies as follows:

The rebirth of Rover Cars John Markham and Rod Ramsey (Rover Cars);

BMW (Europe): Horst Kern (DMB&B, Frankfurt), Hans-Christian Wagner (BMW) and Roswitha Hassis (BMW);

The Transax story: Tom Blackett (Interbrand);

The repackaging of Highland Spring: Ian Hall (Highland Spring) and the Michael Peters Group;

McVitie's Mini Cheddars: Colin Tether (McVitie's);

What Landor did for British Airways: Chris Holt (British Airways) Jane Beadell (Landor Associates) and Richard Ford (Landor Associates);

Sainsbury's Bio Yogurt: Anthony Rees (J. Sainsbury);

Tesco's ambient ready meals: Christine Cross (Tesco);

Premier Brands: Paul Judge (Food From Britain) and Dominic Cadbury (Cadbury Schweppes);

Gordon's Gin: Terry Hanby (United Distillers);

Competitive sparkle – Champagne's strategic response: Stephen Woodward (Ayer Advertising);

The Toshiba brand personality: Morven MacCullum (Toshiba UK) and Wendy Gordon (The Research Business).

Thanks are also due to other contributors who, through their willingness to discuss their views and experiences, provided the practical foundations for this book: Simons Adams (Clarke Hooper Consulting); Marilyn Baxter (Saatchi & Saatchi); John Cannon (Network Management); Barry Clarke (Clarke Hooper Consulting); Pamela Conway (Michael Peters Group); Pat Farrell (Rover Cars); Ian Fryer (H.J. Heinz); Steven Gravelle (J. Sainsbury); Steve Griggs (Creative Research); Mark Harrison (Consumer Connection); Stella Hartley (Prestige); Roger Hobbs (H.J. Heinz); Neville Holland (Royal

Mail); Igor Humphries (NatWest); Tracy Huntley (Clarke Hooper Consulting); Paul Jackson (BSB Dorland); Hymie Lipman (Kingston University); Stuart Mackay (Michael Peters Group); Tony McManus (KP Nuts); Rod Meadows (Dorland Advertising); David Metherell (Pepsico); Fernanda Monti (Esomar); Sue Moore (British Airways); Ed Newton (David Young & Associates); Jason Nicholas (Guinness Brewing Company); Simon Patterson (CRAM International); Nigel Pearcey (Clarke Hooper Consulting); David Pearson (Sony UK); Michael Roe (Research International); Leslie Semper-White (Nicholas Laboratories); Pat Skelly (Webb International); David Smith (Synectics); Roger Stangroom (Rover Cars); Neil Swan (The Research Business); Mark Todd (Toshiba UK); Graham Walker (Sponsorship Consultant); Ian Walker (United Distillers UK); Kate Warr (Handel Communications); Peter Warren (Hiram-Walker, Allied Vintners); and James Waugh (Rawlplug).

Finally, special thanks are always due in the compilation of any book to those who take responsibility for the word processing. In particular, we would like to express our thanks to Janet Parsons and others, without those painstaking efforts in reading our writing this book would not have reached its deadline on time!

1

What is branding?

Definition of a brand

A brand is a product or service made distinctive by its positioning relative to the competition and by its personality.

Its *positioning* defines the brand's point of reference with respect to the competition. This is often determined by price. For instance, Gucci products such as handbags and women's accessories occupy a high price positioning which will attract high income earners who value style, affluence and exclusivity, a positioning which is also associated with other luxury brands like Dunhill and Christian Dior. Positioning may also be determined by product usage. Yogurt, for instance, might be positioned as a healthy breakfast food alongside muesli, or it might be positioned as a children's dessert alongside ice-cream. Positioning, therefore, describes the brand by defining its competitive context.

The brand *personality* consists of a unique combination of functional attributes and symbolic values. Functional attributes describe extrinsic, tangible product properties such as 'hardwearing', 'easy to use' or 'portability', while symbolic values describe intrinsic, intangible properties such as 'friendliness', 'fun' and 'care'. Some brands are mainly (but not exclusively) characterized by functional attributes, for example:

DHL	guaranteed next day delivery
Radion	deodorizes as well as cleans
Duracell	longer lasting batteries.

Other brands are largely characterized by symbolic values, for example:

Levi 501's	sexy and independent
Mini Cooper	lively and impertinent
Coca-Cola	young, fun and sociable.

Getting the balance right is not always easy. In the case of Rolls-Royce cars, for example, the brand personality relies heavily upon its historic reputation for high-quality engineering and craftsmanship, functional attributes which must constantly be protected and reinforced in each new model that is introduced. This means adopting the latest technology and engineering developments in each model. In contrast, the symbolic values of the Rolls-Royce personality include tradition, luxury, class, etc., which need to be constantly reinforced but should remain relatively unchanged. A sudden lurch towards modernity would not be in the best interests of the Rolls-Royce personality!

Sometimes, however, it may be important to change or update the symbolic values of a brand personality while maintaining the original functional attributes. Highland Spring mineral water has offered the same product formulation over many years but its symbolic values have been updated from 'Scottish kilts and tweeds' to 'Scottish sophistication and freshness', more relevant values to today's consumer.

For successful brands, the positioning and the personality are inextricably linked. The positioning defines potential competitors and the personality distinguishes the brand. In the case of Gucci, for example, the price defines the brand's positioning (at the top end of the market) while the personality creates its exclusiveness. The relative importance of positioning and personality will depend on the extent to which a brand is intended for a specific target market or product sector. Thus, where a brand such as Coca-Cola is aimed at the mass market, an exclusive personality is essential. In other instances, such as Gucci, a highly targeted brand, positioning is more important.

Brand proposition

Collectively, the positioning and brand personality may be termed the brand *proposition*. This should constitute the starting point for brand managers charged with the responsibility of developing and/or maintaining a brand in the marketplace.

Davidson (1987) argues that:

> To stand out, you need to have a simple proposition which is easy to understand. ... Brand propositions which are complicated or inconsistent will have no chance.

The proposition often consists of a series of statements. For Sony Walkman these might be :

- 'a brand with technological superiority'

- 'a brand that is reliable'
- 'a brand that offers performance quality'
- 'a brand that is young and zestful'
- 'a brand at the top end of the medium price sector'.

Thereafter, every aspect of the branding process must be consistent with these statements, whether it relates to the communication mix such as advertising and sales promotion, or whether it relates to its pricing and distribution. Despite the number and relative complexity of the brand statements which describe the proposition, these may, very often, be encapsulated in one-line advertising slogans or straplines. For instance, the Sony brand proposition (applicable to Sony Walkman also) is encapsulated in the strapline : 'Why compromise?' Other straplines (1992) include :

'The choice for a new generation'   (Pepsi)

'Pure Genius'   (Guinness)

'Once driven, forever smitten'   (Vauxhall)

Finally, it is worth noting that some writers (Aaker and Shansby 1982; Ries and Trout 1986) do not distinguish between the positioning and personality elements of the proposition. However, in our view, this distinction is vital. For some brands, for instance, it may be desirable to change the competitive set (positioning) but to retain some aspects of the original personality (see Lucozade example in Chapter 3). In other cases it may be more desirable to retain the original positioning, but to update the personality (see the Highland Spring example above).

Consumer–brand relationship

The relationship between the consumer and the brand, or more precisely the consumer's perception of that brand, is key to the brand's acceptance. Ideally, the brand should invite the consumer to 'wear' it, whether it be Levi 501s, Gucci shoes, a Sony Walkman or Johnny Walker Black Label whisky.

The strength of the relationship between the consumer and the brand will reflect the 'fit' between the consumer's own physical and psychological needs and the brand's functional attributes and symbolic values as perceived by the consumer.

Some authors (e.g. Whan Park *et al.* 1986) distinguish three categories of consumer needs. In addition to functional and psychological/symbolic needs, they add experiential needs. These are defined as desires for products that provide sensory pleasure, variety and/or cognitive stimulation. Brands which fulfil these needs present a personality, offering stimulation and/or variety. However, in practice, it is extremely difficult to distinguish experiential needs from physical needs.

Whether consumers actually buy the brand will, of course, depend upon their buying power. The brand may fit with the consumers' needs, both physical and psychological, but unless it is affordable, the brand will remain aspirational.

The closer the 'fit', the stronger will be the consumer's identification with the brand and the stronger the relationship. This explains why the same brand may be accepted by one consumer, but rejected by another. Consumer 'A', for instance, may be attracted to a Volvo because, as a functional attribute, it offers ample space (meeting a physical need) and because of its symbolic values of family caring (meeting a psychological need). Consumer 'B' on the other hand, may reject the Volvo because, as a young, single adult his or her physical and psychological needs are different.

The branding cycle

The process of branding is a continuous cycle of research, planning implementation and control. As Figure 1.1 illustrates, creating a new brand begins with research to identify key consumer needs, both physical and psychological, which are relevant to the product category in order to help develop an appropriate brand personality in terms of its physical attributes and symbolic values. The research will also explore product usage and status and the consumer's perception of competitive brands, their personalities and positionings in order to find the appropriate positioning for the new brand. The information from the research thus provides the basis on which to plan and implement the brand proposition. Successful branding clearly depends upon implementing the correct combination of the components of the marketing mix which, in totality, serve to communicate the brand proposition. Effective communication will then lead to a clear association of the brand proposition with its shortforms, the brand name and strapline which, when combined with distinctive packaging, act as communication triggers. Whether those triggers lead to acceptance or rejection of the brand will, as we have said earlier, depend upon the 'fit' between the brand

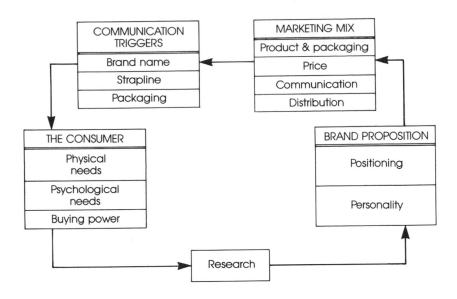

Figure 1.1 The branding cycle

proposition and consumers' physical and psychological needs and buying power. The cycle then continues through research, to monitor the brand's progress. This ensures that changes in the consumer profile and consumer needs are addressed through fine tuning the personality and positioning of the brand.

Unlike products, which ultimately die, brands, if managed effectively over the cycle, will continue to be valuable over a very long time. Matchbox and Corgi toys, for example, have continued long after their original parent companies went into liquidation. Brands also change owners from time to time—Smith's Crisps, for example, have been owned by Nabisco, and more recently by Pepsico.

Brands and profitability

Strong brands help a company to maintain market share in the face of a changing competitive environment. It has been shown that this in turn leads to above average profits. Research by PIMS (Buzzell and Gale 1987), based on studies of 2600 businesses over a long period of time, showed that the percentage return on investment increases as market share increases. For example, it was found that brands with only 10 per cent share of the market were likely to yield, on average, slightly over 10 per cent return on investment, whereas brands with 30 per cent share were likely to yield, on average, in excess of 25 per cent return on investment.

Brand strategy and competitive advantage

The building of the brand's market share is a long-term process requiring, as it does, the communication of a sustainable competitive advantage which distinguishes it from the competition. The speed of technological development and its accessibility make it difficult for most companies to achieve competitive advantage through functional attributes alone. Similarly, sustaining a long-term competitive advantage through cost leadership is also difficult, given the ever-shortening lead times associated with new methods of production and operations. Increasingly, therefore, companies are looking towards the intangible symbolic values associated with their brands as the means of building long-term competitive advantage. Strong brand propositions provide the foundation for growth in brand franchise and market share through the extension of the brand into new product categories and international markets. The use of brand strategies to build competitive advantage are discussed more fully in Chapter 9.

Corporate brands and corporate identity

In recent years, recognition of the strategic value of successful brands has given rise to a growth in advertising devoted to brand owners, the often unheard of benefactors of household names.

Some corporate brands, such as IBM and BMW, are already well known. Such brands represent a monolithic approach to corporate branding insofar as they are used across all products, totally on their own (except perhaps for model numbers). Other corporate brands have achieved prominence through an endorsement approach, lending their name to product brands. Examples of this approach include ICI, Dulux Paint and Kellogg's Rice Krispies. Increasingly, however, it has become necessary for companies to address such audiences as stock markets, environmentalists and potential employees as stakeholders in their future. Corporate branding in this context becomes more extensive and much more complex. The communication of a corporate identity uses a richer selection of communication devices such as uniforms, annual reports, vehicles, etc., to reach all the key audiences affecting a company's future. Corporate brands and corporate identity are discussed more fully in Chapter 5.

Brands as assets

Brands survive because they represent a stream of future income to the owner even when the original company ceases to exist. In this sense they are often held to be realizable, albeit intangible assets. In recognition of this, many companies are including a valuation of their brands as assets in the balance sheet: e.g. Reckitt and Colman, the UK toiletries, household products and food company; Rank Hovis McDougall, the UK flour and baking company; and the UK conglomerate, Grand Met. It is argued that successful brands are the result of millions of pounds of investment spent over long periods of time—a price that would be difficult to justify today in the launch of a new brand, particularly as so many fail to achieve a break-even market share. In view of the very high costs associated with launching a new brand, an alternative strategy may be to acquire an existing brand or brand-owning company.

There is considerable debate as to whether the practice of valuing brands in the balance sheet is reasonable. However, understanding that brands represent a long-term stream of income to the company moves brand management into the strategic arena and puts the operational aspects of the job into an entirely different perspective. It therefore becomes a job for senior management to take firm responsibility. These issues are discussed more fully in Chapter 7.

Brand stretching

As an alternative to brand acquisition many companies have sought to avoid the prohibitive costs of launching new brands and the associated risks of failure by extending the franchise of their existing brand names to new products. This process is known as *brand stretching*. Just how far a brand can be stretched varies considerably and depends upon the strength of the parent brand. It is critical, however, to ensure that the process of brand stretching does not dilute the core values of the brand, thereby weakening its proposition and overall coherence. The bigger the gap between the original product and the product group to which the brand is to be stretched, the greater the risk of failure and consequent damage to the brand. ICI, the corporate brand, has successfully stretched its name across chemicals, paints, petrol, pharmaceuticals and fertilizers. All products have a common chemical base. Perhaps this is why the extensions do not dilute ICI's core values of technical excellence and reliability. In contrast, it has proved difficult for a company such as Cadbury Schweppes to stretch its brands outside confectionery and soft drinks. Brands such as Smash and Typhoo Tea have been sold off by Cadbury Schweppes, who has reverted to its core business. These issues are discussed more fully in Chapter 4.

International branding

The brand franchise can also be extended across international market segments which exhibit similar needs and buying power, and where there are no significant cultural barriers to entry. Extending the brand name internationally, of course, increases the benefits of brand stretching. In some cases this has meant establishing the brand globally. In more limited cases this practice may be restricted to Europe or a selected group of countries. The list below gives the top 10 global brands at present, as measured by Landor Associates (1990) in their brand awareness survey. The names are all familiar and span a variety of product categories from drinks to hi-fi.

1 Coca-Cola
2 Sony
3 Mercedes-Benz
4 Kodak
5 Disney
6 Nestlé
7 Toyota
8 McDonald's
9 IBM
10 Pepsi-Cola

There are few obvious rules about whether or not to 'go global' or to 'go international'. It is often local market factors or company history which determines practicality. For example, if there is no dominant local manufacturer or distributor, then entry into that market with a new, foreign brand is likely to be easier. Thus, major European retailers such as Aldi and Carrefour have established firm footholds in Spain where retailing is highly fragmented and there are no national chains. The multi-national company Heinz, on the other hand, does not have a global brand, largely because the company has grown through acquisition of local food manufacturers each with well-established market shares and a loyal customer base. International branding issues are discussed more fully in Chapter 8.

Brand names

Brand names serve to identify the brand and to trigger the brand proposition. There are three alternative naming strategies, stand-alone (e.g. Persil), endorsed (e.g. Kaliber from Guinness) and family (e.g. Heinz). Increasingly, however, these classifications are breaking down as stand-alone names develop line extensions (such as Persil Washing-up Liquid), endorsed names stand alone (such as Kaliber) and family names become indistinguishable from endorsed names (e.g. Weight Watchers from Heinz). Brand names also serve a legal role that is vital to the brand's commercial success. The brand name is only legally protected from infringement or mis-use by others when it has been registered under the Trade Marks Act. Only then can trade mark owners capitalize on the vast amount of investment in their brands. Thus, brand names become valuable assets in their own right which may be bought, sold, licensed or franchised. For a more detailed discussion see Chapter 2.

Building the brand proposition

The brand proposition may be built and reinforced through different elements of the communication mix, including advertising, sponsorship, sales promotion, packaging and public relations. Advertising may be used, for instance, to create a new brand proposition from nothing as, in the case of the launch of Castlemaine XXXX, or it may be used to revitalize an ageing brand such as Lucozade. Sponsorship such as the Bell's Scottish Open can use associative links to add symbolic values like youth, vigour and health to the brand. It can also be argued that creative sales campaigns like 'Take the Pepsi Challenge' and creative packaging like Phileas Fogg have much more to do with building the brand proposition over time than with effecting short-term sales gains. In contrast, public relations is perhaps best used to overturn negative perceptions resulting from, for example, the *Exxon Valdes* disaster and to replace these with more positive perceptions. See Chapter 3 for a more detailed account of building the brand proposition.

Own-label

Own-label grew as a cost-cutting response to the inflation of the 1970s and early 1980s, typically undercutting branded items by 20 per cent or more. Between 1970 and 1985, the own-label share of the grocery market rose from 20 to 28 per cent although in some stores and some product sectors the own-label share is even greater. Tesco and Sainsbury, for instance, offer 50 per cent own-label goods. Aldi, the ninth largest European grocery retailer, although a relative newcomer to the UK retailing scene, offers 75 per cent own-label items. The own-label concept, it may be argued, is a broader concept than that of brands since it embraces both the store proposition and those of individual product lines. As a result, own-label can build consumer perceptions of the store and the store can build perceptions of own-label. Finally, evidence suggests that own-labels are becoming brands in their own right. Boots Natural Collection is a prime example. The balance of power, however, between own-label and manufacturers' brands ultimately rests with the consumer. If the consumer wants a particular brand and considers the range incomplete without it, then the retailer is obliged to stock it. For a more detailed discussion see Chapter 6.

Summary

A brand is a product or service made distinctive by its positioning relative to the competition and by its personality which comprises a unique combination of functional attributes and symbolic values. Collectively, the positioning and the brand personality may be termed the brand proposition which, in turn, may be encapsulated by an advertising strapline such as 'Why compromise?' (Sony) or 'Once driven, forever smitten' (Vauxhall). Branding is a continuous cycle of research, planning, implementation and control which establishes and maintains the brand. However, it is the brand name (supported by the strapline and packaging) which triggers the brand proposition and once registered under the Trade Marks Act may become a valuable asset in its own right, frequently outliving the original products or company. Development of the overall brand proposition requires careful coordination of the entire marketing mix. The key to successful branding is to establish a relationship between the brand and the consumer, such that there is a close 'fit' between the consumer's own physical and psychological needs and the brand's functional attributes and symbolic values.

Strong brands with a high market share provide the company with a sustainable competitive advantage and above average return on investment. Increasingly, this competitive advantage can only be sustained through the brand personality, particularly its symbolic values. Competitive advantage through technological lead or cost lead is often rapidly eroded. The competitive advantages of branding are increasingly being used to build corporate brands and corporate identities which communicate with wider audiences than just a company's consumers.

In recent years, brand franchises have been extended to cover product areas outside their original product category. Brand stretching, as it is termed, has become a cost-effective alternative for launching a new product in many instances. The brand franchise can also be stretched internationally where common market segments exist across international boundaries and where there are no cultural barriers to entry.

Branding is a major part of modern marketing. The power of successful brands has been realized for some time by manufacturers, but since the 1980s there has been a growing reaction to manufacturers' brands by the retailers. Own-labels, originally regarded as cheap alternatives to manufacturer brands, are now becoming brands in their own right, taking on the positioning and personalities of their stores as well as individual product propositions.

CASE STUDY: The rebirth of Rover Cars

'When Austin Rover became Rover Cars on 4 September 1988, it was most definitely not a cosmetic name change but the culmination of a total marketing strategy.' So said the then marketing director of the Rover Group in a speech shortly afterwards.

The company's philosophy hitherto had been biased towards producing cars they wanted to build and that fitted their financial and industrial plans. There was no clear insight into the marketing opportunities of the company or how to focus all the efforts of the company in the right direction.

All this changed to some extent during the early part of the decade, but took on a major impetus with the appointment of Sir Graham Day as chairman of the Rover Group in May 1986. With a chairman committed to marketing, the process of moving from a product orientation towards a consumer orientation took on real meaning. Indeed, one of Sir Graham's favourite expressions was: 'If you love the consumer to death, you can't go far wrong.' Clearly in any company where the chief executive officer is not fully committed to marketing, effecting significant change, quickly enough, becomes almost impossible.

At Rover, a fundamental change in strategy was developed, known internally as 'Roverization'.

The key to developing a new strategic approach was to develop a full understanding of how consumers purchase cars—establishing the complex relationships between marque and model. A buyer behavioural model was developed which, in its most simplistic form, showed the two crucial stages in purchasing a car: getting on the shortlist and final product evaluation. Typically, consumers shortlist a number of cars by first considering the desirability and imagery of the marque and then by looking at the car's brand image—what does the car say about the person who drives it?

Some of the basic information which was used in developing that strategy was obtained through extensive consumer research, as summarized below.

Marques and brands

The first findings in 1987 related to brands:

The company had a confused image—a schizophrenic blend of Austin and Rover, saying nothing particularly well to consumers individually or together.

Austin was seen as an essentially negative badge and acted in reality as a barrier to purchase. Consumers saw it as being dull and uninteresting, overtly practical and functional, with the virtues of space and economy, but unreliable and for older drivers—aged 55 or more. Not a particularly dynamic base to work from.

Rover, on the other hand, had some genuine qualities. It was seen as prestigious, a quality car, traditional and original. However, it was also seen as being unreliable, uneconomic and for older drivers and, of course, its associations with Austin also had an undesirable effect on its own image. This position was worse when you consider that four of the six models at that time were badged Austin and accounted for around 90 per cent of sales.

So, at the end of the day, Austin Rover products were less likely to get on the shortlist because of the poor marque image and poor brand image. No matter how good the product was in reality, Austin Rover cars were less likely to be chosen than those of the major competitors. For example, the Montego was, in reality, a superior product to the Cavalier and Sierra: it accelerated faster, had a better top speed, was better equipped and had superior handling. But in the consumer's mind it was just a car from Austin, in the medium price sector, which did not rank alongside the others.

In general, marques could be divided into two main types: first, those with a strong reputation for reliability, technology and engineering excellence, seen as being quality marques; secondly, the higher volume marques, not known for their quality and reliability and seen more as managerial marques, in a fleet context.

Among the quality marques, some offered both emotional and rational reassurances. These marques were seen as having high status at low risk and typically included BMW, Mercedes and Saab. If, however, a quality marque was overtly practical and low on emotional support, it was seen as being low risk, but this time with lower status. This was best exemplified by Volvo.

Looking at the managerial marques, those that offered practical strengths were seen as lower status but with low risk. These included Ford and, to a lesser extent, Vauxhall.

Marques with high emotional and limited rational appeal were seen as high status, but a high risk. In 1987, Rover was seen to be in this category, together with the French and Italian executive cars.

The company's first steps were to address the gap between perceptions and reality on Montego, introducing changes to the product which were in line with what customers wanted and communicating this with high-quality, vibrant advertising on TV, in the national press and at the dealer level. Next, plans for future products were reviewed to ensure that new models in the pipeline were truly worthy of the Rover name—that they would meet and exceed customers' expectations. The results became evident in such brands as the Rover 200 and 400, which commanded the high ground in the medium car sectors. People now wanted to own a Rover, both when buying a new car or second-hand car. The ultimate measures of success had been achieved: class-leading satisfaction levels among owners and high resale values. These brands have been developed onwards and upwards, with image-building niche vehicles added to the range, e.g. Rover 220 GTi sports flagship, Cabriolet (applauded as the best convertible in this market segment) and, in late 1992, the Rover 200 Coupé.

Other successes followed: the Rover Metro, launched in 1990, achieved the accolade of the 'best small car in the world'. Customer research showed that the new Rover 800, launched in 1991 to complete the portfolio of new Rover brands, had raised owner satisfaction to new heights and was a fundamental step in the next phase of Roverization—to continue to build the Rover marque values. Reintroduction of the Rover grille, the essence of the company's heritage, played a key role in establishing Rover 800 as the flagship for the Rover marque. The Rover 800 Coupé, yet another new product, not only competed further up-market than any previous Rover, but also raised the profile of the whole company. The result has been to get customers who would never previously have considered a Rover of any type to take the marque seriously.

Roverization, however, is dynamic: 1993 will see the launch of another Rover brand, which will further build the equity and standing of the marque. But this is just the product part of the Rover story—the Rover experience is about much more: 'One name, one standard, everywhere.' It enshrines every aspect of the customer experience, from the point at which you think about your next car, through the process of choosing, buying and then living with your car and the relationship with the dealer, who, to most people, is the face of Rover.

Dealerships

In the minds of the consumer, there is no real differentiation between Rover, the company, and the Rover dealer network. Consumer expectations of a franchise carrying the Rover badge are high. On the whole, however, the Rover dealer network in the mid-1980s was on a par with other mass market motor manufacturers, but did not reflect the prestige marque to which the company aspired.

The task, therefore, was to create a customer-driven ethos throughout the Rover Cars franchise. Based on extensive marketing research findings, the 'Customer Satisfaction Initiative' was developed, to encompass all dealership staff. It included a series of performance measures that would clearly indicate customer perception of dealers and the standard of service provided, in terms of both new car purchase and after-sales support.

Individual dealers were measured against four key criteria:

1 A customer research questionnaire
2 Standards of premises, people and processes
3 Mystery shopper research
4 Distance learning (commitment to specific customer satisfaction training modules).

Individual opportunities for improvement were identified and actioned, while an overall index of dealer performance was derived to provide comparisons between dealers and formed the basis for a significant financial reward and penalty incentive programme.

The Customer Satisfaction Initiative was significantly revised in 1991, to be less prescriptive and encourage increased dealer involvement. The company-measured performance standards were drastically reduced in number, increased emphasis was placed on the customer research and dealer training was focused on quality assurance and total quality management (also providing support to gain accreditation to BS 5750). In addition, a series of 'best practice' process guides were issued to assist dealers to further improve their standards of customer service and support this continuous improvement through self-measurement.

The results were significant: benchmarking research showed customer satisfaction with the Rover network to have improved considerably (both absolutely and relative to the competition) in both 1991 and 1992. Rover and its dealers are not standing still, but the groundwork has now been completed for the rebirth of the Rover marque to be supported through this critical area of customer interface.

Corporate identity

From an Austin Rover identity which was visually uncoordinated and in considerable disarray, a new Rover corporate identity was developed, following considerable research and development. Successfully communicating the core Rover values and embodying 'one name, one standard, everywhere', the Rover identity is most in evidence at the dealerships, but follows through in all advertising and communications, both external and internal.

Within the company, subsequent massive investment in total quality programmes not only transformed production quality and efficiency but also genuinely won over the hearts and minds of Rover's people. The new focus among all employees on quality and customers' satisfaction, in their broadest contexts, inevitably reinforced the Rover message to the world outside.

'Roverization'

Thus, when Austin Rover became Rover Cars it was part of a new marketing strategy designed to address the weaknesses and threats which research had highlighted. To be credible to the public, the name change to Rover had to be made at the right moment. Too early, before the new products were launched or improvements at the dealers were being experienced, and it would have been just another name change. Too late and the opportunity to capitalize on building the Rover image would be under-exploited and confused by old identities.

The process of 'Roverization' was not without its critics at the time, but from the company's point of view the decision to relaunch the Rover marque and drop Austin was a turning point on the road to success. Subsequently, continual improvement to the product range, the dealerships and all marketing actions have followed the Roverization strategy. Rover management now regards the credibility of the Rover marque as beyond doubt, but the company continues to follow the same clear marketing strategy, with defined targets for the years ahead. The marketing management at Rover is now dedicating itself to a strategy for the 1990s: 'Roverization—phase 2.'

CASE STUDY: BMW (Europe)*

Europe '92 : perspectives

BMW is an export-orientated company. Two-thirds of our output is exported. As far as the main export regions are concerned, the emphasis is clearly on the highly developed industrialized countries, i.e. the EC, the USA and Japan. As of January 1st, 1993, however, the ratio

*This case is taken from a paper first presented at the 42nd ESOMAR Marketing Research Congress, Stockholm 1989, by Horst Kern, Hans-Christian Wagner and Roswitha Hassis, where it was awarded an ESOMAR prize. Permission for reprinting this paper has been granted by the European Society for Opinion & Marketing Research ESOMAR.

of exports to domestic sales will be exactly reversed, because two-thirds of our production will then be sold on the single European market.

We believe that key markets should not be left to importers. A manufacturer should rather develop the markets locally and 'be at home' in the markets. This is the reason why today we have a total of 14 subsidiaries in the major car markets of Europe, North America and the Far East.

Even at this stage, BMW has thus already adjusted its distribution network to the single market of the EC—as have many other motor manufacturers. January 1st, 1993, will just mark the completion, in the political field, of what will long have been a reality—at least in major sectors of the motor industry.

The standardisation of technical rules and regulations will certainly be beneficial. Is this also true of the 'standardisation' of our target groups? A superficial glance at the data defining how our customers are structured might suggest that our target groups are already homogeneous anyway.

The education of BMW's customers is above average and so is the number of them who are employed in leading positions, who are self-employed or working in the liberal professions, and who are consequently to be found in the high-income brackets.

Does the 'Euroconsumer' exist?

But are things really as simple as all that? We have nine languages in the Europe of the Twelve. We have eleven different currencies, of varying quality, and it is unlikely that the ECU will be the means of payment even after 1992.

We have highly developed industrialised countries and others which are agrarian—with differences in lifestyles to match. The gap between the various standards of living is huge. In terms of gross domestic product per inhabitant, the wealthy regions are five times better off than the poorer ones.

However important harmonisation may be, the differences in culture, traditions and lifestyle which have grown up over the centuries will persist—and we should be glad about that.

So there will be no Euroconsumer. The administrative act which will take effect on January 1st, 1993, will not level out the peculiar characteristics of the peoples, it will not wipe out the differences in mentality and least of all will it create one uniform language.

Why do we need 'Eurobrands'?

BMW decided to be an exclusive speciality make, a brand which is active in a market segment that accounts for only 15 per cent of the world market. In this exclusive market, only those brands which have established a clear profile for themselves world wide and which take the individual demands of their exclusive clients into account are successful.

It is one thing to create a brand profile which is globally valid. It is a different matter to sell successfully in a specific market. We try to meet these requirements by determining a central and unified brand strategy, but translating this strategy into decentralised and country-specific action. We call this concept 'global branding–local marketing'.

Market research was commissioned to determine the ideal positioning for BMW on a European and at a local level. First, a series of group discussions was held to extract the relevant vocabulary and brand attributes across each country. Then, a questionnaire was constructed using both a common 'core' of statements appropriate to all countries plus a series of country-specific statements to address local attitudes/opinions. In addition, open-ended questions were asked to allow consumers to explain in more detail what they meant by certain words. It became evident later that without these questions we would not have been able to recognise that, for example, Dutchmen who demand the same measure of exclusiveness as some of the Italian car buyers do, have an entirely different idea of the qualities which amount to this exclusiveness.

Results from the survey demonstrate that consumer requirements across five different countries, namely Austria, Italy, Netherlands, France and Switzerland, fell into three groups:

- attributes which are equally important to *all* the motorists of the market segment under study in *every* country and which thus are valid throughout Europe;

- criteria which are equally important to *all* the motorists of *one* country and thus constitute national differences;

- and finally requirements which are equally important to *some* motorists in *all* countries and thus result in target group-specific differences.

Consequently, anyone who wants to offer tailor-made suits for Europeans can manage with one pattern. However, he must weave his cloth according to the local custom and dye it individually.

European pattern

Requirements which are valid throughout Europe are:

- reliability
- safety
- quality
- advanced technology.

We call these criteria *basic requirements*. Cars which are not perceived as meeting these requirements are excluded in the initial stage of the decision-making process from the short list of potentially eligible purchases. On the other hand, a car which meets these basic requirements is considered to be a good car in all countries.

We come across this decision-making pattern in all countries alike.

National cloth

Once the pattern has passed this fundamental test, the next step is to make certain that the choice of cloth suits the national taste and takes the climatic conditions of the respective country into account.

When applied to the car, this means: in *the Netherlands* for example a car gains in attractiveness by means of 'intrinsic qualities', such as solidly produced interior fittings, rather than by externals.

As a counterpoint, let us look at *Austria*. There the car might well, and even should, demonstrate self-assurance. It is certainly supposed to display what its owner can afford and 'who he is'. There, the car is used far more deliberately for presenting oneself to the outside world than it is in other countries.

As a last example, let us look at *Italy*. There, the car is expected in particular to match its driver's personal style. Requirements on design and aesthetic qualities, together with dynamic driving performance, stand out very clearly from the requirement profiles valid in other countries.

In this way, a highly characteristic requirement configuration for each country emerges, which consists of more or less identical basic requirements and a number of country-specific additional expectations.

Does that mean that one and the same car can only be sold with different rates of success in these countries?

In our opinion, the answer is no. In view of the fact that all countries are in agreement regarding the basic requirements, a car which is rated a 'good car' in France will also be recognised as 'good' in Austria and in the Netherlands. Obviously the difference rests in the fact that additional expectations *vis-à-vis* the car are articulated differently from one country to another. Thus the success with which a car is sold in the various countries is ultimately a matter of communication.

Individual dyeing

European pattern and national cloth do not yet amount to a tailor-made suit. Let us not forget that we are dealing with people, despite all the points they have in common as a nation, with individuals who want to express their own personal style.

We carried out a typological analysis across the total of all drivers in all five countries in order to be able better to describe the needs of our

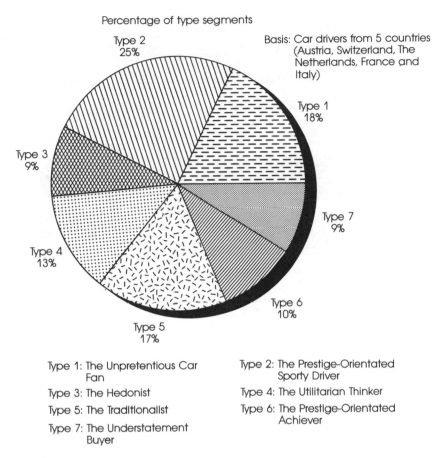

Percentage of type segments

Basis: Car drivers from 5 countries (Austria, Switzerland, The Netherlands, France and Italy)

Type 2 25%
Type 3 9%
Type 4 13%
Type 5 17%
Type 1 18%
Type 7 9%
Type 6 10%

Type 1: The Unpretentious Car Fan

Type 3: The Hedonist

Type 5: The Traditionalist

Type 7: The Understatement Buyer

Type 2: The Prestige-Orientated Sporty Driver

Type 4: The Utilitarian Thinker

Type 6: The Prestige-Orientated Achiever

Figure 1.2 International typology: percentage of type segments. (Basis: car drivers from five countries).

target group within our segment. In this process, the 'requirements on the car' served as the active variables, while socio-demography, attitudes to the car and to motoring, and lifestyles were passive variables.

The solution which was deemed ideal produced seven types. They are represented among the European car drivers as shown in Figure 1.2.

Knowing the sizes and the characteristics of the various types now allows us to determine the core and the fringe target groups of a brand against the background of the strategic guidelines.

But in addition to that we were interested above all in the distribution of the various types in the specific countries.

Obviously there are requirement patterns which are found with equal frequency in *all* countries. They include, for example, the 'prestige-

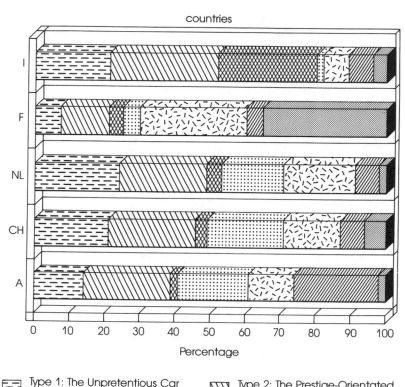

countries

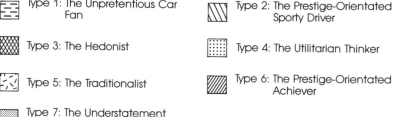

Type 1: The Unpretentious Car Fan

Type 2: The Prestige-Orientated Sporty Driver

Type 3: The Hedonist

Type 4: The Utilitarian Thinker

Type 5: The Traditionalist

Type 6: The Prestige-Orientated Achiever

Type 7: The Understatement Buyer

Figure 1.3 Distribution of segments

orientated sporty driver' and the 'unpretentious car fan'. Thus 'global branding' could have a direct appeal to these two 'Euro-types'.

On the other hand, the different composition of the car-driving population from one country to another shows that a conception of oneself as exhibited, for instance, by the 'traditionalist' and the 'understatement buyer', is shared by two out of three motorists in France and by only one in ten in Italy. This is clear evidence of the need for 'local marketing' (Figure 1.3).

What does this mean for practical marketing activities? We tried to bring out the facts of the case from BMW's point of view.

There are transnational similarities among all customers of the total universe in study as well as among the BMW prospects. It is interesting for us that these similarities among our prospects are to be found on a higher level. In simplified terms BMW drivers demand higher standards with regard to styling, driving performance, modern technology and exclusiveness.

On the other hand we see differences between the car drivers of the various countries which also apply to BMW drivers.

BMW drivers in the five countries have some points of reference in common: this provides starting points for global strategies. However, at the same time they see themselves as children of their nation, just as Germans, Frenchmen or Italians. Hence, local marketing is necessary to address to the target group adequately.

Application of the findings

Thus the results provide many arguments for 'global branding and local marketing'. In addition they allow or invite us to search for optimal strategic guidelines by a clever combination of positioning criteria. The optimum is achieved if these guidelines:

- are attractive to as many members of the target group as possible;
- are coherent and form an integrated whole despite their multi-dimensional character;
- meet the requirements of the corporate identity; and
- provide a unique position ahead of the competitors.

Both the principles of positioning and the research findings were substantial when BMW reformulated its international positioning approach in a more up-to-date manner. While the previous approach (Figure 1.4) had been characterised by a rather mono-dimensional orientation towards technological competence and progressiveness, the new approach (Figure 1.5) is extended by the addition of emotional components. Aesthetic value, elegance, design, exclusiveness and individuality are additional facets which extend the traditionally technical and sporty core of the brand and are thus intended to broaden access to the brand still further.

The most recent studies already furnish proof that a good many of our prospects are ready to look at the BMW brand from the above-mentioned new perspective.

It is true that this development is influenced to a high degree by the new model ranges of the 5 and 7 series which we launched in 1987 and 1988. However, the novelty can wear off very soon. Our competitors are waiting just around the corner to launch their new products. The development of new products is extremely costly in terms of time and money. For this reason, the entire environment surrounding the products, and the posture of the company as a whole must take the common objectives into account.

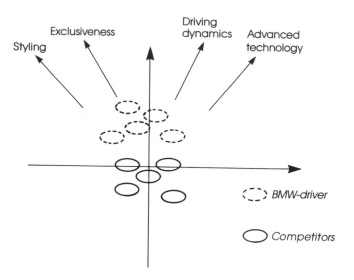

Figure 1.4 Positioning model 1

Thus the positioning competition is increasingly shifting from the product to its environment. An optimised automobile will be no more than the basic prerequisite of success. Creating an integrated whole, a space within which to experience the automobile in its totality, will ultimately decide on success in the market place.

At joint workshops held in every country where the study has been carried out so far, with the participation of the people responsible for marketing at headquarters and in the subsidiaries, with the agencies and the respective research companies, the country-related results were presented and discussed against the background to the new strategic goals.

These workshops proved to be most helpful, because they provided an interdisciplinary platform:

– for scrutinising the situation of BMW in depth and in a complex manner;
– for bringing out country-specific peculiarities and problems;
– for providing a basic approach for global brand management of analyses comparing different countries;
– and last but not least for discussing catalogues of specific pieces of action.

The development of jointly supported goals was thus another step towards resolving the above-mentioned conflict of aims between headquarters and subsidiaries. On the whole, the approach presented here proved to be an extremely suitable means of making the

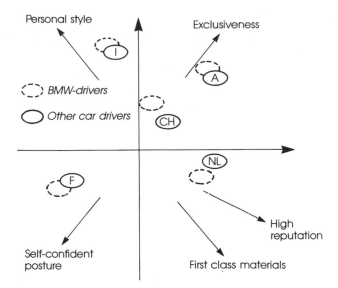

Figure 1.5 Positioning model 2

interesting markets more transparent and thus of extending the basis of international strategic planning.

Headquarters and subsidiaries are both provided with an instrument which enables them to adjust and monitor the market position. Harmony between the resulting goals and action is essentially dependent on a constant dialogue between the people in charge of marketing at headquarters and in the subsidiaries. Market research assumes the function of an important mediator in this interactive process.

Since it was possible thus to satisfy the information needs of strategic marketing planning at headquarters and in the local subsidiaries, there are no longer any obstacles to the studies being repeated regularly. In addition, a continuation of the studies in the USA and Japan is envisaged. An extension to more distant culture areas will presumably confront us with new problems, on which we may be able to report at some later stage.

References

Aaker, D. and Shansby, J., 'Positioning your product', *Business Horizons*, May/June 1982.

Buzzell, R. and Gale, B., *The PIMS Principles: Linking Strategy to Performance*, The Free Press, 1987.

Davidson, H., *Offensive Marketing*, Penguin, 1987.

Landor Associates, *Image Power Survey*, 1990.

Ries, A. and Trout, J., *Positioning : The Battle for the Mind*, 1st edition
    revised, McGraw-Hill, 1986.

Whan Park, C., Jaworski, B. and MacInnis, D., 'Strategic brand
    concept, image management', *Journal of Marketing*, **50**, October 1986.

2

Brand names

Purpose

The brand name should be the trigger to the proposition offered by the brand. It is a shorthand communication of the brand's personality and positioning and, as such, is synonymous with the satisfaction the brand delivers, both functional and symbolic. It is the most obvious means of differentiating one brand from another.

Blackett (1988) specifies three key roles for the brand name. First, it identifies the particular product or service which then allows the consumer either to accept or reject it. Secondly, it communicates messages to the consumer through the descriptive qualities of the name, e.g. Shake 'n' Vac, or through associations built up over time (these may be functional or symbolic messages, or both). Thirdly, it functions as a piece of legal property, protected by law from competitive attack or trespass; the brand name may eventually become a valuable asset in its own right.

Brand names usually fall along a continuum. At one end there are the free-standing and essentially meaningless names like Sony, Radion and Hoover. At the other end there are purely descriptive names like Do It All and Dab-it-off. Somewhere between these two extremes lie suggestive names like Readybrek (instant breakfast cereal), Shift (oven cleaner) and Wash & Go (all-in-one-shampoo and conditioner).

Blackett visualises what he terms the Brand Name Spectrum shown in Figure 2.1, to which we have added our own examples. Clearly, descriptive names communicate easily in the short term. They are 'simple, direct and essentially conservative in tone' (Blackett 1988). However, they are also vulnerable to copying with legal protection of the name being difficult to achieve (see later).

Suggestive names also communicate well—provided that the consumer understands the product area and the relationship of the particular brand to that area. The communicated message is frequently more subtle.

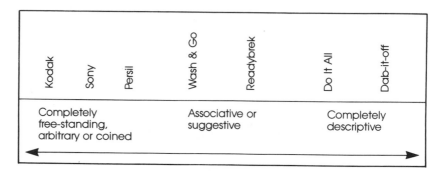

Figure 2.1 The Brand Name Spectrum

Free-standing names, however, present difficulties in communication, at least initially. Their meaning may be, at best, obscure and may even be non-existent. Establishing relevance and meaning to the consumer may take years of investment. Then, however, the rewards may be reaped with an effective and satisfactory take-out by the consumer from carefully crafted, built-in associations. Sony, for instance, is readily associated with 'innovative technology' even though the name itself bears no intrinsic communication qualities. Kodak has built up powerful associations of 'natural colour' and 'consistent quality' while Persil triggers 'family caring'.

To consumers, therefore, the brand name identifies a product or service which allows them either to accept or reject the product. To the marketer, the brand name is also important but serves a different purpose. It acts as the focus for the entire marketing effort, whether in relation to brand maintenance or new brand development. The brand becomes synonymous with the team that drives it.

To both parties, therefore, there is considerable significance in the role and purpose of the brand name. Practitioners interviewed for this book make the following observations.

> The name is critical, vital. It is the name that first triggers in the mind of the consumer.

> A focus for new brand development.

> Your brand name is your point of difference.

> You need to retain the name in association with another memory which is the identity of the brand.

In a business environment, where most elements in the marketing mix are constantly under review, the brand name is usually the only variable that never changes.

Brand-naming strategies

It is convenient to group naming strategies into three categories:

- stand-alone names
- endorsed names
- family names.

Stand-alone names

These are single brand names used for a single product and are, arguably, the strongest naming strategy. Examples include Twix (chocolate confectionery) and Pampers (disposable nappies). Originally Persil, Timotei and Sony would have been considered stand-alone brand names but in recent years this strategy has changed (see below). Stand-alone names are often shorter and, therefore, more memorable. They are also easier to protect legally.

Endorsed names

These use the company name as support for their own brand name. As such, they have an advantage over stand-alone brands in being able to benefit from the proposition of the original brand. They also, however, run the risk of diluting the original proposition.

Examples of endorsed brand names include Cadbury's Flake (chocolate), Bell's Islander (whisky) and Kaliber, made by Guinness. Guinness took a risk when they endorsed Kaliber as their alcohol-free lager; however, their strategy paid off (Slater 1988). Low and non-alcoholic beers enjoyed very little success when first launched in the 1960s. Not only was the taste delivery poor, but there was a severe image problem associated with the product category. Guinness's technology overturned the first problem area, and the Guinness name the second. For the first time a respected British brewer had had the confidence to put its name on a non-alcoholic beer. It gave the new brand credibility through an association with the Guinness brand heritage.

Endorsement is usually used to help establish a new brand. Arguably it reduces the cost and risk of successfully launching a brand with a stand-alone name. Thus, Tab could be said to have failed through the absence of the Coca-Cola endorsement, while the subsequent launch of Diet Coke benefited from it. The ultimate aim of this type of endorsement is to make the new brand 'stand on its own feet'. In some cases, however, endorsement is used to provide permanent support for other brands such as British Airways' Club World. When Club World was first launched in 1988 with its closely integrated design strategy of the new brand logo across every item of the Club World package—headrest covers, bag tags, menu cards and so on—it was decided to link or endorse the desired Club World symbolic values of comfort, relaxation and status with the well-established British Airways' values of quality, safety and internationalism. Undoubtedly, this endorsed strategy led to one of the most successful business class launches in recent years.

In certain cases the consumer's perception of the endorsed brand may also *enhance* the endorsing brand. This is the reasoning behind the policy among car manufacturers to maintain a position in the luxury segment of the market, e.g. General Motors with Cadillac and Ford with Jaguar.

Family names

This describes a fairly homogeneous group of products sharing a common brand name. Examples include Wella (hair products), Rawlplug (DIY products) and Heinz (foods).

However, these categories are not mutually exclusive. Thus Heinz, which is used as a family name in the context of canned foods, is also used as an endorsed name—for example, Weight Watchers from Heinz. Endorsed names sometimes drop the endorsement, as in Kaliber, while stand-alone names such as Timotei have developed line extensions.

Of course, every new company entering the market uses a stand-alone brand name strategy. Sony is a case in point. The name was devised because there was a not unreasonable belief that the original name for the company, 'Tokyo Tsuschin Koggo Kabushiki Kaishi', was impossible to recall (Morita *et al.* 1988). It was, therefore, decided to opt for a four- or five-letter name which was pronounceable, could stand up internationally, but which meant nothing descriptively. In the 1950s and 1960s there was still a strong American influence in Japan as a result of the number of GIs stationed there after the Second World War. One of their common expressions was 'sonny boy'. Sonny, however, when pronounced in Japanese, means to 'lose money'! It was decided to drop one 'n', hence Sony. The name was easy to pronounce and there were no ready-made associations, positive or negative. Today, as the product range has grown, the strategy has changed from stand-alone to a combination of family branding (for example, Sony hi-fi) and endorsed branding (for example, Sony Walkman, Sony Trinitron and Sony Discman).

Successful brand names

While, according to a survey by Landor Associates in 1990, each of the top 10 brands in the UK have founding family names—such as McVitie's, Kellogg's, Cadbury, Heinz—successful new brand names are more likely to result from a consideration of several key factors.

Linguistics

Research by Vanden Bergh *et al.* (1987) of 479 successful brand names over the last 15 years analysed 10 phonetic devices, such as alliteration, onomatopoeia and plosives (hard-sounding consonants like b, c, d) and a further 12 orthographic (e.g. unusual spellings) and semantic devices (e.g. puns, word plays, 'fit'). They concluded that only plosives and semantic 'fit', e.g. Shake 'n' Vac, have any effect at all on successful brand names. Slick (hair styler), Crest (toothpaste) and Active (industrial liquid detergent) are other examples.

Ries and Trout (1986) have identified a different linguistic approach to successful brand names which they term 'phonetic shorthand', reducing the brand name from several syllables to just two—Pan Am for Pan American, Amex for American Express, NatWest for National Westminster are three examples of the successful use of this device.

They also observe the practice of using initials as a method of phonetic shorthand: IBM, TWA, P&G. However, they suggest that only the most well-known companies can afford this strategy since awareness of 'named' companies as opposed to 'initial' companies is almost 20 per cent higher. In UK terms, for instance, how many know what ADL stands for (sponsors of the 1988–92 London Marathon), or DHL or BICC?

Distinctiveness

Practitioners in the field are more likely to consider distinctiveness as the key consideration in the development of a successful brand name, as the following quotes indicate:

> Firstly, the name must be distinctive

> It has to identify and differentiate the product.

Um Bongo, the children's fruit drink, tries to achieve distinctiveness by being innovative and evocative. It supports a 'fun' positioning and also incorporates certain linguistic qualities, such as plosives and soundplay. Kestrel, a brand of lager, is distinctive but for different reasons. It deliberately avoids the conventional Germanic route for lager names and adopts a strong, independent alternative.

Corporate brand names also need to be distinctive. Allied Dunbar, for instance, establishes an apposite Scottish link in an attempt to convey strength, independence and financial confidence.

Adaptability

It is also important when choosing a brand name to consider the desirability of line extensions at some future date. A name too heavily entrenched in a particular product area like Rawlplug, which to many is closely associated with wall fixtures, may experience difficulties when applied to other product sectors like drills. However, with a brand such as Almay (cosmetics), which signifies general symbolic values such as caring and safety, as well as specific product attributes like hypoallergenic, line extension has been more feasible and has taken the brand beyond the female cosmetics area. Almay Skin Care for Men is also alive and well!

International applicability

A further consideration is the ability of the brand name to be used internationally, not only in terms of pronunciation but in terms of its suitability and global availability. Sony, a totally contrived name, achieved this quite easily. Not only has no other international organization used or registered the same name (i.e. the name was globally available), but since the name was intrinsically meaningless, there were no negative associations in any other language.

Other products which may have several different brand names internationally are looking for global uniformity. In the UK, Snickers has debunked Marathon and Chocolate Treats has taken over from Minstrels. In contrast, Oil of Ulay is known as Oil of Olaz in Europe, Oil of Olay in the US and Oil of Ulan in Australia.

The trend towards international standardization would suggest that it is only a matter of time before the Oil of Ulay brand is given a single international name.

Use of logos and graphics

Choosing an appropriate logo and/or graphic support can reinforce the name, as demonstrated in Figure 2.2. McVitie's Boasters in bold

Figure 2.2 Logo designs

typeface and an exaggerated swirl to the 'r' suggests sophistication while Mini Cheddars in bubble logo promotes a 'fun', 'warm' personality for the brand.

Other examples include the National Westminster Bank, which uses a triangular motif suggesting strength, reassurance and solidity and the Jaguar motif on the bonnet of their cars suggesting power and individualism. Like brand names, logos may become enduring assets in their own right. They should therefore be equally distinctive.

Brand name registration

Finally, and very importantly, when considering new brand names it is essential that the brand name and its support logo and graphic motif are registered at home and abroad in order to achieve protection that is legally enforceable against any other manufacturer using the same. Once registered, that name becomes the unique property of the brand owner, and providing registration is renewed at regular intervals, legal protection may be achieved for life (for a more detailed account see the section on 'Trade mark registration' on page 34).

Brand name: creative process

Research into the creative process of brand naming is far from extensive. However, McNeal and Zeren (1981) carried out a study in the USA which identified six particular steps in the name development process. These were:

1 identification of objectives or criteria for the brand names
2 generation of name alternatives
3 screening of alternatives
4 researching consumer opinions
5 trade mark search
6 brand name selection.

This process was then revised by Shipley *et al.* (1988) and tested in the UK among leading marketing managers of companies listed in the British KOMPASS register. Their revised process is set out in Table 2.1.

Table 2.1 Shipley, Hooley and Wallace development process

Step	Object
1 *Set branding objectives*	What is the name required to do?
2 *Select branding strategy*	Will the name stand alone, be a family name or be endorsed?
3 *Specify brand name criteria*	What should the brand name communicate?
4 *Generate brand name ideas*	For example, use a brainstorming or computer generation technique
5 *Screen brand names*	Establish positive and negative imagery and carry out a trade mark search to check uniqueness
6 *Select the brand name*	Select according to branding objectives and criteria

Overall, the Shipley *et al.* research suggested that the revised model for brand name selection was more appropriate. In particular, the separation of 'branding objectives' from 'brand name criteria' ensures that objectives which set out what the brand is required to do are considered separately from criteria which focus on the inherent attributes of the new name. In McNeal and Zeren's model these two categories were combined.

The revised model also includes 'branding strategy' which affects the type of brand name—family, stand alone or endorsed—that will be consistent with the company brand strategy.

Furthermore, the research attempted to identify some key features of each stage in the process. The conclusions were as follows:

- Step 1, branding objectives, identified 'desired image' as the most important branding objective in brand name selection.
- Step 2, branding strategy, showed that 60 per cent of companies within the sample adopted an endorsed branding strategy, 22 per cent a stand-alone name and 18 per cent the family name.
- Step 3, brand name criteria, identified compatibility with required product image, memorability and attractiveness as the top three criteria. It was surprising, however, that pronounceability was ranked tenth when internationality is such a key requirement of practitioners.
- Step 4, brand name generation, identified brainstorming and group discussions as the most common name-generation method, with alternative methods such as word association and the Eureka method (management inspiration) as the next most likely methods. The use of computers to generate names was ranked eighth.
- Step 5, screen brand names, showed that companies typically used four types of screening process—in-house company personnel, specialist agencies, consumer research and, importantly, trade mark search—to establish the uniqueness of the brand and hence its availability.
- Finally, in step 6, brand name selection, 30 per cent of those involved in the final decision were managing directors and a further 18 per cent marketing directors, reflecting a widespread recognition of the importance of the brand name in the marketing process.

Murphy (1990) describes a similar procedure. He stresses the importance of a systematic approach to brand name development and the need to coordinate input from the client side, marketing consultants, copywriters, linguists, researchers, consumers and trademark lawyers. Murphy begins the creative process with a *naming strategy* in which the personality of the brand, its positioning, target audience and international aspirations are identified.

Next, a series of *naming themes* are developed. Murphy speculates on possible naming themes for a new, Japanese, high-performance sports car—themes focusing on the Japanese country of origin, power themes, wild animals or international life-style.

A series of group discussions among people who are selected for their creativity and language skills are then run to develop and expand those themes. Such groups often employ research methods similar to brainstorming exercises which encourage lateral creative thought.

This stage of expanding the naming themes is often also supplemented by computer name-generation techniques.

- First, the names are screened against the agreed naming strategy until there is a shortlist of, say, 200–300 names.
- Secondly, if the name is to achieve international status it must be screened for suitability and acceptance in five or six different languages. This reduces the shortlist to around 50 names.
- Thirdly, the names are subjected to a preliminary legal search to check against duplications. The final 20 or so names are then examined thoroughly for linguistic suitability, pronounceability and legal availability internationally.

With only a handful of names surviving this final test, consumer research is then often undertaken to ensure that no serious negatives have slipped through the last hurdle. The method uses panels of 100 or so consumers who have undertaken this kind of 'jury service' for several years. Other methods may use traditional groups of 'naive' consumers. In the final consumer check for Kaliber, for example, several different spellings were checked—Caliber, Kalibre, and Kaliber—and each was researched against Silver Eagle as an alternative name.

The final test, however, for the last remaining names, must be in the context of the marketing mix where the brand name is set in its packaging livery in a simulated shopping environment. 'Does the brand name work?' Does it 'fit' the desired positioning? Does it communicate the appropriate brand proposition? Can you go up to the bar and ask for 'a glass of …'?

Trade mark registration

Trade marks may be described as words, symbols, signatures, colours and brand names which distinguish one product or service from another, for example the Coca-Cola swirl, the Rolls-Royce double R, McVitie's Hob-nobs brand name. By registering such marks, the company is permitted sole use of that name or symbol, initially for a period of seven years, after which it may be renewed every 14 years.

Registration is not compulsory but is strongly advised. For a relatively modest fee of around £600 in the United Kingdom, it offers the trade mark owner considerable powers and protection, including that of a statutory monopoly. This means that a trade mark owner may take the case to the High Court to prevent any infringement or use of that owner's registered trade mark by any other company or person.

Registration has teeth. Its powers are much easier to enforce for instance than using the common law 'passing off' rights where it is necessary to prove that the defendant is deliberately misleading the consumer into thinking that the defendant's product is the same as the plaintiff's (i.e. the original manufacturer).

The first Trade Marks Act was passed in 1875 when a group of Sheffield cutlery manufacturers wished to enforce their sole use of specific marks on their cutlery. The current act dates back to 1938 but was amended in 1984 to introduce additional legislation for service mark registration.

An example of how tightly the Trade Marks Act may be interpreted is in the context of the Pepsi Challenge, in which members of the public are invited to taste two cola drinks, one is Pepsi, the other Coca-Cola. However, because the Coca-Cola brand name has been registered under most trade mark classifications, it would be considered an infringement of the act if Pepsi used the Coca-Cola name and/or logo in such a way as to 'import a reference' to its proprietor. It can be used neither in comparative nor 'knocking' copy. As a result, on all Pepsi Challenge booths where the taste preference tests take place, no mention or reference can be made to any brand other than Pepsi. Coca-Cola is simply referred to as 'another leading brand of cola'.

The process of registration, which incidentally may be carried out years before a product has been invented and then 'banked' for later use, involves

1 filing an application domestically and, advisably, internationally with the Trade Marks Registry;
2 satisfying grounds for trade mark registration in terms of distinctiveness and uniqueness;
3 advertising application in the Trade Marks Journal to allow for any opposition to be filed; and
4 payment of the registration fee.

This procedure may take two years to complete in the United Kingdom but registration abroad may take as long as six years or more.

Registered brand names may also be licensed or franchised to other users. Heineken, for instance, is brewed 'under licence' by Whitbread while Kall-Kwik and Body Shop operate a franchise system in which franchisees not only adopt the registered brand name but are given the right to copy the franchisor's entire business concept—its shop fittings, staff training, promotional merchandise, accountancy systems and so on. In both instances, it is essential that the trade mark owner maintains strict and legally enforced control over the manner of use of the registered brand name and, in the case of franchises, the manner of its operation.

Overall, therefore, trade mark registration is an essential concomitant of the brand name process. Only then can the brand name be afforded legal status against infringement or mis-use, and only then can trade mark owners capitalize on the vast amount of investment placed in their brands. It is in this way that the brand name becomes a valuable asset in its own right.

Summary

The brand name is the *trigger* to the brand proposition. The brand name is therefore a shorthand communication of the brand's personality and positioning. Brand names can be seen as a 'spectrum' ranging from free-standing names such as Kodak at the one end to descriptive names such as Dab-it-off at the other, with suggestive brand names like Wash & Go in the middle of the continuum.

There are three alternative naming strategies—stand-alone, endorsement and family—though these classifications may be more apparent than real with stand-alone developing line extensions, endorsed names dropping the endorsement and family names picking them up again.

Successful new brand names are likely to result from a consideration of several key factors. Linguistics is an area where research has indicated the importance of plosives and semantic 'fit'. Distinctiveness, adaptability, international applicability, supporting logos and brand name registration are also key to the development of successful new brand names.

Research into brand name creation has identified a series of steps to aid the development process. These include setting branding objectives, selecting a strategy, specifying the brand name criteria, generating ideas, screening the name and ultimately selecting the best according to the original objectives and criteria.

Once selected, it is of paramount importance that the brand name be registered at home and abroad in order to secure its legal protection. Only then can the brand name assume the status of a legal property in which the manufacturer can invest and on which no other manufacturer may trespass. In this way, the name itself becomes a valuable asset in its own right.

CASE STUDY: The Transax story

The Transax service

In November 1986 a revolutionary new service was launched in the United Kingdom which provided a guarantee to merchants that cheques exceeding the drawer's limit will be honoured. This service, which is now called 'Transax' (see logo), is provided to 35 000 retail outlets, including many of the major high street names—Next, Saxone, Austin Reed, Halfords and Ratners. The service guarantees personal cheques and business cheques up to a prearranged store limit, and all cheques are authorized using a free telephone call. If any guaranteed cheque subsequently 'bounces', Transax reimburses its full value to the merchant and then takes steps to recover the amount outstanding. The Transax service is therefore of considerable benefit to customers and merchants alike. Customers gain a further, potentially less expensive, means to purchase higher cost items and merchants gain a further means to stimulate sales which carries no risk and undue expense.

TRANSAX®

Chequepoint checkmate

When Craig and Marjorie Walsh set up their cheque guarantee service in November 1986 they decided to call it Cheque Point Guarantee Limited. The name had a neat, logical ring to it; it described fully the key benefit of the service and even in its abbreviated form— 'Cheque Point' —lost none of its impact and relevance. The name had been suggested by the advertising agency they had hired to help them launch the new service and the agency dutifully checked the name in Companies House to ensure that it was clear to use.

Imagine their horror, therefore, when, shortly after they had launched 'Cheque Point' at a press reception in London, the Walshes received a letter from solicitors representing Chequepoint Bureau de Change, claiming prior rights in the 'Chequepoint' name and threatening action for 'passing off' if the Walshes did not desist. Not being Londoners, neither Craig nor Marjorie Walsh was aware of Chequepoint's chain of Bureaux de Change, which are largely confined to the West End. Nor was it easy to find out who owned Chequepoint Bureau de Change or how big they were (one of the first things you do when litigation is threatened!).

It is worth pausing here to explain what is meant by 'passing off'.

Passing off

The common law tort of 'passing off' is the original form of action for trade mark owners to defend their rights and interests. In its crudest definition, 'passing off' is to ensure that 'nobody has any right to represent his goods (or services) as the goods (or services) of somebody else' (Lord Chief Justice Halsbury, 1896). This is, however, a rather simplistic view, and the outcome of 'passing off' actions can be difficult to predict, as although there is a line of precedence established over many years, essentially each case turns on its own facts and evidence.

To the layman, however, 'passing off' could perhaps be described as a cake that requires certain ingredients for success to be achieved. These ingredients have been established over the years, and were summed up by Lord Diplock in what has become known as the Advocaat case in 1979; he ruled that in order to sustain an action for passing off the plaintiff must prove:

1 that there is a misrepresentation
2 made by a trader in the course of trade
3 to prospective customers of his, or ultimate consumers of goods or services supplied by him
4 which is calculated to injure the business or goodwill of another trader (in the sense that this is a reasonably foreseeable consequence)
5 which causes actual damage to the business or goodwill of a trader by whom the action is brought.

The rights which 'passing off' is designed to protect are only acquired through use in the UK, and as a general rule, the greater the reputation, the greater the rights to protect.

Thus Chequepoint Bureau de Change would need to prove that damage to its well-known business was caused by confusion arising from Cheque Point Guarantee's use of the name. A tall order, perhaps, in view of the dissimilarity of the services provided by the two companies—Chequepoint Bureau de Change only provided foreign exchange services, and Cheque Point Guarantee only provided indemnity service to merchants accepting sterling cheques.

Should the Walshes oppose the action or should they give in and change their name? On the one hand, they had just launched their business at considerable expense and were concerned lest they lose credibility (a vital ingredient in the service they supplied) with their hard-won customers; on the other, they were a tiny organization with limited resources confronting a mysterious opponent of unknown size and determination. They decided to fight.

The hearing

Accordingly, Craig Walsh thought it was important to convince the court that not only did Cheque Point Guarantee Limited offer a very different service from Chequepoint Bureau de Change—and therefore had no interest in competing for its business—but that Chequepoint Bureau de Change's name had little recognition and goodwill, and thus that there was little to 'pass off'. In order to prove the latter, the Walshes commissioned MORI, the well-known market research company, to interview a sample of customers who had just used a Chequepoint Bureau de Change. MORI's interviewers asked the customers whether they could remember the name of the bureau de change they had just used, and only a small minority could do so with any accuracy. Whether this was instrumental or not it is difficult to say, but on the second day of the hearing, having let slip that he still did not understand that you could cash a cheque at a bureau de change—thus questioning perhaps the relevance of the name in this connection—the judge called a recess. It was then that the Walshes were approached by the 'other side' and offered a settlement if they agreed to change their name in six months, a clear sign that Chequepoint Bureau de Change no longer were confident that their case was cut and dried. As the Walshes were not in a position to fight a protracted action (a typical passing off action can take many months to complete, with high costs and no guarantee of a successful outcome), they accepted—albeit with considerable reluctance.

Enter Interbrand!

With only six months to develop a new name and implement this in sales literature, stationery, business forms, window stickers, etc., the Walshes had no time for delay. Shortly after their court case, therefore, they approached Interbrand, the international branding consultancy, with the brief that they should create and register a new name and identity for their business as rapidly as possible.

Interbrand's procedure for developing brand names is entirely pragmatic. It is informed by the simple truth that, to be effective, brand names must help position the product or service they identify in an attractive and appealing way, they must be free of negative linguistic or cultural associations and they must be available to use and protect as trade marks. Given the very large number of trade marks that already exist it is therefore necessary to approach the creation of

a new brand name in an open-minded and creative way. There is
no point in following familiar, well-trodden creative 'routes' because
it is almost certain that someone else has been there first. (Is there
not a close similarity in meaning between the names 'Visa' and
'Access'?)

So the task of developing a name to replace 'Cheque Point' became
not just a creative challenge but a strategic one: there were
fundamental issues of identity and positioning at play and these
needed to be addressed by Interbrand's project team in an
appropriate, but original, manner.

This, surprisingly, was easier than it seemed. Looking back, 'Cheque
Point' was a good name: it was certainly simple and appropriate—but
it was neither particularly distinctive nor precise (as the court case
showed!). It was felt, therefore, that a new name which alluded more
closely to the nature of the service was required, and the creative
team drew up a brief which specified a wide range of ideas, from the
almost abstract 'Green Light' (signifying approval) to the very
descriptive 'Cheque Mate' (reassuringly close to the original name).
Between these extremes lay a fertile middle ground where suggestion
and innuendo could coexist comfortably with the exigencies of
protectability.

It was from this middle ground that 'Transax' emerged. Now, with the
benefit of hindsight, it seems so obviously right; yet it was very far from
Interbrand's thoughts at the outset of the project. Interbrand
brainstormed, using group sessions with word experts; they used in-
house resources (including name-creation software and a Name Bank)
and professional copywriters. All the ideas that emerged from these
processes were passed back to the project team who then developed
a 'long list' of candidate names which met broadly the
communication criteria agreed. Following internal discussion and
preliminary scrutiny by Markforce Associates, Interbrand's group trade
mark legal consultancy, a list of 50 names was selected for
presentation to the clients. Fifty names may seem a lot—but a great
deal of ore has to be fed into the hopper to produce a small amount
of pure gold, the attractive and protectable brand name. It must be
remembered, too, that the clients had just come through a thoroughly
disagreeable and potentially destructive experience, so this time
everything had to be right. And for Interbrand, too, the challenge was
a stiff one. Whatever names were submitted would inevitably be
compared with 'Cheque Point', which now had a significance to the
clients that quite outweighed its utility. Interbrand, therefore, had to
ensure that the creative task was done thoroughly and that all possible
'avenues' were explored to provide the best possible choice.

At the presentation, therefore, names as varied as Assent (rejected
because of the similarity to 'Access', but subsequently used by Barclays
Bank!), Cheqtel (rejected because, while using 'check' or 'cheque'

can produce attractive, relevant names, they were felt to be uncreative and somewhat redolent of the past) and Transax were submitted and discussed at considerable length. Transax was selected as a strong candidate and, together with several others, was then searched for availability as a service mark in Class 36 of the UK Trade Marks Register. In parallel, Interbrand initiated a small market research exercise, designed to establish the relative acceptability of the shortlisted names, taking into account the agreed criteria. This took place with approximately 100 potential users of the service and their selection was overwhelmingly in favour of 'Transax'.

'Transax' meanwhile emerged unscathed from the legal searching process (which took only two weeks or so) and the clients decided to adopt the name—although it has to be said that they still retained a strong preference for 'Cheque Point'!

'Stage Two' of the exercise could now commence. This comprised two important exercises. First, Markforce Associates filed an application to register 'Transax' in Class 36, thus insulating the name by staking prior rights, while solicitors formed Transax Financial Services Limited. Then Interbrand's design team started work on a visual identity for the new name, with the brief that this should be distinctively different from the old 'Cheque Point' logo—and of course 'Access' and 'Visa' with whom it would compete for visibility at the point of sale.

Interbrand's designers developed a wide range of concepts, the best of which are illustrated below. It will be noted that they differ only in the nature of the lines above and below the 'Transax' name, and show that by varying these the whole tone of the design can be changed.

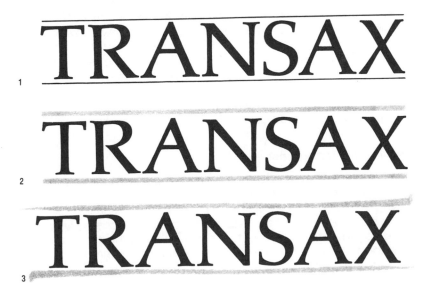

In treatment 1 (thin black lines) the logo appears weak. In treatment 2, the thick lines make it too rigid and heavy. In treatment 3, the informal hand-drawn lines are strong yet relaxed—the preferred effect.

Consider these designs in the context of the Transax service.

Transax guarantees payments of the cheque and, in return, receives a small fee on each transaction. Many customers find it a little unnerving that their 'credit worthiness' is to be investigated by a third party before their cheque is accepted; retailers, on the other hand, want reassurance that Transax is reliable and will stand behind its guarantee. The logo had, therefore, to help in two important respects; it had to reassure retailers and, at the same time, be approachable and not intimidating to consumers. Using fine, delicate lines is somehow unsatisfactory, both aesthetically and practically. The lines make a logo a little weak, and the name somehow floats in space. It is less reassuring than it should be to retailers, but it is still not approachable or friendly to consumers. The use of the stronger lines in the second logo is an improvement, but the overall effect is somehow too rigid and controlled. The third logo better meets the dual objectives. The informality of the hand-drawn lines helps to relax the logo, which would be significant to consumers, yet it is still a strong, reassuring logo from the retailer's point of view. This logo is also more aesthetically pleasing; it is less contrived than the others and more the product of thinking, breathing human beings. So, even a straight line can have both aesthetic and practical qualities.

Not surprisingly, implementing the change of name had its difficulties. First, existing customers had to be reassured that the name change was being made for the very best of reasons and would in no way affect the quality of the service they received. Next, new stationery had to be ordered, brochures printed and window stickers redesigned (try persuading several thousand retailers to strip from their windows a heavily gummed decal and you will understand some of the pleasures of implementing a name change—Transax eventually offered £1 to charity for each 'Cheque Point' sticker returned!). However the task was accomplished with relatively few problems; the 'Transax' name was well received by old and new customers alike, by the ever-growing ranks of Transax employees, and eventually by the owners of the business!

Maintaining the 'Transax' name

'When a man knows he is to be hanged in a fortnight', said Dr Johnson, 'it concentrates his mind wonderfully.' Had he experienced the horrors of passing off, he no doubt would have expressed the same sentiment. Certainly the experience of the Walshes made them acutely aware of the need to protect their 'intellectual property', and this they did with commendable zeal. Not only did they seek to protect, through registration, their interest in the 'Transax' name in the UK and internationally, but they resisted attempts of more than one British financial institution to adopt a similar name for their services!

During the financial year 1990, Transax guaranteed some 5.3 million cheques with a combined value in excess of £700 million, a significant increase over the previous year. Thus growth was achieved despite a period of economic uncertainty and a downturn in high street spending, and underlines the concern that merchants feel regarding security of payment.

Transax is now the largest cheque guarantee company in the world outside the United States, and currently has three overseas subsidiaries, in Ireland, France and Australia. The 'Transax' name is extremely well known and respected among a very wide range of outlets, and the 'Transax' trade mark—the registered property of Transax Financial Services Limited—is inviolable. The strength of the legal title the company enjoys in its brand name and the investment it has made in developing its service means that the 'Transax' name now has considerable value in its own right. However, this is very far from the situation that applied back in June 1986.

Conclusions

What this case illustrates, therefore, is the importance of careful trade mark selection and registration. Unless you lay claim to and protect your trade mark through the provisions the law allows, you will always be vulnerable to the depredations of third parties. Nowhere, arguably, is this more important than in the area of services where the 'product' supplied is of an intangible nature, and the reputation a 'proxy' for the quality of services. Unless these precautions are taken you can never be wholly confident that you alone will reap the benefits from the investment you have made in your business. In a sense the Walshes were fortunate that disaster befell them when it did—at a very early stage in the development of their business. They had the opportunity to start afresh with a new (and Interbrand would argue, a better) identity, and have subsequently built one of the very few enduring new brands on the UK financial service scene.

References

Blackett, T. *Researching Brand Names*, MIP 6.3, 1988.

McNeal, J. and Zeren, L., 'Brand name selection for consumer products', *MSU Business Topics*, Spring 1981.

Morita, A., Reingold, E. and Shimomura, M., *Made in Japan, Akio Morita and Sony*, Fontana, Harper Collins, 1988.

Murphy, J. *Brand Strategy*, Director Books, 1990.

Ries, A. and Trout, J., *Positioning: The Battle for the Mind*, 1st edition revised, McGraw-Hill, 1986.

Shipley, D., Hooley, G. and Wallace, S., 'The brand name
    development process', *International Journal of Advertising*, **7**, 1988.
Slater, K., 'Kaliber, an international success in non-alcoholic beer',
    KAE Conference Speech, 1988.
Vanden Bergh, B., Alder, K. and Oliver, L., *Linguistic Distinction among
    Top Brand Names*, Institute of Advertising Research, August/
    September 1987.

3

Building the brand proposition

A successful brand—one that stands the test of time—is a brand that says something distinctive, and it is this point of distinction that is embodied in the brand proposition. But how do consumers recognize what the brand stands for, and in what ways is the brand proposition communicated? This chapter explores the operational process of building the brand proposition through different communication campaigns. In some cases the emphasis of the campaign is on building the brand personality. In other cases, the positioning and personality are so inextricably linked that the campaign both repositions the brand and modifies its personality.

Advertising

Advertising is often considered one of the most effective media for communicating with the consumer. Very often the consumer is captive, sitting in front of a television screen or reading a magazine. This provides an opportunity to establish a relationship with the consumer—a relationship in which the advertising can communicate both a personality and a positioning.

In Farquar (1990), Ogilvy is quoted as saying: 'Every advertisement should be thought of as a contribution to the brand personality.' For mature brands, advertising may seek to reinforce the existing, and hopefully successful, brand proposition. For ageing brands, on the other hand, there may be a need to reposition the brand in ways that make the brand personality more relevant to its target consumer (who may have changed) or to today's life-style (which certainly will have changed), or to both. However, for new brands there will be a need to create an attractive and distinctive brand proposition from nothing. An example here would be Castlemaine XXXX (lager) which first went on sale on draught in 1984. It was launched into an already crowded market of at least 34 brands and one where the 'continental' heritage had already been smashed by Fosters with its Australian-rooted campaign featuring Paul Hogan, the actor.

Castlemaine XXXX took the Australian dimension in another direction. Whereas Fosters brought Australia to the UK in a series of scenes featuring a macho Hogan out-of-step with British culture, Castlemaine XXXX took the UK consumer to Australia by featuring the Australian outback, singled-minded, hard-drinking Australian inhabitants and, above all, the Australian preference for Castlemaine XXXX, even at the expense of friendship and marriage!

Table 3.1 demonstrates the rapid establishment of the 'Australian' dimension for Castlemaine XXXX from 30 to 91 per cent over a period of six months with significant growth too in both functional attributes and symbolic values. The 'Australian' dimension positions Castlemaine XXXX in the same competitive set as Fosters and other Australian lagers.

Table 3.1   Consumer evaluation of Castlemaine XXXX

	May (%)	June/July (%)	Aug/Sept (%)	Oct/Nov (%)
Identification as Australian (aware of XXXX)	30	74	90	91
Strong in alcohol	21	23	28	27
Particularly good flavour	17	22	27	25
Suitable for sessions with the lads	26	33	37	36
Appeal particularly to younger people	18	30	37	32
A bit different from most	27	27	35	32

Source: Channon (1987).

For mature brands, however, there is the need to reinforce and maintain the existing brand proposition. To quote Ogilvy once more: 'Your advertisement should consistently project the same image year after year' (Farquar 1990).

One way to achieve this is to retain the same advertising slogan over a number of years, for example:

- 'BMW—the Ultimate Driving Machine'
- 'Heineken refreshes the parts other beers can't reach'
- 'Have a break, have a Kit-Kat'

Alternatively, retaining a particular advertising device may achieve consistency in building the brand personality. In the UK, the Tetley Tea Folk, for instance, have featured since 1973. They may be said to communicate 'quality tea from the experts' (functional attribute) as well as 'sharing+neighbourliness' (symbolic values). The Andrex puppy is also an enduring advertising device which communicates functional attributes of 'strength', 'length' and 'softness' together with the symbolic values of 'love' and 'homeliness'.

Eventually, however, the appeal of a mature brand may begin to weaken and it will be necessary to reposition the brand in ways that make it more attractive to existing and new users and relevant to both.

Lucozade is one such brand, 50 years old and originally positioned as an 'aid to recovery'. This defined its competitive set as 'over-the-counter' medicines sold through chemists. It was sickness-related, targeted towards children and by implication for occasional use only. To halt declining sales, a strategic decision was taken to reposition the brand as a source of energy for the more health-conscious consumers of the 1980s, a shift from 'health' to 'healthy' (Hoggan 1988). The competitive set hence changed to include other refreshing drinks. Its point of distinction, however, was maintained through its personality which retained the functional attribute of 'energy' provided through its glucose ingredient. The first television commercial featured a housewife getting through her busy day with Lucozade. Follow-up commercials featured Daley Thompson, the athlete, as a machismo, symbol of energy. Then the brand was 'taken onto the streets' with the introduction of 330 ml cans, a range of flavour variants and a poster campaign that featured the brain teasing letters of

N
R
G

The next development was to promote Lucozade as a drink for 'anyone', as research indicated that the Daley Thompson endorsement was projecting a male bias. There followed the 'Energy for the Human Race' campaign featured on posters and in the women's press.

Progressively, advertising was being used to communicate a changing brand more in tune with today's consumer and today's life-style, while at the same time retaining the core energy-giving values which remain at the heart of the Lucozade brand personality. As a result, Lucozade is now perceived as a healthy, energetic, fun-loving drink which all consumers can enjoy. Arguably, the strength of that brand proposition did much to ensure its own rapid recovery from the tampering scare in 1991.

In these examples, advertising has been used to communicate a positioning and/or brand personality which appeals to the target consumer. If, however, the brand fails to deliver the promise of the advertising, then the brand proposition will totter and fall. Advertising merely accelerates the communication process.

Sponsorship

Brand sponsorship can also be used to build or maintain a brand proposition through the associative link between the event and the sponsoring brand. This has led to massive growth in the sponsorship medium where spend levels have risen from £35 million in 1980 to £325 million in 1991 (Mintel 1991).

The Bell's Scottish Open, for instance, gives the brand (Bell's) significant television exposure and, incidentally, exposure to a product area, spirits, normally barred from the television screen. Television coverage from the Gleneagles course helps reinforce the Bell's brand personality of Scottish tradition and heritage. But, in addition, it helps graft onto the brand personality, symbolic values like 'health', 'open-air freshness' and 'vigour' which help reposition the brand away from an ageing, home-closeted, target market towards a younger, more active sector of the population, moving the brand towards a competitive set which includes spirits like vodka and Bacardi, white rum.

The associative link may be said to work both ways, from sponsored to sponsor (more usually) or from sponsor to sponsored. The next example illustrates the latter. When, for instance, football was suffering heavily and negatively from the combined disasters of Hillsborough and Heysell (1986), Barclays Bank took up sponsorship of the Football League. It provided a much needed 'lift' to the game through its associative link with a 'solid', 'respectable', 'secure' organization like Barclays Bank.

More recently, sponsorship has entered the broadcast medium where there is massive scope for reinforcing or building the brand personality through association with a particular programme.

PowerGen, the UK electricity generator, was the first to enter broadcast sponsorship when, in September 1989, they signed a contract for just under £2 million for a year's sponsorship of ITV's networked weather forecasts. By March 1990, spontaneous awareness had risen from 3 to 37 per cent and prompted awareness from 39 to 59 per cent. Important also was the establishment of a distinct and professional brand personality for PowerGen prior to its flotation on the stockmarket in February 1991 through its association with the professionalism of the weather broadcasters.

Barclaycard's (Visa) sponsorship of 'Wish you Were Here...?' (travel programme) also uses the associative link to build or reinforce its brand proposition, which is particularly apt since three million Barclaycard holders travel abroad annually. It builds the brand's positioning as an alternative to travellers' cheques and foreign currency and also reinforces the brand personality through its association with the quality and profesionalism of the programme.

Sponsorship of any kind, therefore, is a marraige between partners where there is sharing of common values. In Barclaycard and 'Wish you Were Here...?', for instance, there is the opportunity to reinforce travel associations. Where there are differences (Bell's whisky and Bell's Scottish Open, for example) there is scope both to revitalize the brand personality with more desirable and more relevant attributes and values and to reposition the brand alongside 'younger' drinks.

Sales promotion

Sales promotion is often associated with relatively short-term, tactical activities like reduced price, extra product, couponing and free gifts. Such activity is geared towards achieving short-term sales uplifts and cannot claim to build the brand proposition. Indeed, the Harris survey into sales promotion trends (Harris International Marketing 1991) found that 92 per cent of managers evaluated promotions in terms of sales effect. Only a third considered brand image, which forms part of what we have termed brand personality. Research by Ehrenberg (1991) concluded that: 'Consumer promotions have large, immediate sales effects but do not appear to be brand building.' The international study of sales promotion and its effect on sales of established, FMCG products, showed no noticeable effect on sales outside the promotional period, nor did it increase repeat purchasing, i.e. brand loyalty. In other words, sales promotion is short-lived and tactical rather than long term and strategic.

However, Ehrenberg's concept of brand building relates to sales volume and growth, whereas in the communication mix brand building is more likely to refer to the development and reinforcement of the brand proposition.

One sales promotion campaign that can claim genuine brand-building properties was the Heinz Centenary Year in 1986. This campaign demonstrates the range and creative scope available through sales promotion. Under the theme of 'Heinz Meanz Businezz', a programme of seven major consumer promotions was put together encompassing some of the key Heinz brands, such as Heinz Baked Beans, Heinz Soups, Heinz Tomato Ketchup, Heinz Salad varieties and Heinz Sponge Puddings.

- *The Heinz Hundreds* promotion was featured on 55 million cans of Heinz Baked Beans, Spaghetti and Soups. On offer was an equivalent £1 cashback for every seven labels (giving consumers over half their money back) plus the chance to win £100 000 at an award ceremony held at London's Inn on the Park (hotel) and hosted by TV's 3-2-1 presenter, Ted Rogers. At the time this was probably the biggest cash prize ever offered by a food manufacturer in the UK.

- *Feed Baby Free* was the biggest baby promotion ever run. It targeted 1 million mums and attracted 90 000 applications. The offer entailed a full refund for every five labels of Heinz baby food cans and jars. In addition, a free savings book was given to mums, which offered £1 for every 50 labels collected (equivalent to a 2p discount on every item) and which effectively lasted until the baby had moved on to normal family food. Most of the key supermarkets participated in the promotion, including Sainsbury, Boots, Tesco, Asda, Safeway, Gateway and the Co-op.

- *Treasure Hunt* offered a top-prize win of £57 000. Maps of Great Britain flooded the country though the colour press. Using 10 cryptic clues, consumers were asked to place a cross where they thought the Heinz treasure might be buried. At the Grand Final at a beach location in Guernsey, 10 finalists were asked to choose one of the 100 squares, aided only by a low-angle photograph, to reveal the amount of their winnings—£1000, £10 000 or £57 000. Anneka Rice made a celebrity appearance and was also given a cheque for £1000 for her favourite charity, the British Deaf Association.

- *Centenary Give-Away* offered (for the first time) free Heinz products on baked beans, soup and spaghetti, constituting what was described at the time as the 'most generous refund offer from Heinz'.

- *Party of the Century* invited children aged 5 to 16 years to enter a simple competition and tie-breaker to win one of 100 4-day visits to Disney World, Florida, with three relatives or friends. The offer was featured on-pack across a wide range of children's beans and pasta products, including Haunted House, Beans & Sausage, Tomato Ketchup and Macaroni Cheese.

- *A Taste of Yesteryear* offered a replica model T-Ford van for £1.99 plus two labels from Heinz Tomato Ketchup and Ploughman's Pickle. The offer was featured on millions of pack flashes and around 100 000 applications were received.

- *Car-a-Day* was the final 'blockbuster' promotion of the year which featured a free prize draw for a car every day for 100 days. In addition, three Sherpa minibuses were given away to local charities. Described as the 'biggest promotion in the UK trade', Car-a-Day was launched at Longbridge, the main manufacturing plant of Austin Rover, partners in the promotion. The launch event involved a spectacular demonstration of music and sound, laser beams and a selection of Austin Rover cars, which were driven around the conference stage. The promotion was featured on 60 million Heinz labels (see Figure 3.1).

With a budget spend of little more than the previous year, significant sales increases were demonstrated for the Heinz Centenary Year with an increase in volume sales of 4.4 per cent equivalent to an extra 120 million packages or £19 million in added sterling value.

Arguably, however, the key benefit of the range and breadth of these centenary year promotions was to build on the warmth and confidence most consumers felt towards the Heinz brand name (see logo). By strengthening the Heinz brand personality in terms of symbolic values like 'quality', 'reliability', 'care for all the family', the Heinz Centenary Year not only built on its past but invested in its future.

Another campaign that can claim genuine brand-building properties is the Pepsi Challenge. This involves a world-wide programme around a 'blind' taste test between Pepsi and 'another leading cola', namely Coke. The campaign began in Dallas, Texas, in 1975, came to the United Kingdom in 1988 and was simultaneously run in 24 countries around the world including Brazil, Holland, Australia and Mexico.

Figure 3.1 Car-a-Day promotional cans

In 1991, in the United Kingdom, the Pepsi Challenge booths which featured at major shopping centres, and special event rigs at county shows and pop concerts, were redesigned to provide a stronger, more impactful, teen-focused presence (see Figure 3.2). The 'Take the Pepsi Challenge' logo was also redesigned to communicate both diet and regular Pepsi variants. It featured prominently on all the sampling booths, special event rigs, Challenge uniforms and promotional materials, including sampling cups and give-away coupon books.

In addition, there was the noise and razzmatazz of music. There were video shows around the special event rigs. There was also local radio advertising and there were the personality girls in Pepsi-liveried sweatshirts and trousers who were briefed to be: 'professional, fun, warm and enthusiastic'.

The result of all this orchestrated, promotional activity, identified by qualitative research, was to provide Pepsi with 'local, celebrity status'. It demonstrated that Pepsi was 'big', Pepsi was 'confident', Pepsi was

Figure 3.2 The Pepsi Challenge rig

'fighting Coke'. Arguably, this type of sales promotion had a lot more to do with building the brand personality and positioning of Pepsi than effecting short-term sales gains for the brand.

Sales promotion in the 1990s is adopting a much broader role than simply pulling the trigger to buy. The examples above may be said to build and reinforce the brand proposition in a consistent and on a longer term basis than has been hitherto acknowledged.

Pack design

Pack design might be considered an ongoing free advertisement for the brand, both in-store and at home. It used to be known as the 'silent salesman'. Now it plays a much more active role in the marketplace. Not only does it say 'Here I am' but also 'Buy me because you'll like me. I'm your friend'. In other words, the consumer is being given a reason to buy, that reason being its brand proposition.

Good packaging communicates the brand proposition through a series of visual cues such as logo, graphics, colour, layout. Mackay (1990) identifies three types of visual cue with varying contributions to the brand. First, there is the *identifier*, a key symbol which triggers brand recognition, e.g. the 'Captain' on the Birds Eye packs to convey 'warmth' and 'paternalism'. Secondly, the *contributor*, which may not aid brand recognition but may play a more positive role in communicating symbolic values, e.g. the Ochil Hills on the Highland Spring label to communicate 'freshness' and 'purity' (see case study). Thirdly, *passengers*, like the red spot on the 7-Up cans, which are simply there but make no direct contribution to the brand proposition.

Lewis (1991) describes packaging as a 'dialogue with the consumer'. She extols the value of an active pack in communicating the brand personality, first through symbols, e.g. the Fairy Liquid baby (soft and gentle), the Dettol sword (defender of health) and secondly through graphics, e.g. SR, snow and mountains (bright, white teeth) and the Oil of Ulay nurse (professional skin care).

Colour, too, may trigger brand recognition and as a result the associations that go with that brand, e.g. Cadbury purple and Kodak yellow. However, additional visual clues may also be required to prevent the Cadbury purple triggering the Silk Cut brand proposition and the Kodak yellow triggering Hertz (car rentals).

Creating striking packaging for a new brand launch may make a significant contribution to establishing an identifiable brand proposition in the consumer's mind. Phileas Fogg, the brand of crisps and savoury snacks, provides a good example. Its launch packaging involved unique, distinctive, intriguing pack graphics that invited the consumer to perceive its brand personality in similar terms. In addition, as a new product, the distinctive packaging gave it a unique positioning in the marketplace, perceptually quite distant from conventional savoury snacks. Other examples include Body Shop (cosmetics and toiletries) packaging, offering simple, but effective graphics which suggest a natural, no-nonsense brand personality, and Masson Light, a non-alcoholic wine, conveying symbolic values of 'crispness' and 'lightness' through its subtle colour tones and elegant pale green lettering.

Established brands such as Bell's Scotch whisky and Heinz baked beans, also need to 'talk' to their consumers to reassure them of their continued heritage and tradition within a modern context. In these instances, design changes must be subtle and ideally 'unnoticed' by the consumer.

When Heinz beans, for example, updated its packaging, the familiar turquoise was maintained but the Heinz logo was made fuller and fatter, the keystone above the brand name was broadened, and the 'with tomato sauce' was changed from turquoise to gold. The difference in design was hardly noticeable and hence reassured consumers that the brand was still 'their friend', while at the same time bringing it graphically up to date.

Public relations

At the heart of public relations is the issue of reputation and, in the context of this book, brand reputation. In helping to build that reputation, public relations sets out to influence and manage the channels of communication be they magazines or newspaper articles, company reports or television programmes. From these channels of communication consumers form their opinions and attitudes about the brand proposition. Unlike other communication media, however, the task of public relations is very often to overturn negative perceptions of a brand proposition and, to that extent, its role is more challenging.

One such example concerns Research International, the largest ad hoc market research company in the world, also known unfortunately as the 'largest unknown research company'. Its brand personality was described as 'bureaucratic' and 'inaccessible'.

A new brand proposition was developed which defined Research International as 'the most effective and best resourced problem solving research company in the world'.

A major marketing initiative was implemented via a staged press launch of 25 000 stickers and press releases for key marketing and trade magazines. The initiative involved a free HELPLINE, offering research buyers free advice on any aspect of research, whether it be the interpretation of data or the setting up of pan-European research. Using a special exchange which bypassed the normal switchboard, telephone handsets were placed on the desks of 10 top Research International directors, one of whom was always on 'duty' between 9 a.m. and 6 p.m. Monday to Friday. Additional media releases were developed to announce new services and new research techniques being offered by Research International.

In this way, public relations was used to overturn negative perceptions of Research International among research buyers and, importantly, to build a positive brand personality involving functional attributes like 'good resources' and 'international experience' as well as symbolic values like 'warmth', 'innovation' and 'accessibility'.

The need for consistency

Although this chapter has focused on individual contributions to the brand proposition through different elements in the communication mix, the strength, consistency and durability of that brand proposition will depend on the extent to which the communication mix is integrated. It will also depend upon the consistency of the proposition build over time. Changes, where necessary, must be gradual yet consistently built into each communication employed.

Summary

This chapter has examined the operational process of building the brand proposition through the communication mix.

Examples of long-running advertising slogans and devices such as the Andrex puppy illustrate the use of communication media to build and reinforce the functional attributes and symbolic values of the brand. Other advertising examples include ageing brands like Lucozade, where there was a need to increase its relevancy in terms of both positioning and personality to today's consumers, or new brands like Castlemaine XXXX, where there was a need to create a brand proposition from nothing.

Sponsorship, particularly broadcast sponsorship, builds the brand personality through associative links between the sponsored event/programme and the sponsoring brand. PowerGen is an example of a 'new' brand which has acquired a distinct and professional brand personality through its association with the professionalism of the weather broadcasters.

'Take the Pepsi Challenge' exemplifies a sales promotion campaign which has a lot more to do with building Pepsi's 'confident', 'big' brand personality and a positioning that challenges Coca-Cola than with effecting short-term sales gains.

Pack design can be used to project actively a brand's proposition through its on-pack visual cues. The launch packaging for Phileas Fogg is an example of 'unique', 'distinctive', 'intriguing' pack graphics designed to communicate an attractive brand personality, while at the same time giving the brand a unique positioning in the marketplace.

Public relations can be used particularly effectively to turn a negative brand proposition into a positive one.

Finally, the point has to be made that communication of a consistent brand proposition can only be achieved if each element of the communication mix forms part of an integrated campaign.

CASE STUDY: The repackaging of Highland Spring

Market background

The UK mineral water market grew throughout the 1980s at an average rate of over 30 per cent per annum. By 1987 the market was estimated to be worth over 75 million.

Nevertheless, the potential for further growth was seen as astronomical; British consumers still drank under 2 litres per capita per year, which was almost insignificant when compared to our European neighbours (e.g. France 71 litres, Germany 46 litres, Italy 30 litres).

The fast rate of growth, combined with future prospects, made this one of the most competitive markets in the UK. By 1987, over 80 brands were manoeuvring for position, and the battle for market share had become increasingly fierce. Pricing had, in real terms, been falling since 1982 but advertising expenditure was rapidly increasing (more than tripling in the last two years).

Perrier virtually created the UK market and continued to hold an impregnable position with a 40 per cent share of 'Sparkling' (the largest product sector, accounting for nearly two-thirds of sales). Meanwhile, Evian dominated the 'Still' sector with a 30 per cent share. Most other brands (including Highland Spring) were available in both 'Sparkling' and 'Still'. It was believed that, as the market matured, there would be room for only two or three major brands besides Perrier and Evian. Highland Spring was determined to be one of them.

Brand background

Prior to the October 1987 relaunch, Highland Spring was available not only as a brand in its own right, but also as a quasi-own-label (i.e. major multiples were selling the product with a label showing their own name and that of 'Highland Spring').

This situation had arisen partly because of EC regulations which demand that the source of mineral water is described on-pack. The words 'Highland Spring' were being used to describe the source as well as the brand.

By 1986, as competition in the market intensified, Highland Spring 'brand' share was in decline, and the company was becoming increasingly dependent on quasi-own-label for survival. And in a market where increasing competition was already exerting a downward pressure on margins (average price per litre fell from 65p in 1982 to 52p in 1985), Highland Spring Ltd were inevitably making even lower margins on quasi-own-label than on 'brand'.

A difficult choice had to be made. Either (a) the brand would be allowed to die and Highland Spring reduced to commodity status, available only via own-label arrangements (no longer even a quasi-own-label, but now an own-label proper as the words 'Highland Spring' would add no branded values at all in the absence of a brand to feed off); or (b) an attempt could be made to restore the fortunes of the brand itself via significant marketing investment. This latter course, however, would almost certainly require the withdrawal of the Highland Spring name from own-label product, as the continued existence of quasi-own-label would undoubtedly undermine any efforts to build the values of the brand proper.

Bravely (for by this time quasi-own-label made up the bulk of Highland Spring's business), Highland Spring's new management decided, in mid-1986, on the latter course of action.

Accordingly, the Cope Matthews advertising agency was briefed to develop advertising proposals and (at the agency's suggestion) Michael Peters & Partners were briefed to look at the design of the Highland Spring brand identity.

At the same time, negotiations were begun with the major multiples whereby Highland Spring Ltd would continue to supply own-label product, but no longer under the Highland Spring name. This, in turn (to comply with the labelling regulations), meant that separate, dedicated bore-holes would need to be established for each of the major own-label customers, so that each would have its own 'source' of natural mineral water.

It was decided that Highland Spring would be relaunched as a brand in Autumn 1987.

Relaunch marketing objectives

- To reposition Highland Spring as a premium mineral water brand.

- To increase distribution of Highland Spring brand.

- To increase the value of the Highland Spring brand.

- To reverse the brand's declining share-trend and restore it to growth.

- To protect the position of Highland Spring Ltd as a major supplier of own-label product, but no longer under the Highland Spring name.

Relaunch design brief

In the context of the overall marketing objectives, the role of design was to create a stronger, more distinctive brand identity for Highland Spring, positioning it at the premium end of the market as 'the definitive Scottish mineral water'.

The target market was defined as ABC1 adults, aged 25–44. TGI analysis and qualitative research (conducted by The Research Business) were used to help build up a picture of their habits and attitudes relating to mineral water. In summary, it was intended to appeal to health-conscious individuals who liked to think of themselves as sophisticated and discerning, motivated by 'quality of life' as much as by status.

Among mineral waters, Perrier was (predictably) the gold standard—but we detected a slight undercurrent of (perhaps jingoistic) rejection of its overt 'Frenchness'. More importantly, it was found that Perrier's French origins (while undoubtedly endowing that brand with a chic, sophisticated personality) had very little to say about the product itself. The Scottish Highlands, by contrast, could—if treated in the proper manner—lend important credibility to communication of relevant product values (pure, natural, refreshing).

Highland Spring's proposition could then be built around these core product values, supported by the product's origins in the Ochil Hills—a spectacular and unspoilt area at the foot of the Scottish Highlands.

Figure 3.3 (a) Old packaging for Highland Spring

Figure 3.3 (b) New packaging for Highland Spring

The vital thing was to get the brand's personality right; Scottish, but without being 'tartan-tweed'; healthy and vigorous, but at the same time refined and civilized. Qualitative research was a vital tool in helping to define this brand personality.

Consumers found the personality of the old Highland Spring design to be garish, loud, at best 'cheap and cheerful' (Figure 3.3(a)). Using photo collages, these findings were amplified by consumers' image-associations. It became clear that the old design — while communicating 'Scottish' — was associated with quite the wrong kind of Scottish imagery for a premium mineral water. Consumers were picking out images of Scotland 'as seen by Japanese golfing tourists'; loud, brash and invariably old-fashioned imagery of haggis and sporrans and tartan shortbread; 'Jock from down the road'; 'Scottish football supporters'. The Research Business concluded that 'Current Highland Spring has downmarket associations, which lack any connotations of freshness and undermine the product name.'

By contrast, when asked to select imagery appropriate to the 'ideal' Scottish mineral water, consumers put together a collage of clean air, salmon, lochs, malt whisky, subtle tartans and mountain streams.

The resulting image-boards were at the heart of the final briefing to the design team.

The creative solution

Six initial design concepts were created to this brief, and put into qualitative research to provide guidance for design development.

These concepts reflected various approaches in terms of colour and typography, different aspects of Scottish imagery (some more overt than others), varying degrees of emphasis on the product's Ochil Hills source, and different positions and combinations of labels. The bottle shape itself was predetermined, but the various approaches to labelling created apparently different bottle shapes.

According to The Research Business, 'all the new design concepts convey better quality'. However, one concept in particular stood out as best meeting the brief. It succeeded in conveying 'Scottishness, class, sophistication and freshness', and in the words of one consumer 'it looks elegant enough to bathe in' (prompted by which, an 'asses milk' NPD project was briefly considered, but wiser counsel prevailed).

With minor modifications in the light of these research findings (for example, the original concept included long and detailed copy on the lower label, but this was felt to be 'over-the-top') this concept was developed and mocked-up for a further stage of qualitative research, again conducted by The Research Business.

Included in a brand-mapping exercise, with no indication to consumers that this was a test design, it evoked a 'very positive reaction'. Consistently positioned with Perrier in terms of quality and appeal.' It was 'seen to have integrity and individuality' and the minor negatives raised in the first research had now been eliminated.

The developed concept was therefore progressed and became the new Highland Spring brand identity for the relaunch in October 1987 (Figure 3.3(b)).

Evaluation

The new design was subjected to a quantified evaluation against the old design, on criteria distilled from the brief. As Table 3.2 shows, the new design outscored the old by a significant margin on every dimension.

The new design therefore was felt to be effective in helping to achieve Highland Spring's marketing objectives. Thorough qualitative research had helped to define the strategy and guide the design process. And quantified research confirmed that the new design was indeed on-strategy. But would it work in the marketplace?

Table 3.2 Highland Spring design evaluation
(Base=145, consumers ABC1, 25–34, London area: 65% female, 35% male)

	% Agree strongly with statements:	
	Old design	New design
A particularly refreshing mineral water	13	50
A high-quality mineral water	15	62
Pure and natural	39	68
My friends would like it	17	52
For sophisticated people	7	39
A classy design	5	66
For health-conscious people	28	54
Looks cheap	62	6

Source: The Research Business.

In the months following Highland Spring's relaunch, competition in the mineral water market grew even more fierce. Advertising expenditure continued to show dramatic annual increases (Figure 3.4); new brands were launched at the rate of nearly one a month; and pressure on margins continued to be felt as the major multiples' share of sales continued to grow.

Despite the increased competition in the marketplace, every one of Highland Spring's marketing objectives was achieved. In summary:

● *Reposition Highland Spring as a premium mineral water brand*

Average Highland Spring retail price per litre grew +27 per cent between September 1987 and September 1988, despite the overall market price holding fairly stable. Even market leader Perrier only increased in price +5 per cent across the year (see Table 3.3 for details).

Highland Spring's user profile moved from a downmarket bias (compared to 'any mineral water') in 1986 to an upmarket bias in 1988 (see Table 3.4 for details).

In more recent qualitative research, by The Research Business (August 1988), Highland Spring packaging was again examined and 'received very positive reactions from all age groups (many even preferred it to Perrier packaging), communicating an expensive, upmarket, clean and natural drink'.

● *Increase distribution of Highland Spring brand*

Effective sterling store distribution grew from 19 per cent in September 1987 to 35 per cent in September 1988 (see Table 3.5 for details).

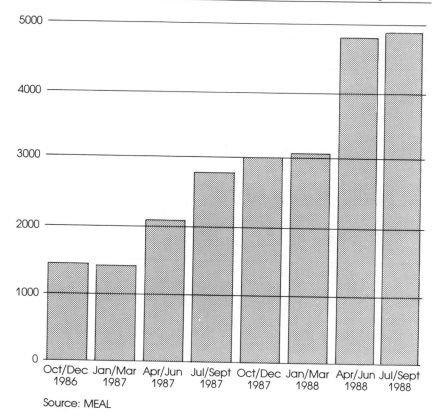

Source: MEAL

Figure 3.4 Mineral water advertising: MAT expenditure (£'000)
Source: MEAL.

Table 3.3   Average retail pricing

	Highland Spring Sept. 1988 v Sept. 1987 Index	Perrier Sept. 1988 v Sept. 1987 Index
UK total	127	105
London	140	104
South	98	104
Anglia	151	108
Wales/Westward	166	105
Central	157	107
Lancashire	127	104
Yorkshire	154	101
Tyne–Tees	104	102
Scotland	123	103

Source: Nielsen.

Table 3.4 Highland Spring user profiles 1986 v 1988

Indices v UK population	1986 Any mineral water	1986 Highland Spring	1988 Any mineral water	1988 Highland Spring
AB	201	176	187	195
C1	126	137	125	127
C2DE	62	66	68	65
15–24	109	93	104	92
25–34	123	141	114	116
35–44	107	108	120	118
45–54	108	119	103	109
55–64	86	78	90	108
65+	68	65	71	65

Source: BMRB/TGI.

Table 3.5 Highland Spring distribution (grocery)

	Effective £ Distribution Sept. 1987	Effective £ Distribution Sept. 1988	(Index)
UK total	19	35	(184)
London	12	36	(300)
South	20	52	(260)
Anglia	6	18	(300)
Wales/Westward	12	25	(208)
Central	17	25	(147)
Lancashire	22	34	(155)
Yorkshire	21	33	(157)
Tyne–Tees	46	57	(124)
Scotland	39	48	(123)

Source: Nielsen.

- *Increase the value of the Highland Spring brand*

Detailed margin information is confidential to Highland Spring, but the above increases in average retail price were profitable to both the retail trade and the company.

- *Reverse the brand's declining share-trend and restore it to growth*

As Figure 3.5 shows, share in grocery grew from 2.2 per cent in September 1987 to 3.0 per cent in September 1988, giving a volume increase (allowing also for rising market size) of nearly +50 per cent. Owing to the price increases, value share grew even faster.

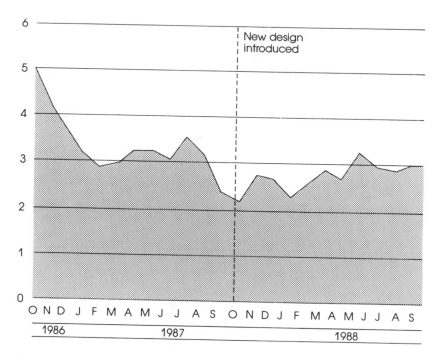

Figure 3.5 Highland Spring volume shares (grocery)
Source: Nielsen.

Table 3.6 Highland Spring shares (off-licences)

	Aug./ Sept. 1987	Aug./ Sept. 1988	Index	6 months to Aug./ Sept. 1987	6 months to Aug./ Sept. 1988	(Index)
Market volume (kilolitres)	2110	2250		3123	3297	
Highland Spring volume share (%)	6.4	9.1	(142)	5.6	9.0	(160)

Source: Stats MR.

In the smaller but nevertheless important Specialist Off-Licence sector (Table 3.6) volume share grew from 6.4 per cent in August/September 1987 to 9.1 per cent in August/September 1988.

- *Protect the position of Highland Spring Ltd as a major supplier of own-label product, but no longer under the Highland Spring name*

Following the withdrawal of quasi-own-label (Figure 3.6), Highland Spring's share of own-label supplies nevertheless increased from 49.8 per cent in September 1987 to 55 per cent in September 1988 (Figure 3.7).

From these results alone, however, it could not necessarily be concluded that the new design was effective in the marketplace. The brand might have succeeded despite rather than because of the design's contribution. It was, therefore, necessary to look at other variables in the marketing mix:

Product

There was no change to the Highland Spring product itself, only to the packaging design. There were no physical changes that could have affected product characteristics.

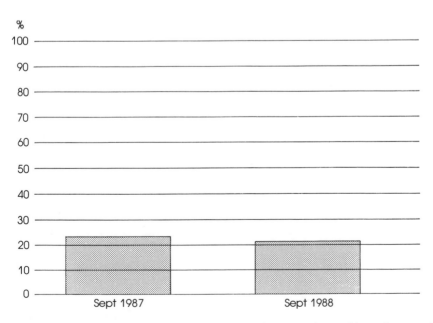

Figure 3.6 Own-label supplied by Highland Spring: volume shares (grocery)
Source: Nielsen.

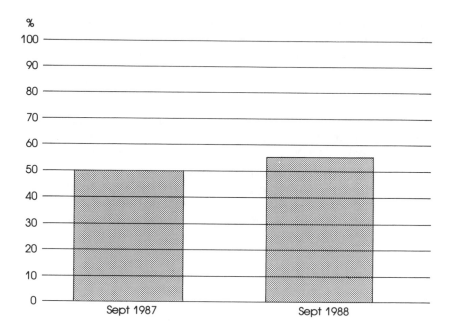

Figure 3.7 Highland Spring Ltd share of all own-label sales
Source: Nielsen.

Table 3.7   Mineral water market regionality

	Total volume Sept. 1987 (%)	Total volume Sept. 1988 (%)	(Index)
London	40.7	43.3	(106)
South	10.0	11.2	(112)
Anglia	7.4	6.5	(88)
Wales/Westward	7.2	6.2	(86)
Central	13.0	11.2	(86)
Lancashire	10.8	10.4	(96)
Yorkshire	5.7	5.5	(96)
Tyne–Tees	1.3	1.3	(100)
Scotland	4.0	4.3	(108)

Source: Nielsen.

Pricing

Highland Spring pricing post-relaunch grew dramatically, whereas competitors' pricing held stable or grew only modestly. Taken together with share data, these figures showed either that Highland Spring was relatively price-insensitive versus the market leader, or that pricing, if anything, would have depressed the volume share gains that might otherwise have been made.

In any event, Highland Spring could not be accused of having 'bought' volume share gains.

Salesforce

There was no significant change in Highland Spring's salesforce or distribution arrangements during the periods under discussion.

Market regionality

Sometimes, significant changes in market regionality can distort overall UK totals. In this case, however, the regionality of the mineral water market as a whole had not changed significantly (see Table 3.7). There had been a slight shift in bias towards London and the South (where Highland Spring's share is above average).

These effects virtually cancelled each other out.

Market seasonality

There are two seasonal peaks in this market — one in summer (June–August) and a smaller one pre-Christmas (November–December). The degree of market seasonality, however, did not differ significantly between 1987 and 1988, and in any case could not in itself explain any differences in Highland Spring's share.

Sales promotion

There was no sales promotion behind Highland Spring at the time of the relaunch. From relaunch to September 1988, the only promotional activity was a low-key leaflet offer ('Buy 4 and send off for a £1 voucher') in Tesco, Gateway and CRS, which ran in May/June 1988.

Consumer redemption was — as always with this kind of promotional device — low, although the promotion was undoubtedly helpful in consolidating distribution and facings in these months. There was no on-pack promotion of Highland Spring.

Advertising

Highland Spring advertised for the first time in November 1987, spending £411 000 (MEAL) in a 4-week burst, followed by a further £665 000 (MEAL) in April–June 1988 (see Table 3.8). However, this

Table 3.8   Mineral water advertising

Mineral water	Expenditure (£000)							
	Oct. – Dec. 1986	Jan. – Mar. 1987	Apr. – June 1987	Jul. – Sept. 1987	Oct. – Dec. 1987	Jan. – Mar. 1988	Apr. – June 1988	Jul. – Sept. 1988
Badoit	32	5	•	21	•	•	33	40
Brecon	38	18	26	•	•	•	66	34
Buxton	•	•	•	•	245	152	456	251
Highland Spring	•	•	•	•	411	•	665	•
Perrier	392	•	532	8	16	•	312	494
Ramlosa	•	•	•	551	110	12	16	•
Spa	142	30	435	564	•	•	854	285
Volvic	•	•	•	•	•	•	321	100
Total	604	53	993	1144	782	164	2723	1204
MAT (Moving Annual Total)	1469	1453	2097	2794	2972	3083	4813	4873

Source: MEAL.

Table 3.9   Highland Spring user regionality, 1986 v 1988

Indices v UK Population	1986		1988	
	Any mineral water	Highland Spring	Any mineral water	Highland Spring
London	165	195	149	156
South	117	145	124	149
Anglia	107	92	106	109
South West	85	56	96	125
Wales & West	70	58	90	76
Midlands	91	55	90	70
North West	90	79	89	66
Yorkshire	58	36	69	51
North East	67	57	60	53
Central Scotland	67	108	67	117
North East Scotland	52	55	70	119

Source: BMRB/TGI.

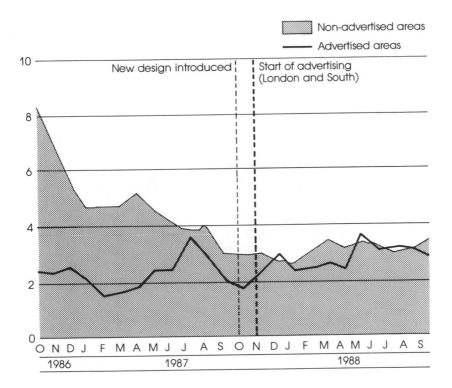

Figure 3.8 Highland Spring volume shares (advertised and non-advertised areas)
Source: Nielsen.

advertising ran in only two TV areas (London and the South). Figure 3.8 shows that the advertising was effective in stimulating a slightly faster share-growth in these areas than in the non-advertised areas. However, this figure also shows a healthy growth trend in the rest of the country where Highland Spring was not advertised, and had (prior to the relaunch) been declining at an alarming rate.

Thus, while advertising had undoubtedly contributed to Highland Spring's success, it could not by itself explain all—or even most—of the gains that had been made.

Further evidence of this is provided by an analysis of changes in Highland Spring's regional user-profile (Table 3.9). This shows that brand usership had strengthened between 1986 and 1988 in most parts of the country. There was certainly no bias here towards the advertised areas.

One further piece of quantitative research was carried out by The Research Business in January 1988: 216 respondents who had never

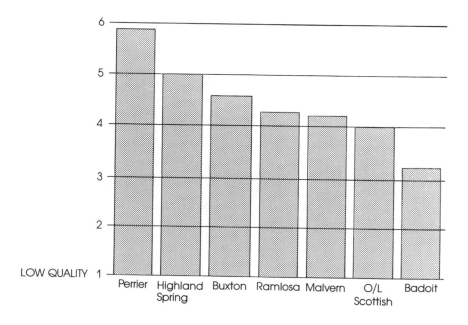

Figure 3.9 Brand ranking on 'quality'
Source: The Research Business.

seen the commercial, but who were prompted only by the bottle designs, were asked to rank Highland Spring and six competitive brands in order from 'High Quality' to 'Low Quality'. Figure 3.9 shows the results.

To quote The Research Business, 'showing a separate sample of respondents the commercial does not have a significant effect on this hierarchy.

Conclusion

Highland Spring's relaunch marketing objectives were achieved. It became, in the eyes of consumers, a premium brand, and this was reflected in its pricing. Distribution, market share and margins all moved from a downward to an upward trend.

All of these positive changes demonstrably started with the introduction of the new design in October 1987, although other elements of the marketing mix also helped, particularly advertising in London and the South.

Of course, *absolute* proof of the new design's effectiveness is impossible. Even the econometric models so widely used in demonstrating the effectiveness of advertising cannot be employed with any confidence in measuring design, because design (a single change at a single point in time) cannot be analysed via time-series data in the way that advertising can, and this is generally considered essential to the construction of a useful model.

The new Highland Spring design was effective in helping to achieve the commercial objectives set for it. It was calculated that the entire design exercise (including the cost of new labelling machinery) paid for itself in well under a year. By contrast, the advertising (even if credited with all the gains in London and the South) was still some way from pay-back.

In 1992 Highland Spring brand is now widely available in all types of outlets and in over 70 per cent grocery sterling distribution. Highland Spring is now the UK's leading mineral water producer.

References

Channon, C. (ed.), 'Castlemaine XXXX Lager. The role of advertising in building a profitable new brand', *Advertising Works*, Vol. 4, 1987.

Ehrenberg, A., *The After-Effects of Consumer Promotions*, London Business School Publication, 1991.

Farquar, P., 'Managing brand equity', *Journal of Advertising Research*, August/September 1990.

Harris International Marketing, *Trends in Sales Promotion*, 1991.

Hoggan, K., 'Back to life', *Marketing*, March 1988.

Lewis, M., *Understanding Brands* (ed. D. Cowley), Kogan Page, 1991.

Mackay, S., *Familiarity Breeds Contentment*, Michael Peters Publication, 1990.

Mintel, *Sponsorship 1991*, Mintel Special Report.

4

Brand stretching

For many companies, particularly in fast-moving consumer goods markets, the risks and costs associated with new product launches have become prohibitive. Media costs have escalated and competition has intensified. Launching new products is, however, not the only expense. The establishment of a successful brand, as we have seen, requires sustained investment over a long period of time if the brand proposition is to be embraced by the consumer. The problem intensifies as it becomes increasingly more difficult to obtain distribution for new products without evidence that considerable promotional muscle will be used to move the products off the retailers' shelves. Furthermore, the success of many major brands in terms of their market dominance has also made it more difficult for new entrants to establish themselves, particularly in markets in which the opportunities for hi-tech, new product developments are limited, such as groceries and soft drinks.

As a result, many European and American companies have, in recent years, sought to overcome the problems of entering new markets by capitalizing on the reputations of their existing brand names wherever possible. In the United States, for example, it has been estimated that around 40 per cent of new products introduced into supermarkets annually between 1977 and 1984 were line or brand extensions (Nielsen 1985), and more recent studies have put the figure much higher (Ogiba 1988). This approach to new product launches is part of a continuum of brand stretching, covering at the one end, line extensions, which are minor product variations usually intended to appeal to other, often overlapping, market segments, and at the other end brand extensions, which use the brand name to embrace new technologies or new product categories. Examples of the former might include the extension of the Coca-Cola line to include Diet Coke, Caffeine-free Coke and Cherry Coke. Examples of the latter include the Japanese brand Yamaha which extends from motorbikes to musical instruments.

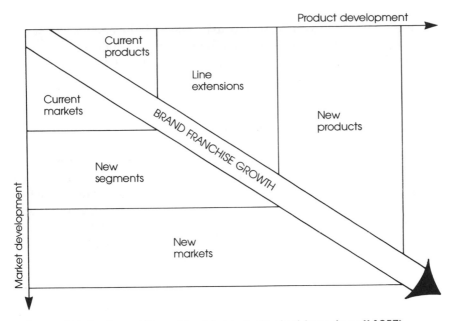

Figure 4.1 The Brand Franchise Matrix (adapted from Ansoff 1957)

The process of brand stretching can be represented conceptually as part of a matrix, as shown in Figure 4.1. The Brand Franchise Matrix is defined by two dimensions.

Along the product development dimension, the brand is stretched to include minor product variations (line extensions) and ultimately completely new product categories. Along the market development dimension, the original brand (and product) is launched into new segments of the existing market and then into new markets which, in the extreme, can result in a global brand. In most cases, the widening of brand franchise is achieved by a combination of both—i.e. the brand franchise grows along the diagonal from left to right. Dunhill, one of the world's leading luxury product brands, is an example of a gradualist approach to the extension of the brand franchise along this diagonal. It has extended the original product brand, cigarettes, into new markets and simultaneously extended the brand to include, first, other smoking-related products such as pipes (a new segment) and lighters (a related product category), and, secondly, completely new product categories such as clothing and male accessories including belts, cufflinks and, more recently, male cosmetics.

Other examples include Ambre Solaire with its range of sun

protection products which are now available globally and Gucci, the luxury product designer label. In all these cases, consumers' familiarity with, and trust in, the original brand have been used successfully to extend the brand franchise.

Stretching can be dangerous

Not all practitioners, nor all writers on the topic of branding, agree that brand stretching is an effective strategy. Procter & Gamble, for example, has, in the past, chosen to create new brands in preference to brand extensions. Thus, its line of washing powder includes Bold (the 'All in One' cleanser and conditioner), Dreft (for woollens) and Ariel (a biological powder). For babies' nappies it has Pampers, for toothpaste it has Crest, etc. However, more recently its washing powder lines have been extended to include grease and odour remover variants (e.g. Daz Ultra and Ariel Ultra) as well as liquid variants of Daz, Bold and Ariel. Arguably, by creating so many successful, independent brands Procter & Gamble has increased its potential for line extensions which, conceptually, do not stray very far from their original brands. However, no use is made of the name Procter & Gamble for brand endorsement, in contrast to its major competitor in the UK, Lever Bros, which endorses all its brands. Similarly, IBM chose not to establish a new brand when it entered the microcomputer market, in sharp contrast to Apple who chose to launch the Macintosh (the Apple Mac) despite their previous success in this market with the Apple brand.

The most ardent opponents of brand stretching are Ries and Trout (1985), who regard most line or brand extensions as a dilution of the original brand proposition, and consider that extensions eventually confuse the customer, leading to cannibalization and a decline in overall market share. The strongest brands, say Ries and Trout, are those that are synonymous with one product, i.e. they have become the generic name for the product. However, there are probably as many brand stretching successes as there are failures. It is not true that all brands that have been stretched have lost market leadership (if they ever had it in the first place). Nevertheless, there are dangers in stretching a brand too far from its original product category, particularly if the brand is very closely identified with that category.

The danger is that ill-considered brand extensions may rebound and dilute the core brand name, rather than confer safety and quality on a new product. Even worse, a failed line or brand extension can damage the original brand by adding new and undesirable symbolic values to the brand personality. Furthermore, these harmful effects can affect future brand strategy, making it difficult to embark upon further brand stretching.

How does brand stretching work?

Brand stretching, first and foremost, enables a new product to use the already well-established functional attributes and symbolic values that make up the personality of the original brand, whether that be corporate or product specific. Clearly, the intended personality of the new product must be the same as that of the original brand, although the positioning need not be. A reputation for quality is an important prerequisite of successful brand stretching, but quality is only one aspect of a brand's personality and positioning. Quality is thus a necessary but not a sufficient condition. Other vital factors might include the perceived modernity of the brand, its perceived innovatory strength and its nationality—how British, German or American is it? Quality needs to be distinguished from positioning, however. For example, Mercedes-Benz, with the strapline 'engineering second to none', has a reputation for quality cars but different model numbers position the corporate brand differently, focusing specific brands (models) on specific segments. For example, the Mercedes 190 is positioned in the low-priced executive segment of the car market.

Secondly, use of an established original brand speeds up the process of establishing product awareness. Creating product awareness can be an expensive process. The use of an established brand name on a new product can help recognition, and reduce the communication cost, by capitalizing on the heavy advertising and promotion expenditure on the original brand.

Thirdly, use of an established brand name reduces the risk of purchase for a first-time buyer. Studies (e.g. Clayclamp and Liddy 1969) have shown that the most important predictor of trial purchase is the use of a known brand name in addition to the level of promotion expenditure.

Fourthly, using an existing brand name to launch a new product makes it easier to obtain distribution.

Finally, by successfully raising brand awareness and reputation among a new market segment, brand stretching can not only strengthen rather than weaken the brand proposition, but it can also increase sales of the original product(s) rather than cannibalize them.

Alternative strategies

As we have noted in Figure 4.1, brand stretching can be represented as a continuum which forms one dimension of a Brand Franchise Matrix. Thus, the simplest, lowest risk strategy is line extension, i.e. minor product changes, such as new flavours (e.g. Heinz soups) or special low-calorie features (e.g. Diet Coke). At the other end of the continuum, the higher risk strategy is to extend the brand to other unrelated product categories. In some cases, this has been successfully accomplished through the use of designer labels such as Pierre Cardin, Gucci and Dunhill, while in other cases it has been achieved through the use of corporate brand endorsement, e.g. ICI. The latter is particularly relevant as the products have quite different competitive advantages that can be reflected in the careful choice and development of product-specific brand personalities.

A 'study' in the United States (Tauber 1988) of 276 brand-stretching campaigns, representing 115 different consumer brands, suggested that seven categories or brand-stretching strategies are used by organizations. These can be seen as incremental stages along the brand-stretching continuum. The seven alternatives, however, omit the line extension option as well as the corporate brand endorsement option. A more complete set of brand-stretching strategy alternatives, building on the results of this research, is given below:

1 Line extensions
2 Same product in a different form
3 Distinctive taste/ingredient/component in the new item
4 Companion products
5 Same customer franchise
6 Expertise
7 Benefit/attribute/feature owned
8 Designer image/status
9 Corporate brands/endorsement

There is a blurred distinction between the simple line extension and our second stretching strategy of launching the same product in a different form, which might also be regarded as a form of line extension.

Arguably, Procter & Gamble's liquid variants of their washing powders, Daz, Bold, Ariel, etc., fit into this second category. The Batchelors range of 'Cuppa Soups' would also come into category 2. Mars Ice Cream is a similar stretching of the Mars Bar into another product form, but unlike Procter & Gamble's liquid detergent, it puts Mars into a new competitive set, the ice-cream market. Thus, stretching strategy number 2 is potentially of higher risk. There is an equal blurring between stretching strategy number 2 and number 3, launching a distinctive taste/ingredient/component in the new item. A distinction has to be made, however, between adding additional flavours to a range of soups for example, which would be a simple, line extension strategy, and launching 'Big Soups' as Heinz did several years ago, which introduced a different concept in soups—the 'meal in a soup' concept.

Clearer light shines between strategies 3 and 4, however. At this point we are firmly in the realms of brand extensions rather than line extensions. When the battery company Duracell launched Durabeam, a range of torches, it used strategy number 4, extending its brand into other products. The risks of this strategy are higher than the others as it not only moves the company into a different competitive set, but also involves it in responsibility for the design and manufacture of products outside its core skills. It is therefore often necessary to subcontract these aspects of the operation. In the UK, for example, Mars subcontract their ice-cream manufacture to Unilever.

Stretching strategy 5, extending the brand to products bought by the same customer franchise, is realistic in the sense that it takes advantage of existing distribution channels and brand awareness, but also further increases the risk as it may not only take the company away from its core manufacturing skills but may also require different marketing and product support skills. Most of the large banks have pursued this strategy by extending their brand to include a range of other financial services, such as life assurance, stock market dealing and housing loans.

Stretching strategy 6 utilizes the reputation of the brand for its expertise. This can often be taken advantage of by corporate brands such as Canon who have successfully moved into copying machines having built up a reputation for the manufacture of photographic equipment.

An alternative stretching strategy (strategy 7) is extending the brand through capitalizing on its main attributes, benefits or features. For example the 'Made Simple' range of books published by Butterworth-Heinemann have, as their competitive advantage, the concept of user-friendly learning. This could be translated into other learning modes such as tapes and videos or into other modes of course delivery that might lead to qualifications. The existence of common benefits, attributes and features (strategy 7) is, as we have seen, central to the success of any stretching strategy and becomes more important in reducing risk the farther a company strays from its original product category. This is taken to its extreme in stretching strategies 8 and 9 which require brand personalities to have strong symbolic values which can transcend extremely different product categories. In the context of designer or image/status brands, examples include Pierre Cardin, Gucci and Dunhill. In the case of corporate brands, examples would include ICI and Bayer, the chemicals companies, and several of the Japanese trading companies, such as Yamaha and Canon.

To stretch or not to stretch?

Like any other marketing decision, the decision to launch a new product or a variant of an existing product using an already well-established brand name has to be seen as providing a sustainable competitive advantage or point of distinction. Choosing to use an established name merely to help gain rapid product awareness and trial will ultimately leave the new product vulnerable to competition.

That competitive advantage will be gained in instances where the proposed original brand has a personality which reinforces real benefits and evokes associations necessary for success in the new marketplace. It is important to avoid negative associations which might emanate from the original brand's personality.

Although the use of an established brand can help market entry and obtain trial, it cannot sustain the position of a product that offers no real benefits, be they functional or symbolic. Brand stretching as a cheap alternative to establishing a new brand is not a method of providing competitive advantage to a product that has none.

Some symbolic values of a brand's personality may well help to establish a new product, but others may not. In using the established brand name, a company runs the risk of embracing both positive and negative associations. It is important when considering the possibility of extending a brand to consider the total personality of the brand and not just part of it. To use only part of it is likely to change the balance of symbolic values associated with the original brand. Vaseline, for example, is a brand associated with both medication and moisturizing skin. It has been pointed out (Aaker 1990) that this brand could choose to extend in either direction: into such products as face and skin creams and soap, or into antiseptics, skin ointments, etc. However, the choice of route will begin to change the original brand personality of Vaseline and therefore potentially limit extension options in the future by biasing the original brand personality in a particular direction.

Nivea, the largest toiletry brand in the world, provides an interesting case history of brand stretching. The brand began life in Germany as a soap in 1906, yet arguably its personality is based upon its association with Nivea Cream. The owners of the brand in the UK have a clear view of the original brand's personality against which to evaluate potential brand extensions (Siddle 1988). The essential attributes and values are that it must correspond with the ideal brand personality and it must:

- care and protect
- be simple and uncomplicated
- be mild
- have natural active ingredients
- have a subtle perfume
- be of high quality
- give value for money
- be blue and white.

Maintaining this personality has enabled the successful launch of a range of sun care products that are number two in the market. Nivea also successfully launched a range of hair care products in Germany in 1984 and now holds the position of market leader in the frequent wash, gentle shampoo market. The latter is a considerable step from the original product category. Its success in the UK has been less notable, probably as a result of its relatively late entry into a market that is already dominated by well-established competitors such as Timotei. In Europe outside the UK, the Nivea brand has now been successfully stretched to include Nivea products for men. This success, in contrast to the relative lack of success in the UK hair care market, underlines the potential advantage of being first into a market. Brand stretching is likely to be more successful and credible in such cases.

The final consideration when deciding on whether to use an established brand to aid market entry or not is obviously the budget. New brands are still being successfully introduced. If a company has the resources to develop a new brand in a product category clearly outside its existing sphere, then it should do so, as this will provide the company with a strategic platform from which to begin line extensions and careful movement along the brand-stretching continuum.

Looking after the original brand

Brand stretching, where it is prudent to choose this option, can only be successful when its original brand is given the necessary support and nurturing. This means periodic reviews of its saliency and relevance to the marketplace. Brands can quickly become old-fashioned and lose their sparkle, as the case of Lucozade illustrates (see Chapter 3). Nivea had similar problems in the early 1970s when lack of investment and changing consumer attitudes resulted in an out-of-date image. This necessitated a substantial brand relaunch aimed at attracting new, younger users, while not alienating the older more traditional buyers. The relaunch was a necessary prerequisite of the subsequent extension of the brand into other product areas.

Summary

Brand stretching, if used correctly, is a means of reducing the costs and risks involved in new product launches, drawing as it does upon the established personality of the original brand. The process of brand stretching can be represented as part of a Brand Franchise Matrix, which is defined by two axes, a product development axis and a market development axis. In reality most brand-stretching exercises move a brand along the diagonal of this matrix, extending it into new product categories and new markets or market segments. Despite the increasing use of brand-stretching strategies, it remains an area of controversy and both practitioners and writers vary in their views as to its efficacy. It is important to the success of stretching strategies that the personality of the original brand be entirely consistent and supportive of the intended brand extension. If successful, the extension will reinforce the original brand, if not it can do long-term damage to the original brand's future. Nine different brand-stretching strategies have been identified along a continuum from simple line extensions to corporate brand endorsements. If used successfully these strategies speed up the establishment of a new product through guarantees of its quality, creating rapid consumer awareness and recognition. Such strategies also reduce the risks to first-time buyers. In the last analysis, the decision of whether or not to use a brand-stretching strategy must take into account the extent to which such strategies will lead to a clear and sustainable competitive advantage for the new product in the context of the budget available.

CASE STUDY: McVitie's Mini Cheddars

United Biscuits is a leading international food manufacturer with an integrated group of snack and convenience food businesses. In the UK and Europe, it boasts a collection of famous brands, including McVitie's biscuits, Terry's chocolate, Callard & Bowser & Nuttals sweets, KP Foods, and Ross Young's frozen and chilled foods. In the USA, it owns Keebler, the number three company in the snacks market in 1989 and the number two in the large cookie and cracker market. Each company is run as an autonomous business. It is with the McVitie's Group that this case study is concerned.

McVitie's have been the market leader in the UK biscuits market for many years both in the branded sector and in the private label sector. Their brands represent 30 per cent of the biscuit market, while their private label sales represent a further 20 per cent. Their oldest brand, McVitie's Digestive, was introduced nearly one hundred years ago, and in 1989 achieved sales of £43 million. Other well-known brands include: Penguin, Cheddars, Hob-nobs, Jaffa Cakes and Carr's Table Water Biscuits.

These products represent a varied collection of different branding devices. The group includes stand-alone brands such as Penguin as well as endorsed brands such as Carr's Table Water Biscuits, McVitie's Jaffa Cakes, McVitie's Digestives, McVitie's Cheddars, Crawford's Custard Creams and McVitie's Hob-nobs.

Tracking study data indicates that McVitie's has the highest recall in the biscuits sector and is synonymous with warmth, cosiness, trustworthiness and a 'nice uncle' image. The promotional strategy has, in the past two or three years, concentrated on below-the-line expenditure with virtually no advertising. The strength of these long-established brands has formed the basis for many successful line extensions, in particular, the introduction of mini versions of several brands, beginning with Mini Cheddars, introduced in the early 1980s.

Cheddars had been a very successful brand in the 1970s and 1980s in a market (savoury biscuits) in which Jacobs dominated and McVitie's had been relatively weak. The original Cheddars was targeted at women specifically and adults generally both as a biscuit for carrying cheese and as a snack base for other toppings.

The idea for Mini Cheddars came not from research but from one person, who identified the opportunity and championed the product development and launch. The only support since launch was a very limited advertising expenditure on London's Capital Radio which ran for four weeks. It was also supported by a large salesforce (the largest in the packaged grocery industry) of about 1000 people.

Table 4.1 Sales index

	1980	1981	1982	1983	1984	1985	1986	1987	1988	1989
Parent brand										
Cheddars, 150 g roll packs	100	98.8	80.4	74.4	68.6	70.8	64.0	60.2	54.8	56.5
Mini products										
Mini Cheddars, single 30 g bags					100	271	306	345	377	494
Mini Cheddars, multi 6 bags per pack					100	554	711	961	1325	1525
Cheese Snips, single bags			100	381	500	444	424	358	303	318
Cheese and Ham Snips, single bags							100	39.5	20.5	10.3
Parent brand										
None										
Mini products										
Mini Cookies, single 30 g bags			100	106.2	72.6	43.9	35.1	37.1	36.9	44.4
Mini Cookies, multi 6 bags per pack					100	348	609	720	614	635

Table 4.2 Biscuit sales by category by volume and value, 1985–89

	1985		1986		1987		1988		1989 (est.)	
	tonnes	£m	tonnes	£m	tonnes	£m	tonnes	£m	tonnes	£m
Sweet										
(e.g. Digestives)	304	430	306	455	306	481	311	507	313	539
Plain and savoury										
(e.g. Cream Crackers)	72	117	72	130	70	124	70	132	69	138
Countlines										
(e.g. Penguins)	68	148	68	166	68	170	80	205	92	240
Chocolate coated/										
chocolate flavoured										
(e.g. Homewheats)	68	89	70	110	70	145	90	172	101	221
Semi-sweet										
(e.g. Rich Tea)	50	40	50	52	49	51	45	46	43	44
Other*	24	37	27	38	27	42	25	37	17	35
Total	586	861	593	951	590	1013	621	1099	635	1217

* Including rusks, crispbreads, oatcakes, cones, wafers.

Source: BCCCA/Mintel analysis.

The success of Mini Cheddars moved McVitie's into the snacks market with the strapline 'Bite size real cheddar cheese biscuits'. A copy of the sales history of the parent brand and its mini extensions can be seen in Table 4.1. Since the launch of Mini Cheddars in 1984, additional flavours have been added to the line, including bacon, marmite and ham. The successful recipe was also extended to include Cheese Snips, a catering product sold to bars, canteens, cafeterias and motorway service stations under the Crawford's family brand.

The success of Mini Cheddars was seen by the McVitie's management as an opportunity to be exploited further. The UK biscuits market had been static in volume terms for several years while the snack market continued to grow. Table 4.2 shows trends in biscuit sales over the period 1985–89.

Mini Cheddars increased biscuits' presence in the snacks category and expanded their share of the children's segment, putting them in competition with extruded potato products such as crisps and savoury snacks. It did not go unnoticed, however, that this was in direct competition with the products of a sister company, KP Foods. The success of Mini Cheddars also led McVitie's to believe that there were opportunities for growth in the biscuit market despite its maturity and high per capita consumption. This success, which resulted in a £35m business, was regarded as an example of what can happen when a large manufacturer exerts its muscle in the marketplace.

Mini Cheddars was rapidly joined by Mini Cookies, a standard crunchy biscuit with chocolate chips, endorsed by Crawfords rather than McVitie's. This addition was launched with very little promotional support but a strong salesforce push. The product was packaged in boxes of six in contrast to a plastic outer and placed at the opposite end of the fixture to Mini Cheddars. Thus, from the consumers' point of view, there was no relationship between the two products. Sales of Mini Cookies grew by 15–20 per cent per year, stimulated by the occasional on-pack price promotion. Sales data for Mini Cookies can be seen in Table 4.1.

The snacks market

More recently Mini Cheddars has principally been found in the crisps/snacks fixture in most multiples despite attempts by McVitie's to retain them in the biscuits fixture. Trade margins for snacks are typically in the 35–40 per cent range in contrast to 20–25 per cent on biscuits. Thus, close identification of Mini Cheddars with the snacks fixture could, at some stage, lead to a demand for higher margins by the trade. Such a classification would also attract VAT which, at present, non-chocolate biscuits do not. The snacks market is also far more price competitive and subject to more promotions to attract attention to individual products that can get lost in a vast repertoire of competing brands and own-labels. On crisps, retail prices are typically 85–90p per six-pack. At present, Mini Cheddars are trading at about 65p per six-pack. Table 4.3 shows sales of snacks by sector for the period 1984–89. Overall sales have only grown by about 5 per cent per annum at current prices.

Table 4.3 Sales of snacks (£ million) by sector at current prices, 1984–89

	Crisps	Savoury snacks	Nuts	Cereal bars	Total
1984	505	205	94	15	819
1985	541	231	103	18	893
1986	585	242	113	22	962
1987	626	261	122	30	1039
1988	657	325	130	48	1160
1989 (est.)	687	374	134	40	1235

Source: Mintel analysis.

A significant feature of the snacks market in recent years has been the emergence of cereal bars. At current prices, sales grew by around 45 per cent per annum over the period 1984–89. These include the brand leader, Harvest (Quaker) with around 25 per cent of the market, followed by Tracker from Mars and Solar (United Biscuits). The original brand, Crunchy Bar from Jordans, still retains about 14 per cent of the market.

The savoury snacks market grew at about 12 per cent per annum over the same period. However, sales in 1988 grew by 25 per cent. The top 10 established brands in this market account for about 80 per cent by value, these include Hula Hoops, Skips and Discos (belonging to KP), Quavers, Tubes and Square Crisps, and Monster Munch (belonging to Smith's) and Wotsits and Ringos (belonging to Golden Wonder). The market is, however, dominated by KP who had 35 per cent share of the market by value in 1988. Growth in the savoury snack market has been particularly vigorous in pubs and off-licences.

Table 4.4 shows the characteristics of consumers purchasing crisps and snacks. The results are taken from a British Market Research Bureau Survey commissioned by Mintel and conducted in June 1989.

'Lunch Box'

Enthused by the success of the 'Mini' concept, McVitie's management began to investigate the extension of this concept to all its core brands (both sweet and savoury) as part of a major development project in 1986. The idea behind Project Snacktime was simple. Take McVitie's most popular biscuit brands and make bite-sized versions that are 'snackable'.

Although the basic concept was simple, development proved to be complex and protracted. The initial response to the development brief from technical/R&D people was that 'it can't be done'. In particular,

Table 4.4 Characteristics of consumers purchasing crisps and snacks
in the last two weeks, June 1989 (Base: 1069 adults)

	Flavoured crisps (%)	Salted peanuts (%)	Hula Hoops (%)	Cereal bars (%)	None of these (%)
All	47	21	18	15	23
Men	43	20	16	11	28
Women	51	21	20	19	18
15–19	71	14	28	29	11
20–24	62	28	22	20	15
25–34	67	26	32	16	14
35–44	53	26	25	22	18
45–54	40	22	7	14	20
55–64	34	19	10	10	26
65+	20	12	6	4	44
AB	35	17	13	17	27
C1	49	25	18	16	21
C2	48	18	21	17	22
D	56	25	18	16	18
E	44	19	15	8	28
London/TVS	45	20	20	17	21
Anglia/Central	50	20	18	16	23
Harlech/TSW	49	21	18	16	25
Yorkshire/Tyne–Tees	49	19	15	15	21
Granada	44	20	17	11	27
Scotland	52	24	22	11	22
With children	69	24	34	22	13
No children	36	19	9	12	27

Source: BMRB/Mintel.

for technical reasons, it was impossible to replicate the taste and
texture of Hob-nobs and Chocolate Homewheat in a bite-sized
biscuit.

The response from marketing was to ask the questions, 'What can we
do as a bite-sized snack?' The answer was: 'Anything you like, with the
dough that is used to make Mini Cheddars.' The technology was
already in place to produce different flavours and unusual shapes of
single-bite snacks like Mini Cheddars.

Marketing development pressed ahead. Several agencies were
commissioned to research the concept and various product
possibilities for inclusion in a 'lunchbox' range.

The conclusions from one agency can be summarized as follows:

- There was potential for a range of bagged snacks positioned for the lunchbox.
- The range had the potential to appeal to both current lunchbox users and non-users.
- There were no indications that a lunchbox positioning would restrict usage of the products, but would merely act as a 'hook' to purchase, as the packaging format made the product ideal for 'on-the-hoof' eating, car journeys, etc.
- However, the new products were likely to be substituted for other current McVitie's products rather than be an additional inclusion.

Where do we go from here?

Armed with these encouraging research results, and encouraged by support for the project from the advertising agency handling the product group, the junior brand manager responsible for the project decided to proceed. It was her chance to make her mark in her first management role within the company. Plans for the launch were formulated. By the Spring of 1989 they were ready for launch — £2.7 million having been invested in new packaging machinery at Ashby. The family brand name for the new range was to be 'Lunch Box'. It would be targeted at mothers with young children. There were four products altogether:

- Mini Cheddars
- Mini Cheddars with Bacon Flavour
- Mini Stars — a light crispy potato star biscuit
- Mini Cookies — chocolate chip bite-sized cookies.

Of these, only Mini Stars was new to consumers. The other three were to be relaunched under the 'Lunch Box' umbrella. The launch plan envisaged merchandizing the savoury products on the snack fixture where trade margins of 30–40 per cent are expected, while Mini Cookies were to be merchandized on the biscuits fixture with expected trade margins of 20–25 per cent. The planned 'Lunch Box' promotion is shown in Figure 4.2 on page 90.

It was at this point that a new marketing manager joined McVitie's. Having briefed himself thoroughly on all aspects of the proposed launch, he raised a number of points that caused consternation among those involved in the launch. These were:

- Mini Cheddars were a brand in their own right, liked by the whole family. The 'Lunch Box' proposition was mainly focused on the child market.

- It ignored the whole basis of the Mini Cheddars success, namely the proposition 'here is a biscuit we've made a mini version of'.

- It was not clear if it should be merchandized as a new range, and if so whether it should be with snacks (which are savoury in general) or with biscuits.

Figure 4.2 The planned 'Lunch Box' promotion

- As a snack a new range would attract VAT and trade margins would be expected to be higher.
- This range would be interpreted by KP Foods as a direct attack.

It was clear that some aspects of the proposed 'Lunch Box' strategy had not been sufficiently thought through and as a brand extension scheme it was flawed in its current form. As a result the project was halted.

References

Aaker, D., 'Brand extensions: the Good, the Bad, and the Ugly', *Sloan Management Review*, **47**, Summer 1990.

Ansoff, I., 'Strategies for diversification', *Harvard Business Review*, September–October 1957.

Clayclamp, H. and Liddy, L., 'Prediction of new product performance: an analytical approach', *Journal of Marketing Research*, **9**, 1969.

Nielsen, A.C., *Testing Techniques,* **1** (1), 1985.

Ogiba, E., 'The dangers of leveraging', *Adweek*, 4 January 1988.

Ries, A. and Trout, J., *Positioning: The Battle for the Mind,* 1st edition revised, McGraw-Hill, 1986.

Siddle, G., 'How Smith & Nephew have managed to extend the Nivea brand. . . profitably!', speech at KAE Conference on Product Development, 1988.

Tauber, E., 'Brand leverage: strategy for growth in a cost control world', *Journal of Advertising Research*, August–September, 1988.

5

Corporate brands and corporate identity

Corporate brands

In many instances the company is the brand. Companies such as Bosch, Heinz, IBM, Cadbury and Christian Dior use their corporate name across their entire product range. However, the way in which the names are used differ. There are, broadly, two different approaches: monolithic and endorsement.

In a monolithic approach, the corporate name is used to encompass several different sectors or market segments. Thus Christian Dior covers products ranging from perfume to clothing, while Bosch includes domestic appliances as well as motor vehicle components. In other cases, such as IBM, the corporate name is used across market segments from PCs to mainframe computers. The weakness, however, is that the monolithic approach does not allow a company to develop specific brands for specific market segments, making a company vulnerable to competition from highly targeted niche brands with more relevant personalities and more precise positionings.

An example might be IBM, who has been threatened in the microcomputer market by companies such as Apple and Toshiba whose brand personalities might be regarded as more user-friendly and whose positioning is distant from their competitor, IBM.

The second approach is to endorse other brands, as in the case of McVitie's Hob-nobs (biscuits), Boots Natural Collection (cosmetics), Cadbury's Wispa (chocolate) and ICI's Miracle Gro (garden plant feeder). As we have seen in Chapter 4, corporate brand endorsement, as a form of brand stretching, may speed up the process of establishing product awareness and, thereby reduce launch costs which, in today's environment of escalating media costs, is particularly desirable.

These two approaches are not necessarily used exclusively but are increasingly used in combination with the third naming approach (described in Chapter 2), family branding. The company, H.J. Heinz, provides an example. It uses a family branding approach across many of its food products including soups, baked beans and pasta products, but uses its corporate brand to endorse its other brands such as Weight Watchers (a family brand).

The promotion of corporate names either in their own right or to endorse product brands has increased in recent years, a fact that is reflected in the increasing amount of money devoted to corporate advertising. One reason for the increase in the use of endorsement *per se* is an increase in awareness of the value of brand stretching. However, there are two other reasons for the generally higher profile that corporate brands are being given.

Social responsibility

The first is in response to the pressures on companies to behave in a socially responsible way. As a result, there has been an increase in advertising publicising the virtues and social awareness of individual companies. The UK company ICI provides an example of an organization trying to present a caring image with the message 'world problems, world solutions, ICI world class'. Similarly, Shell has steadily built its reputation as a trustworthy company, through its 'You can be sure of Shell' campaign reinforced by Shell guides to the countryside. This reputation spreads to its brands, through a policy of endorsement. It also, of course, influences non-marketing areas such as recruitment and corporate culture, which are referred to later in this chapter.

The stock market

Secondly, there has been increasing pressure for companies to pay attention to their own brand proposition as the owners of a portfolio of brands. The case of the UK confectioners, Rowntree, which was taken over by Nestlé, provides an example of the dangers of investing too heavily in building a coherent portfolio of brands at the expense of the company's own identity. The danger is that financial markets perceive brands as wealth-creating assets and ignore the strengths and skills of the corporate owner and architect of the successful brand portfolio. One of the largest UK corporate advertisers, and arguably one of the most successful UK corporate brands in recent years, is the Hanson Trust. By publicising their success in the United States — 'the

company from over here that's doing rather well over there'—
Hanson attempted to establish itself as a successful, winning
company. However, it was particularly significant that, at the same
time, Hanson was bidding for another relatively anonymous
corporate brand owner, Imperial Group. The fact that the bid was
ultimately successful, despite a counter campaign by Imperial with
the line 'Famous brands doing famously', is a further example of the
growing importance of corporate campaigns in the battle for company
survival. Using the corporate name to endorse company brands aids
the process of making shareholders aware of the brand assets owned
by the company.

Corporate identity

Corporate identity has been defined as 'the branding and packaging
of an entire company' (Murphy 1990). Corporate brands should not,
however, be equated with corporate identity. The process of
communicating a corporate identity goes well beyond the creation of a
corporate proposition for consumer audiences alone. As we have seen
above, it aims to reach other key audiences in order to communicate
'the unique capabilities of a company.... that distinguish the
organisation and determine its ability to create value in the marketplace' (Smith 1990). It is also about declaring the future direction for
an organization. Thus Alan Brew, from the corporate identity firm,
Landor Associates, defines it as 'the visual communication of strategic
intent' (Brew 1988). However, we must also include verbal
communication in this definition as the link with corporate culture
and the behaviour of employees.

The communication of a corporate identity requires that an
organization should consistently reflect its strategic intent through all
its interfaces with the various audiences it seeks to serve. In addition
to the sign at the factory gate or office entrance, these interfaces
include company vehicles, employees' uniforms, stationery, and
sponsorship events. Relevant audiences include shareholders,
suppliers, government agencies, banks, employees and potential
employees as well as immediate customers. The consistent
communication of corporate identity can build and reinforce among
employees the correct corporate culture. Effective corporate identity
thus relies on visual communication as well as verbal communication
and corporate behaviour.

Managing a consistent corporate identity involves consistent
management of the corporate culture so that the values of the identity

can be delivered to the various audiences. This process begins with staff recruitment. For the Toyota Motor Company this includes a series of tests to determine applicants' willingness to accept the Japanese emphasis on teamwork, loyalty and flexibility in addition to their literacy and technical knowledge.

In some cases the customer may not be a relevant audience for communicating corporate identity. How many customers, for example, are aware of the company Associated British Foods (the owners of the seventh biggest brand in the UK), Silver Spoon (white granulated sugar) or MD Foods (the Danish owners of Lurpak butter)? It may not be necessary for customers to be aware of the owners of their favourite brands, but to shareholders, employees and other key audiences, it is vital that they understand

- what the company is

- what the company does

- how the company does it.

'What the company is' can be summarized in a set of statements which describe its size, profitability and scope as well as its values. 'What the company does', or should do, is to deliver customer satisfaction through the provision of specific products and services. As has been pointed out (Smith 1990), of course, all products are in some respects providers of services. Thus, cars transport, TVs entertain and inform and food prevents hunger and provides sensual as well as social enjoyment. 'How the company does it' relates not only to functional attributes, such as the mode of delivery (e.g. Avon cosmetics deliver direct to customers), but also to symbolic values which can include, caring, professionalism, friendly service or hi-tech.

The building of a corporate identity is a much more complex process and offers a richer variety of alternative media than product brand building. It is also more pervasive because it requires consistent and effective communication with several audiences. As a consequence of the corporate identity process, it is possible that the 'take out' by different audiences will be different, and quite rightly so. For example, the symbolic value 'hi-tech' may be an important signal to both consumers and investors, but profitability (a functional attribute) is probably only relevant to investors or prospective investors.

Non-consumer audiences

The importance of establishing a clear identity with non-consumer audiences is particularly important for new companies. This is highlighted very clearly in a UK management buy-out that was one of many in the latter half of the 1980s. The company was Premier Brands (see Chapter 7), which was established as the result of a management buy-out of the food and beverages division of Cadbury Schweppes. The subsequent building of a corporate identity for the new company was described by Paul Judge, the managing director, in the following way (see Judge 1988).

> ... a corporate identity was required which would be suitable and usable on all aspects of corporate communication. The new corporate identity needed to portray the revitalised image of the new company, totally separating it from its past association with Cadbury Schweppes. But it was also required to convey a commitment to quality, service and standards given that the new company had no track record. It was also an entity to be focused on by the new company's employees in order to instil a unity of purpose and sense of belonging.

> We needed to demonstrate on the one hand the emergence of a new, vibrant force in food manufacturing but on the other, a company with quality people, quality products and quality services based on long experience in food manufacturing. The corporate identity involved the design of a logo, typeface and company colours and needed to have the ability to transpose across everything from letter headings and business cards to sales brochures and lorries.

> The company logo is based, quite simply, on our bar code. It is the mark of a technological age—an age in which nothing stands still. It reflects the dynamics of both the markets in which we operate and of the company. It also underlines the company's links with the grocery trade.

> The corporate identity had to be consistently and uniformly used from the first day of the new company to build up, as quickly as possible, recognition and awareness of the company. A design manual was produced which was not purely to be used as design guidelines but also set down the rules on how to use all aspects of the corporate identity.

> Having developed a corporate identity, the next stage in the marketing plan was to consider the advertising and promotional support programme required to launch the company. The first step was to identify the key audiences who needed to be informed of the existence and development plans of the new company and then to decide on the best advertising medium to communicate this message.

> The key audiences are not those normally associated with the launch of a new product, but it was necessary to gain the

confidence of all of these groups to ensure the success of the new company. Continued financial support and City backing was required, not only from the banks who were initially financing the company but other banks and City institutions who may become involved in the future and who will assist in the flotation of the company. The trade needed to view Premier Brands as a going concern with business continuing as usual; our customers expected their orders to be delivered on time and to the same quality, and our suppliers had to be confident they would be paid.

The media would be required to regard the company as new and revitalised and be clearly informed about the structure, activities and aims of Premier Brands. Finally, our employees who had lived through a very unsettling time since the first announcement in January needed to be reassured regarding the venture. It is worth noting that we decided not to aim the corporate body of Premier Brands at the consumer; we already had an enormous consumer franchise with our existing brand names of Typhoo, Chivers Hartley and of course Cadbury's.

Mission statement

Just as the focal point of the brand-building process is the brand proposition which sets out clearly the attributes and values making up the brand's personality together with its positioning, so the focal point of the corporate identity-building process must be the organization's mission statement. The mission statement should provide a clear statement regarding the purpose and direction of an organization's activities. The object of the mission statement is to inspire employees and to fix the organization in the minds of its key audiences in exactly the same way as a proposition should work for a brand. General and imprecise mission statements will fail to inspire and fail to distinguish the organization from its competitors. A mission statement should therefore detail:

- the organization's core skills in terms of the activities in which it is prepared to compete;
- its markets or the market segments it intends to serve, including: the geographic spread of the organization's operations — is it fully international or just local?;
- the organization's points or points in the supply chain (e.g. as an oil company Philips Petroleum limits its activities to exploration and bulk delivery of oil products and is not in forecourt retailing, while Elf is prepared to cover the entire range of oil industry activities from exploration to retailing);
- the organization's values and cultural ethos.

Mission statements, like brand statements, should in theory be written to last and should not be revised unless circumstances change significantly. The mission statement, of course, should provide the starting point for all major decisions taken by an organization. The purpose of a corporate identity is to encapsulate the spirit of the mission statement through visual and verbal communication. The core of that identity must be those values in the organization that provide the threads of continuity for its development and adaptation. In some instances, however, companies also change their corporate identity to reflect a change in its skills and product/service offering.

Corporate values

The rapidly changing corporate environment that has typified the last three decades has inevitably necessitated changes in organizational missions and their associated corporate identities. Table 5.1 shows the corporate values associated with some recent corporate identity programmes in the UK together with their logos.

In the case of British Telecom, the company had gone from public to private ownership and, as a result of deregulation, was competing for business in other European countries. Consequently, the new visual identity was required to move the company away from the old image of a local public utility. As in many recent corporate identity revamps, the new identity involved a change of name. The change to simply BT avoided the limiting aspects of 'British' as well as the much used 'Telecom' title. The redesigned logo, the piper, was meant to represent two aspects of communication: listening to and transmitting sound.

The McVitie's logo represents a change in the corporate identity of UB (United Biscuits) brands. In this instance the new name was capitalizing on the established heritage of the company's leading brand, McVitie's. While there are good reasons for doing this, there are also dangers. UB Brands also owned several other well known brands such as Ross Young's foods and Carr's Table Water Biscuits (see McVitie's Mini Cheddars case study in Chapter 4). It could be argued that by adopting the name of only one brand in its portfolio, it was narrowing its identity in terms of the perceived extent of its business.

In contrast, PowerGen was a new company created from the privatization of the Central Electricity Generating Board for England and Wales. As another ex-public utility, PowerGen—according to Michael Peters, the design company—needed to show itself as 'a human company that cares about customers, staff and the

Table 5.1 Corporate values and corporate identities

Company	Corporate values	New logos
British Telecom	Softness, accessibility, international appeal, service	
McVitie's	Warmth, professionalism, family values	
PowerGen	Strength, dynamism, integrity, flair, dependability	
Trusthouse Forte	Strength, choice	

Source: Marketing Week (7 June 1991).

environment, harnessing energy in a responsible way'. Hence, the logo expresses man's control of energy and PowerGen's control of potentially dangerous generation processes, plus the importance of working through people.

In the case of Trusthouse Forte, the new identity not only reflected corporate values, but was also intended to move the company away from close identification with one aspect of its business. For Trusthouse Forte, this was a close association with middle-ranking hotels. The new logo attempted to give the identity a broader application across the individual businesses making up the corporation.

The corporate identity building process

Wally Olins, from one of the UK's largest corporate identity consultancies, Wolff Olins, lists four stages in the process of building corporate identity (see Olins 1989).

Stage 1: Research and recommendations

This stage involves four audits. The first is the identity audit which involves the application of some of the techniques outlined in Chapter 10, including group discussions, projective tests and depth interviews. These are usually with informed individuals from different audiences including customers, suppliers, investors, the media, commercial partners and employees. The outcome of this audit should be a comprehensive picture of the organization's identity as currently perceived, which can be contrasted with both the identity of competitors and the ideal corporate identity.

This stage also includes a design audit of the organization and its constituent subsidiaries and divisions in terms of how they communicate themselves through their names and graphics. This is complemented by a communications audit which explores how the organization communicates and listens, and to whom. Finally, this stage involves a behaviour audit covering the organization's general approach to business from the point of view of outsiders and insiders.

The outcome of these four audits should, according to Olins, be a very clear idea of:

- how the organization is perceived by different groups of people with whom it deals, and why;
- the firm's goals and vision (which may or may not be embodied in its mission statement);
- an identity brief: 'what identity—structure, positioning and personality—would achieve these goals?'

Stage 2: Creation of new identity

At this stage, the consulting agency will set about fulfilling the brief, which may involve changing the name or modifying the old one and applying it more widely, devising and testing a new logo, changing typefaces and presentational style. This new 'visual' identity then needs translating in a communications strategy to introduce the new identity and a programme to change the behaviour of the organization.

Stage 3: Developing the detail

Effective corporate identities should be credible, distinctive and coherent and, most important, should be consistently portrayed throughout the organization. Consistency means getting the detail right so that each interface between the organization and its audiences is the same and each encounter builds upon the last. Thus, there needs to be a shared identity which permeates everything from promotional offers to management training, and from telephone answering to the presentation of the annual accounts.

Stage 4: Launch and implementation

This is a critical stage, but is also an opportunity to consistently communicate, perhaps for the first time, what the company stands for to all its audiences.

Choices have to be made at this stage about whether to launch regionally, nationally or internationally, whether to go for total, immediate transformation or to take a gradualist approach. The decision may, of course, depend upon the financial resources available. Whatever the approach adopted, however, the launch should involve staff training through conferences, seminars and courses designed to win commitment and enthusiasm.

Summary

There are two broad approaches to corporate branding, the monolithic approach which uses a single corporate name across all products, and the endorsement approach, which uses the corporate name to add value to the company's product brands.

The development of a corporate brand is, however, more complex than the development of a product brand involving, as it does, the communication of an organization's corporate identity to many key audiences. The growth in importance of corporate branding has been caused by three factors: the need to reduce the costs and risks of new product launches; the need for organizations to be seen to be socially responsible; and the need for companies to communicate with investors. The effective communication of a corporate identity to employees, through staff recruitment and selection, uniforms, delivery vehicles, etc., can also reinforce desired company culture and ensure that the organization fulfils its mission. Like product branding, however, it is important not only to ensure consistency of values across all interfaces and activities, but also to update the corporate identity regularly to reflect changes in the company and its environment.

CASE STUDY: What Landor did for British Airways

On 3 December 1984 two sleek and shining Boeings—a 747 and a 737—taxied across the tarmac at London's Heathrow Airport to be scrutinized by an invited audience of 200. The event was the unveiling of the new

British Airways corporate identity, intended to signal a set of new-found values within the airline to provide visual confirmation of its strategic coherence as it moved towards privatization the following February.

British Airways was the free world's largest airline with a total of 167 aircraft at that time. Under the chairmanship of Lord King, a 1981 loss of £39 million had been turned into a profit for 1983/84. The turnaround had been given further impetus by the appointment of Colin Marshall from Avis as the new chief executive in February 1983. Cost-cutting and rationalization were accompanied by a new marketing strategy based on service. During the summer of 1983, 15 000 customer service staff were put through a two-day 'putting the customer first' programme, catering was substantially improved and a new advertising campaign by Saatchi's was proclaiming BA as 'the world's favourite airline'.

But the BA board felt that BA's corporate identity (its visual image) was badly out of joint with its new service-led strategy. As a result of deregulation, competition between airlines was increasing, foreign travel was expanding and the air transportation market was becoming global. In order to be a successful player in this global market, BA had changed its corporate philosophy and was changing its corporate culture, its organizational structure and the way in which it managed operations. These feelings were voiced by Colin Marshall and were echoed by Stuart Luxon, BA's general manager marketing services, who, reflecting on the new visual identity, said:

> We needed something to signal that changes were taking place, something distinctive and broad enough to reach all markets. The existing identity had been good, but there was tremendous pressure to get things moving, and we had left it for as long as we could.

The job of overhauling the BA corporate identity was given to Landor Associates, the world's largest design consultancy who previously had done similar work for Alitalia, Singapore Airlines, Thai Airways, Ansett Airlines of Australia and SAS. The latter had also been the centre of a financial turnaround, and in 1983 had become 'Airline of the Year'.

The starting point for Landor was BA's statement, 'Our corporate goal is to become the best airline in the world', which emerged during the first phase of analysis in Landor's four-phase methodology. In this period the BA organization was analysed, its current position against competition established with the use of perceptual maps and its goals identified and defined.

There were four basic reasons why BA wanted to change:

1 To reflect the new management structure.
2 To reflect the new character of the airline.
3 To support the new advertising strategy with its emphasis on technological capability and electronic-style precision.
4 The imminence of privatization.

The objective was to brand the total experience from baggage tags to aircraft, producing a totally unified and integrated system of names, graphic identities, livery design, ground equipment, interiors, sales shops, ticket counters, printed materials, uniforms and lounges.

By November 1983 the work of phase one was complete. A review of all aspects of BA's identity had been made once the strong, valuable image elements were identified and isolated. BA's position as the UK flag carrier was important strategically to the airline and had to be retained. But use of the existing stylized Union Jack on the tail of the aircraft created problems.

Apart from BA's own feelings about the Carnaby Street quality of the strongly coloured flag symbol, Landor's view was that, as the dominant visual image of the airline, it did not transfer well to other aspects of BA's identity (shops, printed material, etc.) and was an inadequate device for a single central identity. There was, it was felt, also an associated marketing problem. The large Union Jack in strident primary colours, together with the single word, British, was seen to be an over-aggressive nationalistic statement which was strongly negative, particularly in some parts of the Commonwealth.

A five-point design platform was developed between Landor and BA, on which the design brief was built. This was:

1 Putting the customer first reflected in BA's emphasis on service.
2 Distinctiveness from competition. BA and its competitors had a similar look which consisted of white fuselage with strong nationalistic images.
3 Discontinuity from the past. BA was anxious to signal change.
4 Pride of origin. Taken to indicate values rather than nationalism.
5 Precision and professionalism. Extolling the technological innovation and competence of the airline.

By mid-January, two prototype designs were produced, one of which became the final choice, with the other representing an intermediate design between the original and the new design. All three were tested by market research in ten countries chosen by BA — UK, US, France, Germany, Japan, Australia, India, Kenya, Saudi Arabia and South Africa. The image attributes tested were: reliable, distinctive, modern, exciting, warm and British. The findings were analysed by Landor's research affiliate. They revealed that the final design scored better than the then existing one on all image attributes except 'warm' where the difference was so negligible as not to be statistically relevant.

The new design was refined as part of phase three and presented to the BA board on 6 July 1984. Following agreement to go ahead, the fourth phase, a two-year programme of implementation, then came into effect including remodelling of seats and the redesigning of much of the aircraft interiors.

The new design

According to John Diefenbach, Landor's president at that time, the new design (see Figure 5.1) was based 80 per cent on 'precision and professionalism' and 20 per cent on 'pride of origin'. The red

Figure 5.1 (a) Old design for British Airways

Figure 5.1 (b) New design for British Airways

speedwing, a thin red line terminating in a downward tick which runs the length of the fuselage, was developed to encapsulate the hard-edged qualities of precision. The speedwing, together with the new colours of midnight blue, silver and grey, constituted the dominant graphic image used on all BA's activities.

The flag on the tail and the dark blue undercarriage, which were identified as core attributes from the old design were absorbed into the new design in order to protect the fanchise which at the same time established change. The flag was modified into a more muted secondary design element and a crest was introduced to soften it further as a hallmark of 'quality and grace'. The word 'Airways' was reintroduced and picked out on the fuselage in a typeface called Basilia. With an eye on privatization, 'British Airways' was thought to be a more commercial proposition.

The results

Both BA and Landor felt pleased with the outcome. Following privatization and the associated new corporate identity, BA increased market share by

- broadening customer awareness;
- appealing to the business traveller;
- projecting positive brand attributes; and
- branding the total experience.

In addition, through establishing a coherent and comprehensive set of standards and controls for media investment, it reduced costs.

Finally, in 1985, BA was named 'Airline of the Year'. BA and Landor are still working together in creating an ongoing programme of corporate and brand identity management structures.

References

Brew, A., Special Report: 'Corporate identity, evolution of an idea', *Marketing*, 22 September 1988.

Judge, P., 'Launching and developing Premier Brands', Paper to KAE Conference on Product Development, 1988.

Kotler, P., *Marketing Management, Analysis, Planning and Control*, 7th edition, Prentice-Hall, 1991.

Murphy, J., *Brand Strategy*, Director Books, 1990.

Olins, W., *Corporate Identity: Marketing Business Strategy Visible through Design*, Thames & Hudson, 1989.

Smith, P., 'How to present your firm to the world', *Journal of Business Strategy*, January/February 1990.

6

Own-labels

Towards a definition

Own-label products include retailer brands sold, for example, by Tesco foodstores, Do It All DIY stores, Next clothing and the Abbey National building society. They may be offered either without branded competition like Next and Abbey National, or they may share shelf space with branded items in a mixed-branding strategy, like Tesco and Do It All.

However, own-label is not confined to the retail sector, but is used also by wholesalers. Nurdin & Peacock's Happy Shopper brand and the symbol group Mace (owned by Booker Wholesale Foods) are two examples. A useful working definition of own-label products is provided by Morris (1971) who defines it as:

> Consumer products produced by, or on behalf of, distributors and sold under the distributor's own name or trademark through the distributor's own outlet.

Retailer perceptions of own-label have traditionally focused on the functional attributes of the brand, such as performance at lower prices. Brand managers also perceived own-label as functionally driven and hence lacking in symbolic values. More recently, however, retailers have begun to introduce symbolic values into own-label lines with a strategy that increasingly threatens the competitive edge of manufacturer brands. This shift in strategy is illustrated quite clearly in the following quotations taken from interviews conducted by the authors.

- 'Parity at a cheaper price' and 'Products which give you what the label says but no more'—traditional own-label.
- 'Brands in their own right with a lot of inherent values' and 'Retailer values—the reassurance of the retailer'—modern own-label.

This shift in strategy has partly fuelled the dramatic growth of the retail-packaged grocery sector, with Asda, once known as the store that stocked only branded items, now offering 8000 own-label lines, and Sainsbury, one of the first into the own-label sector, adding at least 1000 new lines each year.

Evolution and growth

With some exceptions, such as Boots, Sainsbury and Marks & Spencer, who have offered own-label lines for over 100 years, own-label could be said to have begun in the 1970s as a cost-cutting response to inflation with prices typically 20 per cent below branded items. This was achieved through bulk purchasing, zero to low advertising and a product quality that was clearly inferior to branded lines. Whereas in 1971, own-label accounted for 20 per cent of sales, own-label now accounts for a third of all sales, and higher in the case of Waitrose (40 per cent) and Sainsbury (50 per cent) (Mintel Special Report 1991).

In the UK there has been a consolidation of retailer power among the major multiples who in 1989/90 were responsible for 63 per cent of sales, with 47 per cent concentrated in the top five: Sainsbury, Safeway, Tesco, Gateway, and Asda.

It may be argued, therefore, that this shift of power towards the major retailers has fuelled the growth of own-label and provided them with an important power base on which to build their own store identity. As one advertising executive observed:

> When you buy own-label, you buy into (the store) and everything (that store) means to you.

A leading design consultant makes a similar point:

> Supermarkets realize now that if they do a good job in terms of positioning and building up (own-label), then it will automatically do a good job in building up the good image of the supermarket.

There are principally two sectors where own-label has flourished. First, it has flourished in those markets where there has been no more than two or three dominant brands in the sector. In the yogurt market, for instance, there are only two major players: Nestlé's Chambourcy brand (with Nouvelle and Bonjour) and Express Food's Eden Vale brand (with Ski and Munch Bunch). It has allowed own-label to establish a strong and significant presence in the market, which may now be as much as 50 per cent of sales. It has led a Chambourcy spokesperson to comment:

> In the not too distant future, there will be room for only one brand alongside own-label.

By contrast, the petfood sector has over 20 brands in the canned meat sector alone. Pedigree Petfoods sells 11 brands, including Pedigree Chum and Wiskas, Spillers a further four with Bounce and Choosy. Quaker has two brands, Chunky and Felix in addition to H.J. Heinz's 9-Lives and Morrell's Butch and Cat's Choice. There is simply no room for own-label to establish significant market share which currently stands at a mere 6.6 per cent (source: AGB Television Consumer Audit).

Secondly, it has flourished in markets like chilled desserts and ready meals whose varieties have short life cycles. The speed with which supermarkets can develop, test and put on-shelf new product initiatives can rarely be matched by manufacturers who are traditionally more cautious and, to some extent, more precious, about their brand portfolios.

Manufacturers can only respond with one of two strategies. Either they invest in their own brands and secure a unique position within the marketplace on the strength of their brand's personality or, faced with squeezed margins and possible de-listing, they cooperate with retailers and service the own-label sector. In practice, many manufacturers do both. KP, for instance, manufactures potato hoops for most of the major retailers including Marks & Spencer, though none is allowed to adopt the brand name of Hula Hoops. McVitie's and Rank Hovis McDougall act similarly, and successfully service both the own-label sector and their own branded lines.

Nevertheless, for the present, it seems to be the retailer who makes the decisions. Some years ago, The Henley Centre for Forecasting (1982) quoted a major retailer as saying: 'We now see ourselves as the customer's manufacturing agent rather than the manufacturer's selling agent.' Three years later (Randall 1985) a quote states: 'Who needs brands? We certainly don't; the customers don't; so why should they exist.' The same article also quotes a rather pragmatic managing director of a canned food manufacturer as saying:

> Let's say I have a new product; Sainsbury and Tesco have over 50 per cent of the London market. London is so important that, if they won't accept my product, it simply isn't worth launching.

In reality, own-label often provides the manufacturer with an opportunity to off-load excess capacity and secure a larger market share (although not brand share) at reduced advertising and distribution costs. To the retailer, own-label offers control over the product, its supply, quality and formulation, in addition to control over price and margins, items per product line and shelf allocation.

Store loyalty

Retailers also argue that own-label products enable them to establish a competitive edge either through price differentiation or increasingly through quality, which in turn builds store or chain loyalty. This premise, however, is not entirely supported by research in this area (Uncles and Ellis 1989) which suggests that own-labels do not play a significant role in building and maintaining store loyalty. In particular, a study by Uncles and Ellis of the market for ground coffee in the United States concluded that own-label products 'are bought first like any other brand with a similar market share. Some buyers remain loyal to one chain and one own label, but most will buy elsewhere.'

As with purchases of manufacturers' brands, own-label buyers are a mix of sole buyers and multi-brand buyers. In this particular study, data for Safeway outlets show that around 48 per cent of own-label coffee purchasers were sole buyers over a year, i.e. bought nothing else. This compares with 54 per cent who were sole buyers of the brand leader, Folgers, 23 per cent for Maxwell House and 38 per cent for the product category as a whole.

However, these purchases only accounted for 17 per cent of own-label sales. Sole buyers were thus found to be light purchasers.

More than half Safeway own-label purchasers also bought other brands of ground coffee, representing 83 per cent of own-label sales. It was found that purchases were duplicated primarily with the brand leader, Folgers, followed by Master Blend, the extent of the duplication declining as the brand's penetration declined. Thus, own-labels compete primarily with the major brands in the market. Similarly, customers were observed to behave in the same way with regard to the purchase of own-label products from different chains. It was found that 29 per cent of those buying Safeway own-label also bought from other competitive chains and that duplicate buying from other chains tended to decline as the market share of the chains declined.

UK retailers may argue, however, that the Uncles and Ellis conclusions reflect the US retailing scene rather than the UK. What is clear, however, is that the operational and cost-related benefits referred to earlier—such as control of quality—have forced the own-label ceiling to beyond what was thought to be a maximum of 40 per cent of product lines with Tesco and Sainsbury both offering around 50 per cent of their goods as own label.

Tiered retailing

Own-label has not always been the only alternative to manufacturer brands. In 1976, Carrefour, the leading international food retailer, introduced a range of 50 'Produits Libres'. This was the first step into third-tier retailing: manufacturer brands, own-labels and now 'generics'. De Chernatony (1988) defines 'generics' as:

> Retailer controlled items which are packed in such a way that the prime concern with the packaging is product protection with minimal concern for aesthetic appeal, and displaying only the legal minimum amount of information.

In the UK, International (now Gateway) was the first retailer to launch a generic range, 'Plain and Simple', in 1977. This was followed by Carrefour's 'Brand Free' in 1978, Fine Fare's 'Yellow Pack' in 1980, Tesco's 'Value Line' in 1981 and Argyll's 'BASICS' in the same year.

UK generics, however, were a lot less functional than their continental counterparts. They adopted brand names, they sported bright, impactful packaging and used above- and below-the-line promotion. As a result, generics or 'neogenerics' as Hawes and McEnally (1983) termed them, had a lot more in common with own label. Nevertheless, they did offer a considerable price benefit, typically 40 per cent below branded items and 20 per cent below own label. Price differentials, however, have to be recognized in order to be effective. De Chernatony (1987) found that price differentials within different product categories varied enormously. In the washing-up liquid market, for instance, there was a 44p difference between brands and generics or a 165 per cent price differential! In kitchen towels, however, there was only a 13p difference or 22 per cent price differential between brands and generics. Yet there was no significant difference between consumer perceptions of price differences between the two product categories. De Chernatony concluded that: 'Any product range launched on a low price platform needs to have the magnitude of the price reduction clearly advertised to consumers.' The concept of three-tier retailing can therefore be challenged.

De Chernatony (1989) explored consumer perceptions in six product fields: three where advertising spend had increased (bleach, toilet paper and washing-up liquid) and three where advertising spend had fallen (aluminium foil, household disinfectant and kitchen towels). Consumers were asked to evaluate three brands, three own-labels and a minimum of two generics within each product category using image-batteries.

A cluster analysis applied to the data revealed that manufacturer brands are consistently perceived differently to own-labels and generics, but that own-labels and generics are perceived similarly. These perceptions hold true despite different levels of advertising support.

Three points need to be made here.

First, the data provide reassurance to brand managers that servicing the own-label sector does not necessarily inflict a mortal blow upon a brand. This echoes research by the Henley Centre for Forecasting (1982) which concludes that 'It still seems somewhat premature to proclaim the funeral rites for the brand.'

Secondly, despite the evidence that less supported brands are in no greater danger of being 'merged' with own-label, it is perhaps over-optimistic to assume that continual lack of investment will not weaken the brand. Years of brand investment have no doubt contributed much to a brand's resistance.

Thirdly, the term 'generics' was applied to some products which, in reality, were not generic at all, but 'own-labels'. As indicated earlier, UK generics did not conform to the definition of a true generic insofar that they were better packaged and better supported than their continental counterparts.

By 1987, all generics had been withdrawn from the UK marketing scene. Not only was the consumer failing to respond to a three-tier retail structure, but there was the very real risk of damaging the store's positioning by its association with a third-class product.

The own-label proposition

Originally, own-label entered the market on a 'cheap and cheerful' basis with consumers accepting inferior quality for cheaper prices. The packaging was drab, the product lines were 'me-toos' and the performance was patently below branded equivalents.

However, by the mid-1980s, retailers realized the importance of own-label in communicating the personality and positioning of the store through their own product lines. Arguably, own-label had potentially become the most important image-building tool in retailing. In many cases, the packs became brighter, the products more innovative and the performance every bit as good as their branded equivalents. Quality became the name of the game—quality with good value prices. This was and continues to be reflected in straplines such as:

'Good food costs less at Sainsbury'
'It 'Asda be Asda'
'Where good ideas come naturally' (Safeway)

Today, quality is such a key requirement that it is almost taken for granted. Sharoff (1991), president of the New York-based Private Label Manufacturers' Association, says: 'The UK consumer has a far higher expectation for quality than her counterparts in other countries.' Quality may be the result of many different factors, either store-related or product-driven or through association, e.g. celebrity endorsements.

The massive store redevelopment programmes of the major retailers are evidence of the importance of store enviroment as a quality signal to the consumer. Wide aisles, spotless interiors, coffee shops and clock towers are all part of the 1990s one-stop shopping experience, which has played a major role in the rejuvenation and move upmarket of 'Today's Tesco', for example.

New product development has also been influential in the communication of quality through own-label lines. Product sectors, like chilled recipe dishes and ready-to-eat meals, command premium prices with no obvious branded equivalent. In these product sectors, it is own-label that leads and the manufacturer brands that follow. Product sectors—which may not necessarily be new but embrace a certain set of values such as Tesco's 'Green' range (environmentally friendly), Boots' Shapers (calorie control) and Sainsbury's Nature's Compliments (naturalness)—again help to maintain and promote the quality positioning for the store.

Quality through association is more varied. It may be achieved through celebrity endorsement: Hannah Gordon (actor), for example, featured in Safeway's advertising during the late 1980s; the galloping gourmet, Robert Carrier, did the same for Tesco and, more recently, Dudley Moore (actor). Educational links may also be used to bolster quality perceptions of a store. For example, Asda sponsors a Chair in Business Studies at Oxford Brookes. Tesco has developed case study packages for use in schools and colleges and through its Customer Services Department answers as many as 2000 requests a week for information from students. Charity links and sponsorships (particularly of the arts) also help maintain a quality positioning through association. If consumers 'rate' the activity or the celebrity then they are more likely to 'rate' the other partner in the association—in this case the store and the store's own-label.

The own-label proposition is, therefore, a much broader issue than that of brands. Whereas a brand's proposition is essentially product specific, the own-label proposition embraces both that of the store and its own-label lines. As a result, own-label products can help build consumer perceptions of the store, and the store can build perceptions of own-label lines. It is a two-way process.

Personality

Retailers will speak of their own-label personalities in the same way as brand managers speak of their brands as being:

'warm'
   'friendly'
      'reassuring'
         'trustworthy'.

Brand managers, however, may be less complimentary in their perceptions of own-label! Certainly, projective tests, reveal a much more superficial personality for own-label. When brand managers were asked to complete a quotation balloon on how they felt as an own-label product they revealed the sentiments shown in Figure 6.1.

Other projective tests, where the consumer is asked to personify a store as a breed of dog, might reveal the following: Boots, a golden retriever, dependable and gentle; Tesco, a terrier, unpretentious and tough, Sainsbury, a pointer, leading the way. Thus, despite a similar positioning of quality and value for money among major UK retailers, they can, nevertheless, project different personalities.

Perceptions of own-label can also vary geographically, as a spokesperson for Sainsbury indicated:

> We can recognize a difference between heartland and hinterland. The south-east is heartland and the north-east, typical of the hinterland. The company started in Drury Lane and spread out. Croydon is important in our history as a middle-class suburb. You don't have to try too hard to launch a store in the south-east. You can assume people know what Sainsbury stands for. But in Sunderland, we have a completely different job to do. (You have) to get rid of some of the prejudices—large, successful, arrogant southern retailer thinking they can show us how we should buy food. It is the same personality. We don't trade differently, but it takes more time to convince people (in the hinterland) than in Tunbridge Wells (heartland).

In order to reduce the less favourable perceptions in the north, Sainsbury decided to include more friendly, almost frivolous phrases in the launch advertisements for Bio Yogurt (see the case study at the

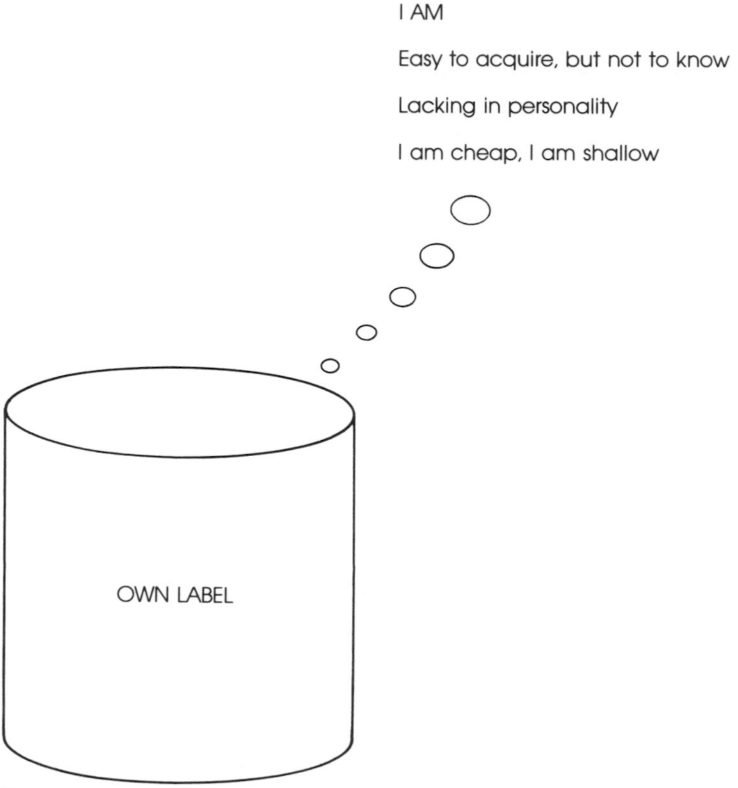

I AM

Easy to acquire, but not to know

Lacking in personality

I am cheap, I am shallow

OWN LABEL

Figure 6.1 Projective test to reveal perceptions of own-label by brand managers

end of this chapter), for example, 'Kind of good for your tummy and yummy.' Such copy aims to 'warm' the Sainsbury personality for those people who might otherwise have considered the store as 'cold and clinical'.

Own-label consumers

Who is the typical own-label purchaser? Evidence is now growing that as own-label moves from a 'cheap and cheerful' base to one of quality and value for money it is attracting a different kind of shopper. Sharoff, of the New York-based Private Label Manufacturers' Association, sees her as 'between 35 and 44 years old with children. She lives in the southern half of the country and is certainly not strapped for cash' (*Super Marketing* 1991). He has also discovered that 'the person with more limited disposable income tends to shop at stores projecting lower images of themselves and with fewer own-label products'.

The trend, it would appear, is for own-label products to appeal to the more self-confident, middle-income groups who like to feel they have made a 'smart' purchase, either in terms of value for money or in terms of innovative product lines.

Design

The importance of pack design in the evolution and growth of own labels became more generally recognized in the 1980s when retailers began to see design as a means of communicating with their customers. The pack could be used both to reflect its product contents and, more significantly, to convey the corporate identity of the store.

Tesco, for instance, has used well-designed own-label products as a means of divorcing itself from the old 'pile it high and sell it cheap' reputation and of introducing a much more upmarket feel for its range of own-label products. This, in turn, has helped reposition Tesco and increased its consumer credibility.

Design literacy among the public has heightened the need for design specialists. Most retailers have several design houses working into them. Sainsbury, for instance, has 12–15 consultancies at peak design times (i.e. the summer months when Christmas work is in hand), but this drops to a core of six consultancies during the lighter winter months. Further evidence of the importance of design is shown in the regularity of design meetings (typically once a week or once a fortnight) attended by senior management.

According to Burnside (1990), own-label design must fulfil two functions: '(It) must reflect the product while perpetuating the corporate image of the store.' This balance, however, is not always easy to achieve. Some stores are very poor at reflecting a distinct house style, as can be seen from the similarity in packaging of various brands of shampoo, e.g. Timotei (Elida Gibbs), Often (Safeway) and Frequent Wash (Boots).

Further evidence of this similarity in design comes from the Mintel Special Report (1991), quoted earlier. It claims that only just over half of respondents in their survey recognized the Marks & Spencer own-label (St Michael) with Sainsbury and Tesco tying on 48 per cent. This contrasts quite dramatically with awareness of national brands like Heinz, Kellogg's, Nescafé and Persil, all of which scored above 90 per cent. It perhaps results from the fact that the own-label proposition is not only very similar across all the key multiples, but that its purpose is to reflect the proposition of the store as well as that of its products.

Despite this, design can offer an opportunity to create a specific identity for the product. This is how the Sainsbury designer explained the creative rationale for the Bio Yogurt pack.

> We tried to avoid the usual yogurt cliche's—especially in a market where there was a health benefit. We wanted to avoid the 'socks and sandals' route and go for the high tec yogurt—a new age yogurt. We used interesting typography, silver ... whereas the (main competitor) Onken has a meadow—very obvious.

Since own-label does not enjoy the level of promotional support of most manufacturer brands, it could be argued that own-label design must work a lot harder to achieve a worthwhile share of voice.

Sainsbury's designer echoes this thought: 'The Sainsbury's design should be the design that the brand didn't have the courage to go with' (Burnside 1990).

Product innovations

Another area where own-label has, perhaps, stolen a march on manufacturer brands is in the area of new product development. Traditionally manufacturers set the pace and own-labels followed with what was often an inferior 'me-too' version. Increasingly, however, own-label has taken on the entrepreneurial role, leaving the manufacturers to follow suit. Fensholt (1988) observes:

> Retailers have captured the product development lead—we are in the chief role. It's the manufacturer who has to second guess it.

Retailer product development initiatives enjoy several operational advantages over manufacturers. First, they have immediate access to stores, which means they can capitalize on as wide a geographic distribution as national brands without the need for super-hyped selling procedures. Secondly, they automatically receive a high allocation of shelf space—sometimes twice as much as manufacturers' brands. Thirdly, the performance of new product initiatives may be quickly and accurately assessed through EPOS (electronic point of sale) in which electronic scanners monitor sales at the check-outs.

Retailers such as Tesco and Sainsbury also operate consumer test centres to develop and monitor the response to new products. Traditionally, the product was put through a three-way test against the brand leader and another competitive own-label. Increasingly, however, new products are tested monadically, i.e. only the test product is evaluated, since there is no comparable me-too line with which to compare its performance.

Increasingly, too, top retailers work in partnership with suppliers, who may also be manufacturers of branded goods. Whereas, before, the product brief might have been given to five or six potential suppliers, each of whom raced to come up with the 'contract winning' goods, it is becoming common for retailers to enter into a 'partnership' arrangement. This means that the resources, expertise and specialist knowledge of the market may be pooled for the mutual benefit of both the retailer and the supplier. However, although retailers may often instigate the concept development process by brainstorming or synectics (see Chapter 10), they rarely develop the products themselves.

One consequence of this carefully managed and often well-researched new product development process is that there are said to be few new product failures, once the product goes on-shelf: 'The approach is to develop one product very carefully, rather than throw 10 at the wall and hope one sticks' (Fensholt 1988).

New product initiatives by retailers can be seen as an important strategic tool for establishing a significant own-label presence in areas that brands have failed to capture.

Brands in their own right

Some own-labels may be said to have become brands in their own right. Boots is perhaps a prime example. The first into own-label in 1877, it still operates a mixed-branding strategy, offering a range of goods, specifically promoted as 'Boots Brands' alongside manufacturer brands. Examples include: No. 7, a range of cosmetics; No. 17, a range of teenage cosmetics; Shapers, a range of diet-controlled food and drink items; Bodytone, a range of health-care items; and Natural Collection, a range of exotic and beautifully packaged toiletries. Through a strategy of brand name endorsement (Boots No. 7, Boots Natural Collection) product ranges capitalize on both the corporate values of the Boots family name and the individual values of the product itself.

Natural Collection, for instance, may be said to offer functional attributes of exotic, natural ingredients while at the same time offering the symbolic values of sensuality, delicacy and femininity. It is these product-specific attributes that distinguish a brand from own-label, and on these grounds Boots 'Natural Collection' qualifies as a brand in its own right. It is perhaps only a matter of time before these brands are offered in stores other than those under the corporate umbrella: Boots Natural Collection in Debenhams, for example, or Boots Shapers in Waitrose.

The balance of power, however, between own-label and brands ultimately rests with the consumer. If the consumer wants a brand and considers the range incomplete without it, then the retailer is obliged to stock it. Mintel (1991) points out that: 'Retailers acknowledge that brands create demand and provide a point of reference for its own-label lines.' The own-label–brand relationship is, therefore, mutually dependent.

Summary

Own-label includes both retailer brands such as Tesco and Do It All as well as wholesaler brands such as Nurdin & Peacock's Happy Shopper. The own-label phenomenon grew as a cost-cutting response to the inflationary 1970s and was fuelled by the consolidation of retailer power among the major multiples. To the retailer, own-label offers control over the product, its supply, quality, price and formulation. To the supplier (who is often also a manufacturer of competitive brands), own-label offers an opportunity to off-load excess capacity, secure sizeable market share and reduce advertising and distribution costs. Therefore, there are advantages to be gained on both sides of the equation.

The rise and fall of generics in the UK reflect the possibility, identified in research, that not only did the consumer fail to distinguish between own-label and generics but that a cheaper, third-tier retail structure can damage overall perceptions of the store.

Own-label has moved from a 'cheap and cheerful' basis in the 1970s to a 'quality' and value-for-money positioning in the 1980s and 1990s. The own-label proposition, it is argued, is a broader concept than that of brands since it embraces both the store proposition and those of individual product lines. As a result, own-label can build consumer perceptions of the store and the store can build perceptions of own-label.

Despite a similar positioning across all the major multiples, it may be possible to identify different personalities between stores, e.g. 'dependable' Boots, 'unpretentious' Tesco and Sainsbury 'leading the way'.

The typical own-label consumer is now thought to be in the middle income group with the sort of self-confidence that makes an own-label purchase look like a 'smart' purchase.

Own-label has been seen to take the new product development lead, particularly in sectors like chilled desserts and ready-to-eat meals with retailers able to capitalize on immediate access to stores, high allocations of shelf-space and test centres which monitor the consumer response.

Finally, evidence suggests that own-labels are becoming brands in their own right, with Boots brands being a prime example. The balance of power, however, between own-label and brands ultimately rests with consumers. If they want a particular brand and consider the range incomplete without it, then the retailer is obliged to stock it. The own-label–brand relationship is, therefore, mutually dependent.

Case Study: SAINSBURY'S Bio Yogurt

Introduction

Sainsbury's Bio Yogurts comprise a range of natural and fruit flavoured yogurts made from wholemilk and special 'live' cultures, believed to aid digestion and dietary balance. Natural yogurt is available in 150 g and 500 g sizes while the three fruit-flavoured varieties (strawberry, blackcherry, peach and passion fruit) are available in 150 g pots.

Bio yogurts, or biologically activated yogurts—the names originally denoting the new strains of mild cultures used, but now virtually interchangeable—are well established on the continent. In Germany they were launched 15 years ago and their share of total yogurt sales is now in excess of 75 per cent. In France, this culture was launched 5–6 years ago and now has a 15 per cent share.

Several attempts had been made to launch the product in the UK with only limited success. Onken, a family firm and one of the major suppliers of dairy products in Germany, started exporting natural Bio Yogurt to the UK in September 1988. In spite of no advertising support, sales grew. Chambourcy launched their equivalent product, a 4-pack set yogurt in 1989. The advertising support was based on a 'life-style' concept, using the brand Activ. This has not as yet been very successful. Loseley launched a range that was intiailly confined to health stores although distribution has since broadened.

Apart from Loseley, which was very low key, none of the brands had launched into the UK market with the explicit health and mildness message.

The plan

Sainsbury's felt that none of the previous attempts to develop this new sector had been properly executed. Their message was two-fold:

- New mild taste
- Potential health-giving properties of this new culture.

Sainsbury's, therefore, attempted to attract two target consumers:

- People who did not buy yogurt due to its sharp acidic taste.
- Existing consumers who would trade-up in price to a wholemilk yogurt with health benefits.

One option discussed was to put the new culture into the standard yogurt range. Sainsbury's, however, felt that it would be a mistake to change the core range which was selling extremely well, the danger being that it could alienate more people than it attracted.

The strategy was, therefore, to create a new market sector, in the same way that Sainsbury's introduced *fromage frais* into the dairy market in 1984. Bio must thus not be perceived as just another yogurt; it had to taste noticeably different.

Product development

The search began for the right product.

In line with the development of *fromage frais* and in view of the fact that Sainsbury's were particularly strong in the natural yogurt sector, it was decided to start with natural yogurt and develop fruited flavours later. Sampling was made of full fat, low fat and fat-free natural yogurts, German, French and English, simply to discover which yogurts were preferred. The continental yogurts tended to be different from standard Sainsbury's yogurt: cleaner and milder, less acidic in taste. The natural yogurt, for example, could be eaten straight from the pot without the addition of sugar or flavourings.

After the initial sampling, the selection was narrowed to a single German, French and UK supplier. Further, the UK supplier was instructed to copy the smooth, clean texture of continental biologically activated yogurts. Further sampling showed that the potential product, in order of preference, was German, French and UK.

As this was to be the beginning of a new market sector, Sainsbury's considered ways it could subsequently be developed. They needed:

- volume
- a variety of sizes; singles for trial and choice, plus multi-packs and/or large sizes
- a choice of fat level
- layered fruit yogurt, as a point of distinction.

Reviewing the three potential suppliers

Supplier 1 from Germany was unwilling to supply the exact branded wholemilk product but offered reduced fat levels. The reduced fat levels tasted good—noticeably different from Sainsbury's standard yogurt—but wholemilk tasted the best and if they were to develop a new market they needed the possibility of all options.

There was the possibility of single 150 g portions and 500 g pots. For the fruited product, a layered fruit yogurt was proposed. However, the fruit layers did not taste good to an English palate; this could be changed if the yogurt supplier were put in touch with a fruit supplier who had a good understanding of Sainsbury's requirements.

The French yogurt from Supplier 2 was also good although the wholemilk version was not as delicious as that of Supplier 1. Again, the fruit was not considered good for the UK market. As the product was produced on Erca machinery (highly automated production lines), the costly setting-up process meant that long production runs were necessary and the producer was unwilling to interrupt the line to change the fruit when Sainsbury's could not, at this early stage, commit to large sales volumes. In addition, multi-packs produced this way tended to look similar on-shelf unless the design was striking.

Supplier 3, from the UK, was flexible in production methods and packaging but the product itself was consistently more acidic than the continental yogurts; it had a closer resemblance to standard Sainsbury's yogurt.

Supplier 1 visited Sainsbury. They were particularly anxious that their own brand should grow and felt that the best way was not to duplicate products in the market. Sainsbury's told them that it would be a long and costly exercise to establish a new brand in the UK and that with 70 per cent of business in own-label they would be more successful to work on own-label. Sainsbury convinced them that their standards of operation were every bit as high as their own, and that even if consumers were to recognize the Sainsbury yogurt as their product, this could only enhance the little-known brand rather than detract from it—such was the authority of the Sainsbury brand. Supplier 1 was persuaded to supply Sainsbury with both natural and fruited yogurt.

Packaging

Sainsbury admired the silver foil metallic designs which distinguished biologically activated yogurts in the French market; this would, however, necessitate sourcing a special pot. The relatively new process of therimage on yogurt pots was available only in limited supplies from one printer in the German market and was still not available in England. Sainsbury also had to source a re-usable lid for the 500 g pot, as, in Germany, 500 g were apparently consumed in a single serving!

Design

While waiting for checks to be completed, technical information to be supplied, the factory-vetting visit, shelf-life tests, fruit supply approval, etc., the Sainsbury designer was put in direct contact with the printer who produced the therimage labels—which were to be applied by heat, stretched and fused onto the pot. The printers produced samples of tints of the various metallic effects that could be achieved. A design was then produced which took advantage of this new process. The design brief was to convey a clean, modern and different yogurt.

Figure 6.2 Launch advertisement for Sainsbury's Bio Yogurt

Pricing

Both the early and the more recent pricing levels set by suppliers of branded 'live' culture products showed a premium against standard yogurt prices. For instance, Chambourcy Actif low-fat products were showing an 8 per cent premium over standard low-fat yogurts while Loseley live yogurts sold at a massive 50 per cent more than the equivalent low-fat Sainsbury range. Sainsbury, however, wanted to create a mainstream market and therefore kept the price premium to a minimum. This also fulfilled the normal Sainsbury requirements to undercut any branded alternative.

Promotion

The product was launched on 21 January 1991 with a special introductory price and an explanatory leaflet. The leaflet was displayed in-store on the 4-foot eye-level run of shelving which had been arranged by merchandising to display the new range. The leaflet described the benefits and the new flavour as well as providing some serving suggestions and recipes to encourage customers to try. Public relations sent a copy of the leaflet, together with a letter, to provincial publications nationwide. The four 150 g pots were sent by courier to each of the top 30 London publications.

A programme of in-store demonstrations organized for the spring enabled customers to sample the new yogurt. This was also linked to a price promotion. Bio also featured in the corporate advertising campaign which used products to demonstrate that the Sainsbury brand is innovative, different and constantly working on new ideas (see Figure 6.2). Sainsbury's management felt that Bio Yogurt fulfilled this brief.

Case Study: TESCO's ambient ready meals

Tesco is one of Britain's largest multiple retailers with 380 superstores and supermarkets. About half of its turnover is generated from own-label products, with approximately 1700 lines undergoing development at any one time.

This case study details the steps taken in the new product development programme for ambient ready meals which may be defined as:

> A new range of ready meal products available from the grocery shelves which do not need to be stored in the refrigerator or freezer and they have a minimum nine-months shelf-life. They are heat processed and contain only natural ingredients, no artificial additives or preservatives.

At Tesco the development of a product is always the responsibility of a product team consisting of the buyer, the marketing manager, the food technologist and the product evaluation officer.

The *buyer* is responsible for getting new products into the business and ensuring that own-label products will make a profit.

The *marketing manager* examines the market and looks at future trends as the means of generating ideas for new own-label product developments.

The *food technologist* is responsible for the technical quality of the product, examining ingredients, checking and approving factory premises and assessing the most appropriate production technology for manufacture of the product.

The *product evaluation officer* (PEO) develops the product in tasting sessions. Being the food expert in the team, the PEO raises awareness of healthy eating, green issues, etc., and produces back-of-pack cooking instructions.

Various other departments are also involved in the product development process; for example the nutrition department, which produces all the nutrition information and assesses whether products qualify for healthy eating logos; the legal department, which authorizes and checks all the information on the pack; the laboratories, which conduct chemical microbial and shelf-life tests. Design and marketing departments are also involved.

Looking at the actual development—how does it all start?

Product concept generation

Ideas for new products are generated from many different sources:

- An examination of the market may reveal a gap, where something could be developed.
- A change in market trends, e.g. towards vegetarian products, may provide concepts for future development.
- Other ideas may result from a study of the competitors' products, brainstorming sessions and discussion groups.

However, in the case of ambient ready meals, the concept was very unusual in that the packaging concept was developed before the product itself.

Packaging concept

On a visit to one of the packaging suppliers, a Tesco buyer became very interested in a new packaging development. This consisted basically of a plastic tray with a sealed foil lid, allowing in-container sterilization. A product could therefore be heat-treated and sealed in the packaging with no further need for refrigeration or freezing.

Traditionally, ambient ready meals have been available in dried or canned form. Canned meals tend to suffer from a poor image in comparison to frozen and chilled meals; and there is also the disadvantage of weight. In a can, 40 per cent of the contents are liquid, which may contain many of the product's nutrients and yet it is often discarded. Dried food, on the other hand, may require the addition of artificial additives and preservatives and does not always give convenience for the consumer in rehydrating and cooking.

The plastic tray with sealed foil lid provided an opportunity for a 'superior' ambient ready meal with none of the disadvantages of either the canned or dried forms. The buyer saw a possible use for the packaging to house ready-made meals. The packaging idea was looked at more closely.

The product team brainstormed the idea to see whether it had potential. The team were at first apprehensive as both the product and the packaging broke new ground and represented a risk.

Nevertheless, having looked at the market, the product team could see a gap. Ambient ready meals would certainly have advantages over canned, dried, frozen and even fresh ready meals. But what did they want ambient ready meals to deliver? What began to emerge was the need for a high-quality product, lean meat, no additives and convenience in use. The marketing manager drew up a New Product Development brief and circulated this to all relevant departments. It included the following issues:

- Was it to be part of a range?
- What were the desired pack size/weight/number of servings?
- What was the proposed shelf-life?
- What was the target market?

One to four weeks is the usual timescale at the concept stage. However, with the ambient ready meals, one year was spent totally on developing the packaging before the food concept was developed. A commercial brief was raised by the buyer, justifying the product for own-label, in terms of expected turnover and profit, including design and development costs.

Product development

Once the packaging was complete, it was taken to a selection of food suppliers to enable them to suggest some product ideas around core recipes like beef stew and dumplings, which already sold well in the chilled food sector.

It is the job of the food technologist to establish which suppliers can technically produce the desired product for Tesco and the jobs of the PEO and buyer to visit each supplier to brief them as to what is wanted. Up to four different suppliers may be given a brief since more than one might eventually be required to meet consumer demand.

The product is developed, checked, amended and re-checked several times, until it is found to be acceptable to the product team. With the ambient ready meal, tasting took place at head office every week until a range was finally decided upon.

During the development process, safety is a key factor to consider. It was decided that the ambient ready meal range would not contain any artificial additives or preservatives, and therefore the processing of the product had to ensure total microbiological kill. During production, the ready meals were held at 121 °C for 30 minutes to ensure this.

Total processing time took one hour, which includes heating, holding and cooling the product.

A nine-month shelf-life was initially put on the ambient meals, although in fact they were still edible after two years. The reason for this was that some oil separation can occur after one year in products that contain cheese, although there is no flavour detriment.

Shelf-life testing was carried out both at the supplier's factory and at Tesco's laboratories. Average shelf-life testing takes three months; for ambient ready meals it took two years. During this time the design department worked on the packaging and artwork.

The development process for ambient ready meals was very lengthy owing to the product and packaging being totally new concepts. It was not just a case of developing a product and putting it in a can. The packaging and seals were all new, which made a technological development as well as a product development. A lot of work was involved to ensure that there were no problems.

The product development process at Tesco usually takes 26 weeks at least, if all goes smoothly! However, for ambient ready meals the total development process took approximately three years.

The final stages

The PEO completed a product development brief which outlined the final details of the developed product, including a description of the product, details of the supplier, details of the shelf-life and an approval of the supplier's premises by the technologist. At this stage the new development was assessed for the earliest feasible launch date. Launch times do need careful planning, to coincide with seasonal purchasing trends. With ambient ready meals, there was a need to accelerate the development in the last few months in order to be first into the market. Tesco knew they had a good-quality product and did not want another manufacturer or retailer to launch a poor-quality ambient meal first as this could destroy customer confidence in all ambients thereafter.

Product testing

A date was also allocated for testing the product in the Consumer Advice Centres. Once a product is found to be acceptable to the head office product teams, the developed product has to pass a quality approval test through Tesco's six Consumer Advice Centres or home placement prior to launch. Exceptions to this include such products as raw vegetables, seasonal canned fruit and vegetables and unprocessed raw cuts of red meat, poultry and fish, where quality relies on technical specifications. Cheese, wine and tea products usually have specialists to approve product quality.

The Consumer Advice Centres are used to assess the acceptability of all new products to Tesco customers prior to launch, using professional market research techniques. For these tests, the following information is needed: age quotas, usership details, cooking and presentation instructions and benchmark details when applicable.

Market researchers recruit customers to take part in taste panels according to strict quotas determined by Tesco's sensory experts. All products are tested 'blind' to ascertain only the physical characteristics of the product. The sensory department arranges with the supplier for the samples to be manufactured and delivered to test locations. Samples are also sent to head office from the same production to ensure that the standard is the same as that previously agreed with the supplier. Samples not arriving at test locations or delivered out of temperature specification are rejected. Chilled foods, for example, must arrive at a temperature between 2 °C and 4 °C and frozen foods at −18 °C minimum.

Respondents are instructed to judge the attributes of appearance, aroma, flavour, texture, overall preference and the acceptability to their household. At the end of the assessment the results are fed, through an optical mark reader (OMR), to a computer which records all the scores. This is then transferred, via telephone link, to head office where it is analysed. All descriptive data (comments) are sent back to head office for fast analysis, i.e. three days.

A report is issued by the sensory evaluation department on whether the product has passed or failed. This is based on:

- the results of the statistical analysis
- consumer comments
- the consumer services officer's report.

Results from the test can lead to any one of the following actions:

- The product is fully acceptable and can be launched.
- The product fails to match the benchmark on minor points, is improved and tested again at head office before launching.
- The product fails to match the benchmark, is improved and undergoes further Consumer Advice Centre testing before launch.
- The product fails considerably and is cancelled and removed from all records.

With the ambient ready meals there were no major failures. Some, however, failed on appearance. These were redeveloped and approved by the head office team.

A 'Label Copy Specification' was also raised by the PEO, together with the marketing manager, which outlined all the information to be included on the packaging, e.g. cooking instructions, ingredients list, nutrition panel, bar codes, etc. All the information had to be approved by the legal department, once the product had passed its test, and then passed on to design to progress final artwork.

The ambient ready meal development was probably one of the most costly products developed, not only from the point of view of packaging development cost, but also the amount of staff hours put into the development of the product.

On-pack information

At Tesco, the aim is to provide nutritional information on all own-label products so that people can see exactly what they are eating. In any new product development, the principles of less fat, sugar, salt and more fibre are adhered to all the way through the development process.

The technology used to produce the ambient ready meals allowed the development of healthier products with no artificial additives or preservatives. The process also retained more of the natural flavours of the ingredients and did not, therefore, require any flavour enhancers.

Cooking instructions are also important. They can help the consumer to prepare and cook food more safely to maintain optimum quality. Instructions on the ambient ready meal packs were to boil for 12–15 minutes or microwave for 3 minutes. Recipes may also be developed by product information officers to put on-pack, within healthy eating guidelines. There was no need to refrigerate or freeze, and shelf-life details were also added.

Following completion of the on-pack specification, the artwork is produced and photographs are taken. The artwork is then approved.

The ambient ready meal packaging was produced with a lot of colour, a lot of photography and a varnished finish to the pack. This was to help communicate the product as a high-quality item within the convenience sector.

Packaging in relation to green issues

The plastic packaging used was in itself recyclable, but the barrier film over the plastic, which prevented oxygen getting to the product, was not. Tesco, however, is looking to change this for the future. The cardboard sleeve cannot be made from recycled board owing to its direct contact with the food in the current design. Again, this is the subject of a re-evaluation.

Product launch

A leaflet accompanied the launch, which included a coupon offer to encourage sales. Once a product is launched, the product team and Consumer Advice Centres keep a constant check on the quality of the product to ensure that it is to the quality the customer requires. In this way, Tesco ensures that nothing goes on the shelves unless the customer wants it.

By the end of 1991, retail sales reached £33 million; by the end of 1992 a similar level of sales was achieved and for 1993 the forecast is for sales to grow to £35 million, as a result of increasing microwave ownership and an increasing need for high-quality, convenience foods.

References

Burnside, A., 'Packaging and design', *Marketing*, 15 February 1990.

De Chernatony, L., 'Consumer perceptions of the competitive tiers in 6 grocery markets', unpublished PhD thesis, City University, 1987.

De Chernatony, L., 'The Fallacy of Generics in the UK', *Marketing Intelligence and Planning*, **6** (2), 1988.

De Chernatony, L., 'Marketers and consumers' concurring perceptions of market structure', *European Journal of Marketing* **23** (1), 1989.

Fensholt, C., 'Minding the store', *Supermarket Business*, November 1988.

Hawes, J. and McEnally, M., 'An Empirically derived Taxonomy of Brands', paper presented at the 1983 conference of the Southeastern American Institute for Decision Sciences, 1983.

Henley Centre for Forecasting, *Manufacturing and Retailing in the '80s: A Zero Sum Game*, 1982.

Mintel Special Report, *Own Label in Packaged Grocery Retailing*, 1991.

Morris, D., 'The strategy of own brands', *European Journal of Marketing*, **13** (2), 1971.

Randall, G., 'The battle for brands', *Management Today*, November 1985.

Super Marketing 'Own label: What the customer is looking for', *Super Marketing*, 12 April 1991.

Uncles, M. and Ellis, D., 'The buying of own labels', *European Journal of Marketing*, **23** (3), 1989.

7

Brands as assets

The brand-building process, as we have seen, requires substantial investment over a long period of time but, if successful, yields a positive cash flow over the long term. Brand building can therefore be regarded as part of a company's capital investment and, as a consequence, it has been argued that brands should be treated as intangible fixed assets for financial accounting purposes. However, while it seems generally accepted that brands have 'economic value', the accounting profession has expressed considerable misgivings about recording such values in published financial statements. There is, nevertheless, considerable debate between marketers and accountants, and indeed within the accounting profession itself, about the issues of both theory and practice that the practice of the capitalization of brands raises.

The regulatory framework

There is widespread acceptance that the practice of brand accounting is within the existing regulations as set out by the Companies Acts, the Statements of Standards of Accounting Practice (SSAP) prepared by the Accounting Standards Committee (ASC) and, more recently, the financial reporting statements produced by the Accounting Standards Board (ASB), the ASC's successor. It is worth noting that the work of the ASB is being supported by work on the development of a conceptual framework including the determination of a definition, and alternative approaches to the valuation of fixed assets. At present, however, there is a distinct difference between the required treatment of acquired as opposed to home-grown brands.

Acquired brands

In the case of acquired brands, the regulations (SSAP 22, Accounting for Goodwill, 1984) require that separable assets, which include intangibles such as brands but not goodwill, should be identified and valued at 'fair value'. The latter is defined as 'the amount which the acquiring company would have been willing to pay for the asset had it been acquired directly'.

The important factor here is the restriction of recognition to separately identifiable assets. If a brand can be sold separately then it may be recognized as an intangible asset in the accounts.

Home-grown brands

The treatment of home-grown brands remains controversial and unresolved. There are no definitive accounting regulations, only a number of non-binding recommendations which take the view that valuations cannot be used unless some reasonable approximation of the cost of the asset in question can be made. Provision exists which enables the use of 'modified historic-cost' to value certain intangible fixed assets, where it may be difficult to identify specific monetary transactions associated with their development. Clearly, for most brands, it is difficult to identify precisely the historic costs associated with their development. Modifications can be on the basis of current cost or market value, neither of which is defined in the regulations, although current cost is generally defined as 'value to the business' of the asset or opportunity cost. The principle of separably identifiable assets also applies in the context of home-grown brands.

Brands and goodwill

The brands debate could be regarded as a very British affair as it partly results from the way in which goodwill is treated in UK accounting practice which encourages the immediate write-off of goodwill to reserves. The effect of this increases gearing (the ratio of fixed interest funding to ordinary shareholders funds) and thereby weakens the balance sheet. In contrast, in North America and the rest of Europe, goodwill is carried as an asset in the balance sheet and amortized through the profit and loss account. Accounting for home-grown brands is prohibited by law in almost all countries with the notable exceptions of Australia and the UK. It has been argued that if UK accounting regulations followed general international practice requiring goodwill to be carried and amortized, the pressure for brand accounting would be reduced (Barwise *et al.* 1989). As it stands, it is argued the substantial costs of writing off the goodwill of acquired companies is encouraging companies to evaluate their acquired brands in order to reduce the goodwill component, thereby reducing the effect on gearing and restoring the shape of the balance sheet. Furthermore, by valuing home-grown brands, companies are able to further restore their weakened balance sheets.

The brands debate

The 'brands debate' emerged in 1984 when the Australian company News Group included publishing titles, which had resulted from the acquisition of a publishing company, in its balance sheet, thereby avoiding the need to write off the goodwill from the acquisition. In the UK, this was followed in 1985 by the capitalization of the Airwick brand in Reckitt & Colman's annual accounts. Other companies followed in rapid succession. In 1988, the UK company Grand Met capitalized the Smirnoff brand following their acquisition of Heublein in the previous year. It continued this practice after its acquisition of the American Pillsbury Corporation in 1989. In its 1988 accounts, Guinness valued their acquired brands (including Johnny Walker, Dewars, Bell's and White Horse Scotch whiskies and Gordons and Tanqueray gin) at £1695 million. Guinness also recognized the value of brands in an associate company in which it held a 20 per cent stake, Moët Hennessy Louis Vuitton which owned such brands as Dom Perignon, Veuve Clicquot and Moët & Chandon champagnes, Hennessy Cognac, and Christian Dior and Givenchy perfumes.

New ground was broken, however, when in 1988 the British flour and food company Rank Hovis McDougall (RHM) included its home-grown as well as its acquired brands in its balance sheet. More than 50 brands were included (including Mother's Pride and Hovis bread, Paxo stuffing, Saxa salt, Bisto gravy browning, and Robertson's jams) amounting to £678 million and representing 59 per cent of the company's total assets.

The Nestlé case in the same year highlights a different aspect of the same phenomenon. In this case, Rowntree, a UK company with tangible net assets of around £300 million and a pre-bid capital value of around £1 billion, was acquired by the Swiss company Nestlé for £2.3 billion after a hard-fought battle with competitors, Jacobs-Suchard. The excess value placed upon Rowntree by Nestlé represented an evaluation of various intangibles, including such brands as Rowntree's Kit Kat, Rolo and Quality Street. Other intangibles probably included the strategic value of preventing a competitor such as Jacobs-Suchard from owning these brands.

Under current UK accounting rules the premium paid for the net tangible assets of Rowntree came under the category of 'goodwill' and, as such, had to be either written off to reserves (the more popular option), severely weakening the balance sheet, or amortized, which would severely affect short-term profits. Both alternatives took no account of the strategic benefits of the acquisition. In the extreme, the acquisition of highly valuable brands by acquisitive companies such as Nestlé could lead to a balance sheet without reserves or with lower earnings per share, yet the company might have become strategically extremely powerful. There are many other examples of companies who have acquired valuable brands and have faced such problems having written off goodwill. These include the communications company WPP and the food and detergents company Unilever.

Cases such as these fuelled a debate which still continues. However, in considering this debate it is important to maintain a clear distinction between the marketing management issues and the financial accounting issues. From the marketing manager's point of view, placing a value on each of the company's brands (and no less importantly on competitors' brands) is of vital importance if sensible decisions are to be made about:

- the identification of potential acquisitions and divestments
- brand licensing/franchising
- the allocation of resources for brand building
- the performance of brands over time.

From the point of view of the company's directors, on the other hand, the important factors are:

- the need to provide a realistic picture of the business for the stock market
- the need to minimize the impact on both the balance sheet and the profit and loss account of goodwill write-offs
- the need to keep gearing at acceptable levels
- the need to deter predators looking for 'cheap' acquisitions.

While these are all desirable reasons for brand valuation from the corporate viewpoint, they raise some important practical as well as theoretical issues which have to be resolved by both the accounting and the marketing professions. These issues concern, first, the rules governing company financial reporting, secondly, the actual valuation process and, thirdly, how brand assets should be dealt with as regards amortization subsequent to valuation.

The 'brands debate' does in fact raise fundamental issues about the role of financial statements, asset recognition and valuation which go well beyond the scope of this chapter. These issues are dealt with more fully in other publications (Barwise et al. 1989) and only a summary has been provided here.

Brand equity

The evaluation of brands is an extremely important issue in marketing management (as opposed to financial management) in most countries. In the United States, in particular, it has become a major research area. The impetus for this work, in common with the brands debate in the UK, comes from the enormous pressures on companies to deliver short-term profits together with the difficulties which companies have in demonstrating the long-term value of brand building and the enhancement of what is called *brand equity*.

Brand equity has been defined (Aaker 1991) as:

> ... assets and liabilities linked to a brand, its name and symbol, that add to or subtract from the value provided by a product or service to a firm or to that firm's customers.

It is important to note, however, that it represents not only the capitalized value of the expected net earnings from the existing brand franchise (its operational value), but also the value of the brand as a stepping-stone for future options such as brand extensions (its strategic value). As a concept, it focuses the management's orientation away from short-term financial goals towards the development and maintenance of assets as the providers of a true sustainable competitive edge.

The assets (and their associated liabilities) which form brand equity will, of course, vary according to the product category and the nature of associated consumer behaviour. However, it has been suggested (Aaker 1991) that these can nevertheless usefully be grouped under five headings:

- Brand loyalty
- Name or symbol awareness
- Perceived quality
- Brand associations other than perceived quality
- Other proprietary brand assets.

Brand loyalty

One of the main objectives of developing awareness, perceived quality and brand associations is the building of brand loyalty. Apart from the obvious benefits of creating a steady stream of future revenue from loyal customers there are other benefits which include the ability to withstand competitive attacks from new brands, the ability to survive short-term interruptions in supply, and the ability to survive changes in government legislation. In recent years, the food and drink industry has come to realize the strength of its branding in a very specific way as a result of unexpected problems associated with product quality (e.g. Perrier) and product contamination by third parties (e.g. Heinz Baby Foods and, more recently, Lucozade in the UK). All these brands have survived short-term disruptions to supply as a result of the strength of their propositions in the marketplace, reflected in both distributor and customer loyalty and the consistency of purpose in developing brand equity.

Name or symbol awareness

An example of a brand whose value was potentially affected by changing name awareness was the Mars Confectionery product Marathon, which in the UK had its name changed to Snickers, the name used in most other countries. The substantial investment in advertising and promotion represented a liability on the brand equity at least in the short term. In contrast, there were longer term benefits of adopting an international name, including standardized packaging and advertising as well as increased international awareness of the product. The re-naming in this case was nevertheless successful. The trick lay in keeping the same packaging while changing the name. In this way awareness and brand equity were maintained through careful management of the process.

Perceived quality

An example of how changes in perceived quality affect brand equity is provided by the UK car company Rover. Until the 1960s, the Rover marque was held in high esteem in the UK and Rover cars were a status symbol of note. Loss of individual identity in a large, poorly regarded British Leyland Corporation, combined with serious problems of quality control, led to a relatively sudden decline in Rover's perceived quality and, as a consequence, market share fell. Today the company would argue that Rover's perceived quality has been reinstated, but at what cost in updated production methods, engine design, quality control and promotional expenditure?

There has been a substantial increase in the financial liabilities associated with Rover's brand equity as a result of the years of neglect. It is claimed that the resultant long-term cash flows from the 'Roverization' policy, as the rebirth policy was called, are resulting in a net increase in brand equity.

Brand associations other than perceived quality

Aaker suggests that it is frequently the successful development of brand associations going beyond the vague concept of quality that create the brand's sustainable competitive edge. In our terminology, these associations are those that focus on the symbolic values of the brand personality. For example, in the cola market, Pepsi has sought to create this edge through developing associations with fun and vitality (quality is taken for granted). One of the ways in which it has sought to do this has been through the sponsorship of rock concerts by Tina Turner, Rod Stewart and, more recently, Michael Jackson.

Careful selection of appropriate sponsorship can help build and sustain brand equity. A further example, that of Sony's sponsorship of the TV coverage of the 1991 Rugby World Cup in the UK, at first glance has a less obvious brand equity value. However, research suggests that this sponsorship significantly raised awareness of the Sony brand. It is difficult, however, to see how this decision supports the Sony brand personality which in other forms of promotion may be presented as providing 'technological know-how innovation and reliability'. The decision may have brought brand exposure, but in the longer term may have done little to build brand equity.

Other proprietary brand assets

These include patents, trade marks and distributor relationships. Clearly, the use of patents can keep competition at bay, especially while a brand is becoming established. This is a particularly important feature of the ethical drugs market where the marketing liabilities with which a new brand begins can be extremely high. Trade marks, once registered, prevent competitive mis-use of the brand name, its logo and graphic symbol. Similarly, where sales of a brand are restricted to specific distributors to the exclusion of competitors, this too can enhance the brand equity.

Brand valuation

The problem

The concept of brand equity is an attractive one. However, if it is to be fully operationalized as a management approach, a value has to be determined for the equity at any point in time. It has so far proved extremely difficult to do this, owing partly to a lack of consistent historical information about the components of brand equity such as awareness, perceived quality, etc. The problem is also attributable to the difficulties of relating such measures directly to changes in expenditure levels, profitability or long-term shareholder value. It has been suggested, however, that no brand should be considered for inclusion in the balance sheet which does not have a sustainable competitive advantage (Doyle 1990).

Many approaches have been proposed, such as:

- the use of price premiums which the brand commands over competitors
- the use of customer preference information
- the use of stock price movements
- the use of replacement cost, i.e. the actual cost of developing a substitute brand
- the use of discounted expected future earnings.

However, no single variable is likely to capture in full the value of such a complex entity as a brand. Such approaches also ignore the additional difficulties of assigning costs to brand development. From an accounting point of view there is no doubt that capitalizing the costs of development improves profitability, whereas capitalizing some notional value of a brand does not.

However, brand valuations based solely on the total cost of marketing, advertising and R&D totally ignore the consumer's valuation of the brand and the fact that a lot of money has been spent on unsuccessful brands. Equally, there exists no market for brands, whereby a market value could be determined by the amount third parties are prepared to pay for the brand name. Such valuations would, in any case, contravene the UK Companies Acts. Similarly, valuing a brand on how highly consumers regard it ignores the importance of financial viability and whether consumers would be prepared to purchase it. On the other hand, valuations based upon discounted future cash flows are likely to be highly unstable and, consequently, on their own would be unacceptable for balance sheet purposes. Other benefits of strong brands—such as their ability to command premium prices or their leverage potential with the distribution trade, making them a springboard for the sale of brand extensions and other products—are even more difficult to measure. There thus seems to be no single variable that can be used to determine a brand's value. This is not surprising given the complexity of the brand-building process and the variety of benefits that successful brands provide.

As a result, several composite methods have been used to evaluate brands for the purposes of both financial and management accounting reports. However, as far as can be ascertained, such methods remain largely based around either an income-based approach (e.g. premium pricing potential) or an expenditure-based approach. In the case of Guinness and RHM the brand valuation is based upon an earnings multiple approach. Other organizations base it around discounted future earnings, or an approach based upon the aggregate cost of building the brand, including advertising, marketing and R&D. The methods used are similar to those used in accounting for other tangible assets when such valuations are to be used for balance sheet purposes. For reasons of confidentiality, however, companies are reluctant to provide details of their valuation methods and calculations.

The Interbrand approach

A widely publicized method, the basis of the RHM approach, is that developed by Interbrand Group plc (Murphy 1991), which focuses on the systematic determination of an earnings multiplier. In this system, earnings are represented by a three-year weighted average of post-tax profits. The determination of the multiple is derived from an in-depth assessment of the brand's strength. The brand's strength is represented by a composite of seven weighted factors:

- *Leadership*   The extent to which a brand leads a market sector
- *Stability*   The length of time a brand has been established in the market
- *Market*   The stability of the market sector in which the brand operates, its susceptibility to technological and fashion changes
- *Internationality* The extent of the brand's international coverage
- *Trend*   The direction of the long-term trend of the brand as an indicator of its relevance to consumers
- *Support*   The amount and consistency of the support given to the brand
- *Protection*   Whether the brand has a registered trade mark and the extent to which other legal protection exists.

The brand is scored for each of these factors and the resulting scores are weighted to determine an overall percentage score—'the brand strength score'. The higher the score, the higher the multiple to be applied to the earnings.

According to Murphy (1991), the relationship between the brand strength score and the multiplier is an S-curve. The perfect brand (i.e.

scoring 100 per cent) is equated with a risk-free investment. However, in reality brands do not operate in a risk-free environment. Thus, the highest multiple that is applied in such cases is lower than that for a risk-free investment and can vary between businesses and industries. It is also necessary to take into account the price/earnings (P/E) ratios of the industry in which the brand sells. The expectation is that the strong brands should have multiples greater than the average P/E ratio in the industry, and vice versa. According to Interbrand, the multiplier for 'a notional perfect brand is twenty times average annual brand-related earnings, although the multiple attributed to an average brand is substantially lower than this'.

Despite the apparent rigour of this approach, the essential subjectivity of the measure is a cause for concern, particularly as it affects the weighting given to the seven factors and the relationship between the brand strength score and the multiplier, and hence the shape of the S-curve itself.

This approach to brand valuation does not fully address the problems of measurement listed at the beginning of this section. In particular it excludes variables related to the strength of the brand's proposition, awareness, esteem, etc. It is important here to make the connection between an evaluation of a brand as an asset at a point in time and an evaluation for brand-building purposes. Our attention should not only be focused upon the historic and present position of the brand alone, but we must also be concerned with, and be able to evaluate, the impact on brand equity of alternative brand strategies. In order to do this we require data with sufficient variation to enable us to measure relationships, for example, between changes in brand proposition and sales/profitability.

Nevertheless, users of this methodology, such as RHM, have had their accounts audited as showing a true and fair view. In fact, it is argued that the approach is similar to that used by companies accounting for other intangible assets, which has excited some criticism in accounting circles.

Depreciation of brands

Most assets depreciate without investment, and brands are no exception. Failure to invest in the appropriate level of marketing support will lead to the eventual decline or failure of a brand, although in the short term those brands may continue to generate profits and maintain share.

From the accounting perspective, all fixed assets (with the exception of land) will normally have finite lives and therefore should, according to UK regulatory bodies, be depreciated or amortized — not, however, as an indication of loss of value but as provision for their replacement. However, amortization does not seem to have been the generally accepted practice as far as brands and other intangibles have been concerned. As might be expected, this has not been met with approval by many accountants. Companies such as Guinness have, nevertheless, supported their policies by stating that they do not consider brand assets to have finite lives. Nevertheless, it may be prudent to make provision for their replacement, as some brands, e.g. Watney's Red Barrel, may not go on for ever!

Similarly, RHM have argued that their brands' lives are indeterminate; thus a policy of regular amortization would be misleading requiring, as it does, some arbitrary choice of period over which to write off the asset. Such a practice, it is argued, would lead to an inaccurate amortization charge to the profit and loss account resulting in an inaccurate profit figure. However, it has been pointed out (Norton 1990) that the practice of making no charge to the profit and loss account would seem to be equally misleading. Brands' fortunes can sometimes take a tumble, albeit unpredictably, and it would therefore seem necessary to make some charge against profit in the eventuality of a decline in the brand. Brewing companies, for example, while not providing for depreciation on their licensed estates and hotels, charge maintenance and repair against profit each year. The cost of maintaining a brand's equity through advertising and other direct marketing costs has a parallel here. But even this practice is controversial and is really only permitted while the conceptual framework is being finalized. A distinction also needs to be made here between regular revenue expenditure to maintain a brand and ad hoc capital expenditure to develop or reposition a brand. This may not be an easy task in many organizations!

However, notwithstanding these problems, whether a brand's value is to be included in a company's financial reports, or whether it is solely to be used in the estimation of brand equity for managerial purposes, does not affect the importance of trying to recalculate regularly both the value of the brand and the resources directly allocated to it.

Summary

The 1980s have seen the development of a major debate about the value of brands as assets both for the purposes of financial reporting and managerial decision making. On the financial side, the debate will continue for some years and will be part of the more general considerations about the standardized treatment of goodwill. There are already increasing pressures, as more international acquisitions take place, for such standardization to be similarly international. Until this has occurred, there will continue to be efforts by acquisitive organizations to reduce the impact of acquired goodwill on their balance sheets by making special provision for clearly separable intangible assets such as brands. For this reason alone, work will continue on the development of more satisfactory methods of brand valuation. However, the increasing recognition of the importance of successful brands, and the concept of brand equity to the long-term profitability of many companies, will also sustain efforts in this area.

Few companies have as yet placed a balance sheet value on their home-grown brands, the most notable being the UK foods and flour company Rank Hovis McDougall. Outside the UK and Australia this practice is indeed contrary to accounting regulations. However, the practice of valuing brands and the concept of brand equity are equally applicable to home-grown and acquired brands.

CASE STUDY: Premier Brands

In 1977, Cadbury Schweppes undertook a strategic review which recommended that the company should concentrate on its confectionery and soft drinks businesses world wide, while treating the foods and Jeyes businesses as cash cows. In 1984, Dominic Cadbury was appointed as chief executive and the company again looked at its strategic priorities. It was decided that if the company were truly to focus on the two chosen areas, confectionery and soft drinks, it should sell the foods and Jeyes businesses and re-invest the proceeds behind its priority areas. Both the Cadbury and Schweppes brand names were around 200 years old with well-established personalities, Cadbury's representing chocolate and plain dealing and Schweppes representing fizzy sophistication.

In the last quarter of 1985, the sale of the Jeyes business was announced. After discussions with many potential trade buyers, the best solution for the disposal was determined to be three separate management buy-outs for the three constituent parts of the business. In addition, in 1985, rumours of takeover bids for Cadbury Schweppes had been rippling through the City of London. In September, the group reported a loss of £1.8 million for its North American operation in the first half of the year and prospects there were not expected to improve until 1986. Given that the US was the group's key growth area, the share price should have fallen, but instead it started to float upwards fanned by takeover speculation. Food companies in the US with established brand names had already been acquired by predators (e.g. Philip Morris paid $5.75 billion, three times the book value, for General Foods, while R.J. Reynolds had paid $4.9 billion for Nabisco Brands).

In January 1986, speculation was further fuelled by the subsequent announcement that the group's 1985 pre-tax profits would fall to around £90 million compared with £124 million in the previous year. At the same time, the group also announced that an £82.5 million buy-out of the group's Beverages and Foods Division had reached 'an advanced stage of negotiation'. The decision to sell the Beverages and Foods Division was first and foremost a strategic one. The poor performance and City speculation merely put pressure on all parties to get on with it.

The Beverages and Foods Division

The Beverages and Foods Division, Cadbury Typhoo Ltd came into being as a result of the 1969 merger between the family-controlled, public company Cadbury and the more independent public company, Schweppes, when each was trying to grow through diversification in the UK. Cadbury's had used its expertise in marketing confectionery brands such as Dairy Milk to introduce Marvel (dried milk) and Smash (dried potato) into the UK. Previously it had developed chocolate biscuits (such as Chocolate Fingers) and cocoa beverages (such as Cadbury's Drinking Chocolate, Cocoa and Bournvita). Schweppes had used finance from its fizzy drinks to acquire Typhoo tea, Kenco coffee and Chivers Hartley preserves, canned fruit and vegetables.

The Division was divided into four business centres, namely tea, beverages and whiteners, foods (biscuits, chocolate spread and instant potato) and Chivers Hartley (preserves and canned foods). In addition, coffee, which had become part of the Division in early 1985, was operated as part of the catering business. In total the Division produced over 150 000 tons of food product annually, distributed primarily through UK packaged grocery markets. Many of its brands were household names that had been part of the British way of life for more than four generations and the Division was a market leader in many product categories.

Typhoo tea was responsible for about half of the Division's profits and one-quarter of its turnover, but was only number three or four in the tea market. The tea business was extremely vulnerable to market fluctuations which were passed on to the Division.

Beverages and whiteners included hot beverages such as Drinking Chocolate, Cocoa and Bournvita as well as whiteners such as Cadbury's Marvel and Coffee Compliment and Kenco Coffee Top.

On the food side, the company had used the Cadbury's Dairy Milk Chocolate heritage to revitalize its chocolate biscuits business. Biscuits were one of the largest packaged food markets in the UK, comparable with frozen foods and fresh vegetables. The biscuit business had, also

Table 7.1 Cadbury Schweppes plc — 1985 long-range plan: Beverages and Foods Division

CURRENCY £million	Actual 1983	Actual 1984	Budget 1985	Forecast 1985	Plan 1986	Plan 1987	Plan 1988
Market : Total tea							
Total market volume (tonnes)	156 500	150 700	148 400	147 300	146 600	145 800	145 100
Total market value (RSP)	421.2	553.4	632.6	623.1	678.5	715.9	735.9
Branded company volume (tonnes)	20 356	18 873	20 120	20 230	21 490	22 230	22 170
Branded company volume share % (TCA)	13.5	13.1	14.1	14.2	15.2	15.7	15.8
Sector : Packet tea							
Sector volume (tonnes)	59 800	53 400	48 400	48 100	44 300	40 700	37 500
Sector value (RSP)	141.4	175.9	183.1	182.4	198.6	209.6	215.4
Branded company volume (tonnes)	8 927	7 405	7 350	7 080	6 550	6 050	5 600
Branded company volume share % (TCA)	15.7	14.6	15.2	14.2	14.3	14.4	14.4
Sector : Tea bags							
Sector volume (tonnes)	96 700	97 300	100 000	99 200	102 300	105 100	107 600
Sector value (RSP)	279.8	377.5	449.5	440.7	479.9	506.3	520.5
Branded company volume (tonnes)	11 429	11 468	12 770	13 150	14 940	16 180	16 570
Branded company volume share % (TCA)	11.9	12.1	12.6	13.2	14.6	15.1	15.3
Market : Beverages							
Total market volume (tonnes)	19 950	19 250	18 350	19 050	18 750	18 500	18 400
Total market value (RSP)	41.8	44.3	43.3	47.0	48.0	50.5	53.8
Branded company volume (tonnes)	6 081	5 654	5 640	5 680	5 625	5 405	5 255
Branded company volume share % (TCA)	31.1	28.5	29.8	28.9	29.1	28.3	27.5

Table 7.1 – *continued*

CURRENCY £million	Actual 1983	Actual 1984	Budget 1985	Forecast 1985	Plan 1986	Plan 1987	Plan 1988
Market: Whiteners							
Total market volume (tonnes)	26 550	25 900	27 100	24 900	24 200	23 800	23 450
Total market value (RSP)	56.8	57.4	63.0	58.1	59.7	61.5	64.1
Branded company volume (tonnes)	6 655	6 831	7 002	6 725	6 010	5 720	5 490
Branded company volume share % (TCA)	19.7	22.4	21.8	23.0	20.8	20.0	19.4
Market: Retail fresh ground coffee (Pre-packed only – excludes beans and bags)							
Total market volume (tonnes)	6 732	8 420	9 132	9 700	11 400	13 100	14 750
Total market volume (RSP)	35.0	45.5	55.6	59.0	70.0	80.0	90.0
Company volume (tonnes)	1 428	1 516	1 611	1 615	1 700	1 850	2 000
Company volume brand share %	21.2	18.0	17.6	16.6	14.9	14.1	13.5
Market: Catering fresh ground coffee							
Total market volume (tonnes)	5 975	5 975	6 000	6 000	6 100	6 200	6 300
Total market value (MSP)	27.7	31.6	35.7	35.7	40.3	45.1	50.0
Company volume (tonnes)*	3 352	3 243	3 273	3 066	3 250	3 362	3 424
Company volume brand share %	56.1	54.3	54.6	51.1	53.3	54.2	54.3
Market: Packeted chocolate biscuits							
Total market volume (tonnes)	56 800	55 700	58 600	54 200	53 500	53 000	53 000
Total market value (RSP)	90.5	96.1	100.2	99.3	103.9	107.0	111.3
Branded company volume (tonnes)	6 152	6 556	7 050	7 050	7 350	7 400	7 450
Branded company volume share % (TCA)	18.6	20.4	21.0	23.0	24.0	24.5	24.5

Market : Instant mashed potato

Total market volume (tonnes)	9 100	9 400	8 700	8 700	8 500	8 500	8 500
Total market value (RSP)	17.7	23.0	21.8	22.3	23.0	24.3	26.0
Branded company volume (tonnes)	3 141	3 346	3 200	3 200	3 145	3 145	3 145
Branded company volume share % (TCA)	36.1	33.2	36.8	36.8	37.0	37.0	37.0

Market : Total preserves

Total market volume (tonnes)	106 600	103 600	101 800	100 100	96 800	93 800	91 200
Total market value (RSP)	99.2	101.8	104.2	102.4	104.1	105.8	107.9
Branded company volume (tonnes)	23 664	24 008	24 450	24 690	24 900	25 200	25 250
Branded company volume share % (TCA)	24.0	23.3	24.7	25.6	26.6	27.9	28.7

Sector : Jam

Sector volume (tonnes)	59 400	58 100	57 000	56 400	54 700	53 100	51 700
Sector value (RSP)	57.1	58.6	60.0	60.0	61.4	62.7	64.1
Branded company volume (tonnes)	13 404	13 493	13 550	13 677	13 700	13 800	13 850
Branded company volume share % (TCA)	24.4	22.9	24.8	25.3	26.2	27.2	28.1

Sector : Marmalade

Sector volume (tonnes)	47 200	45 500	44 800	43 700	42 100	40 700	39 500
Sector value (RSP)	42.1	43.2	44.2	42.4	42.7	43.1	43.8
Branded company volume (tonnes)	10 260	10 515	10 900	11 013	11 200	11 400	11 400
Branded company volume share % (TCA)	23.6	23.9	24.6	26.0	27.2	28.8	29.6

*Includes catering own-label, catering coffee bags, catering one cup filters and cash and carry packs.

expanded into chocolate spreads and the savoury snacks market. In addition, the biscuits business centre's product portfolio also included Cadbury's Smash.

The Chivers Hartley business centre produced 105 products including preserves, canned fruit and vegetables. Major product lines included Hartley's pure fruit jams, Chivers conserves, Rose's and Chivers marmalades, Chivers jellies, Chivers and Hartley's mincemeat, Hartley's canned fruit and vegetables, and Moorhouse's traditional preserves.

In mid-1985, as part of the annual planning cycle, each product area had prepared market and company sales projections for the next three years. These are shown in Table 7.1. However, following the preparation of these plans, the Division experienced a further deterioration in its financial performance, which is summed up in the managing director's commentary to the 1986 budget as follows:

> This 1986 budget commentary is being finalised at a time when the projected 1985 financial performance has now deteriorated to an even more unacceptable level than that forecast in the accompanying schedules. The most recent problems, associated with tea pricing and a deteriorating margin situation in the preserves market, have this period resulted in a further £1.5 million reduction in forecast trading profit to a revised figure of £6.5 million for the year. This results in a return on assets (ROA) of less than 10 per cent and highlights once again the vulnerability of the Division, with its present portfolio of products, to fluctuations in the tea market.

Table 7.2   Revised estimates of 1985 out-turn by business centre (£m)

	Actual 1984	Budget 1985	Forecast 1985
Business centre contribution			
Tea	14.0	17.3	12.3
Foods	6.6	6.5	6.2
Beverages and whiteners	11.2	10.9	11.9
Coffee	4.9	6.4	5.7
Miscellaneous catering	0.5	0.5	0.6
Chivers Hartley	7.1	7.4	6.5
Profit improvement	–	1.2	–
Divisional services* (including selling expenses of Kenco, Cadbury's, Typhoo)	(30.3)	(33.0)	(33.2)
Regional/group charges	(3.4)	(3.7)	(3.5)
Trading profit	10.6	13.5	6.5

*The main increases 1985 on 1984 are due to redundancy, stock financing and over-riding discount.

Table 7.2 shows the revisions to the expected 1985 out-turn by business
centres as a result of the continuing deterioration. Table 7.3 compares the
1986 budget with the 1984 actual, the latest 1985 forecast and the 1986 plan.

Table 7.3 1986 budget summary

	Actual 1984	Forecast 1985	Budget 1986	Plan 1986
Tonnes ('000)	156.1	156.5	154.1	172.2
	(£m)	(£m)	(£m)	(£m)
Net sales	271.2	282.4	265.5	333.8
Trading profit	10.6	6.5	11.0	14.5
Half year trading profit	4.7	3.7	5.0	5.8
Capital expenditure	4.3	5.2	12.6	13.4
YE* operating assets	73.5	72.2	73.2	90.0
Operational cash flow	8.7	8.2	10.0	4.8
Property revaluation		0.4		
ROA (%)	16.0	9.0	15.0	16.2
Employees (average FTE†)	4347	4164	4172	4349

*Year end
†Full time equivalent

The background to the sell-off

As a result of the deteriorating financial position of the Beverages and
Foods Division, Cadbury Schweppes undertook a major review of the
business centres within the Division. The conclusions from this review are
summarized below.

Hot beverages

Individually, the Tea, Coffee, Bevs./Whiteners businesses, and the
retail and catering sales forces lack the functional integrity required
to warrant the independence with which they have operated in
the recent past. Together, however, they are capable of showing a
satisfactory return by any standards.

Foods

On a self-standing basis, this business has been bankrupt for years.
It has been kept afloat by injections of scarce resources, but still has
a negative net present value (NPV) with no prospect of ever
achieving a reasonable return in its own right, as presently constituted.

Chivers Hartley (CH)

This business has a stand-alone NPV which is positive, but falls
significantly short of its book value. The Histon* redevelopment is

* Histon was the major preserves factory in which about £5 million had been invested.

now perceived to have been based on a false premise, viz. that the higher costs of the 'pure fruit' strategy would be recovered through selling price premiums.

Logistics (computing and distribution)

This cinderella business has a stand-alone NPV in excess of its book value—assuming, of course, a mix of business roughly as at present. Roughly speaking the economies of scale brought about by adding in CH volumes are equivalent to the gap between CH's NPV and book value.

As a result of this review the group's chief executive, Dominic Cadbury, was presented with a list of five strategic options.

OPTION 1   Sell the Division as an ongoing concern.

Advantages

1 Assuming sale of at least asset value—£80 million of positive cash flow, with the profit loss made up by interest savings.
2 Less risk and complication compared with partial divestment—employee problems, the 'domino' effect, i.e. selling off the most profitable parts leaves an even lower ROA.
3 Leaves the group with no ongoing problems, i.e. Moreton,* biscuits, service departments, which will be costly to eliminate.
4 A popular 'City and Investors' move which would help the group's public relations image at a critical time.

Disadvantages

1 The need to franchise out the Cadbury name on cocoa beverages, biscuits.
2 The complication of reaching a satisfactory arrangement on chocolate biscuits—salesforces, countlines, etc. Chocolate biscuits were packet biscuits (e.g. 150 g packets) which were seen as a grocery item, but there was some blurring with multi-packs of regular size biscuit bars. The Division also made Bar 6 and Snack at Moreton, which were really more chocolate bars than biscuits and were sold by the Confectionery Division.
3 The need for a manufacturing/supply agreement for beverages supplied by Chirk. Chirk was the main cocoa-processing factory, operated by the Confectionery Division, where the cocoa, Drinking Chocolate and Bournvita were made almost as a by-product of the chocolate-making process.
4 Head Office, Franklin House, complications with shared staff, mainframe computer and confectionery services.
5 The loss of very experienced/above-average senior management resource.

---

* Moreton was the largest factory with 3000 employees, on Merseyside, and seen as a difficult site to manage if split up.

OPTION 2   Retain existing business — same objectives/no major investment.

Advantages

1 Retention of skilled and experienced presence in UK food grocery trade which could have benefits in the future, if/when a third leg to the group's strategy is felt necessary.
2 Ability to 'milk' the business to provide a positive cash flow for a year or two plus profits in the order of £10 million per annum.
3 Retention of a major UK presence in hot beverages — a logical extension of a chocolate business.

Disadvantages

1 £80 million of assets tied up in a business making an ROA below group targets/needs.
2 High risk factor of fluctuating profitability in the volatile commodity markets of tea, coffee, preserves and canned goods.
3 High cost of further rationalization to compensate for low margins — redundancy, closures, etc.
4 High cost of supporting major brands against international competition — Typhoo, Kenco, Hartley. If no support, the value of the brands to the group will quickly become much less.
5 The fundamental problem of biscuits remains unlikely to be resolved.

OPTION 3   Sell Chivers Hartley — retain the rest of the Division.

Advantages

1 Release of £20 million plus of assets from a business realizing only a 12 per cent ROA.
2 Popular move within the City/shareholders.
3 Makes a small improvement in the ROA of the rest of the Division.
4 Eliminates the problem area of Montrose.*
5 There is a minimum knock-on effect on the rest of the Division provided we can continue to serve the logistics end of the Chivers Hartley business — a key issue. Chivers Hartley was managed from Histon with its own sales team and its own buying and technical teams. So it could be separated successfully as long as the volumes sold through the distribution depots and the central invoicing could continue for a given period.

Disadvantages

1 Only goes part of the way towards resolving the divisional issue.
2 If the continuation of a logistics service is not part of the deal, there will be knock-on effects to the rest of the Division.
3 With the recent deterioration in Chivers Hartley profitability and increased pressure on margins in the preserves market, obtaining asset value for the sale may be difficult.

*Montrose was the Chivers Hartley canning business in Scotland. Canning was a very competitive business and Montrose made little money.

OPTION 4   Divest of the biscuit business.

Advantage

1 A major drain on the profitability of the Division would be eliminated (£10 million plus of assets) allowing greater concentration/investment in the more profitable hot beverage business.

Disadvantages

1 There is no clear, practical method of divesting quickly which will not involve the group in a *major* write-off of assets or high redundancy costs.
2 Any form of selling the business or associating with another company will involve the franchising of the Cadbury name on *Cadbury chocolate* products and some intricate agreement on chocolate biscuit countlines.
3 Biscuits and Moreton are so interdependent—any sale would have to involve some form of agreement on the ownership/utilization of the site.
4 The sale of the biscuit business would lead to a major restructuring of the Division involving high rationalization costs.

OPTION 5   A major investment in growth food sectors.

Advantages

1 This could be complementary to divestment from, say, Chivers Hartley and biscuits, thus reducing the need for a major rationalization of the Divisional infrastructure.
2 The group retains a presence in a third sector of a major industry and one which would give more flexibility in moving into 'trend' areas— health foods, snacks, conveniences, etc.
3 A major presence in that beverages could be retained and developed.
4 Economies of scale by utilization of the existing infrastructure should give an acceptable return on investment.

Disadvantages

1 There is an inevitable risk factor attached to further investment in the UK grocery market.
2 This would be seen by the City/investors as a major change in group strategy—not likely to be popular.
3 Any major investment would divert funds from the mainstream businesses.
4 Any acquisition would involve asset stripping.

After considering the available options, Cadbury Schweppes decided in 1985 to concentrate on its core businesses of confectionery and soft drinks and to sell the Beverages and Foods Division in the UK, Ireland and France. Purchase criteria were set and trade buyers were sought.

The potential purchasers

Five food companies among others were initially regarded as potentially interested in purchasing the Division at an acceptable price, i.e. asset value or above. These were Nestlé, General Foods, Douwe Egbert, Imperial Foods and Nabisco. Potential purchasers were evaluated on the following criteria:

1 Willingness to pay a price above asset value
2 Ability to finance and complete the purchase
3 Potential for conflict caused by having to franchise the Cadbury name to a competitor
4 Willingness to purchase the entire Division
5 Level of experience in the UK
6 Likely level of employee and factory rationalization
7 Level of potential threat as a predator for all of Cadbury Schweppes.

The value of the business

The value of the Division was estimated using several different methods which resulted in a range of between £40 million and £78 million. The valuations excluded the export business and Chivers Ireland which were in other divisions and the Division's French operation. Their exclusion amounted to around £6 million. The valuations also took no account of any premium which a purchaser might pay for the strategic value arising from synergies in operations and product portfolios.

In preparing the valuations, due account was taken of the revised trading profit for 1985. As a result, the 1986 budget figure was revised downwards by £1.5 million and the plan figures for 1987 and 1988 were reduced by 45 per cent.

The results of the different methods were as follows:

Valuation based on:

	£(millions)
Cash flow projections (16 per cent discount rate)	40–52
Book value of assets	66
Earnings in: 1984 actual 1985 forecast 1986 projection	50–78
Cadbury Schweppes capitalization, pro rata to trading profit	68

The buy-out

On 13 January 1986 a management team led by the planning director, Paul Judge (who had been managing director of Cadbury Typhoo in 1982–84), announced a bid for the Division of £82.5 million. To many people, the opportunity to transform the Division was not apparent. Its financial performance was distinctly unimpressive, geographically it was scattered across the country and many of the brands were in need of revitalization. However, the public announcement that the Division was to be sold had provoked a lot of interest and finally two counter-bids emerged to the proposed buy-out. This led to a revised bid by the buy-out team on 11 March 1986 of £97 million (including £70 million for net operating assets and £27 million for goodwill) plus an option for Cadbury Schweppes to acquire 10 per cent of the new company's shares on flotation. Eventually, after reviewing the offer, Cadbury Schweppes accepted, and the new company, Premier Brands, started trading on 13 May 1986.

References

Aaker, David A., *Managing Brand Equity*, The Free Press, 1991.

Barwise, P., Higson, C., Likierman, A. and Marsh, P., *Accounting for Brands*, London Business School for ICAEW, 1989.

Doyle, P., 'Building successful brands: the strategic options', *Journal of Consumer Marketing*, **7** (2), Spring 1990.

Murphy, J., *Brand Valuation: A True and Fair View*, Hutchinson, 1991.

Norton, J., 'A brand new asset? Recent trends in the financial reporting of intangible assets', *Sundridge Park Management Review*, **3** (3), Spring 1990.

8

International brands

International brands have been around for a very long time. Some of the oldest international brand names are American; for example, Ford, Hoover, Kelloggs and Coca-Cola. There are also many old European international brands such as Philips, Rolls-Royce, Michelin and Chanel. There is no doubt that this phenomenon continues to grow with the more recent emergence of brand names such as Benetton, Sony, Honda and Heineken. The top 10 world brands in 1990, according to a survey by Landor Associates (1990)* were: Coca-Cola, Sony, Mercedes-Benz, Kodak, Disney, Nestlé, Toyota, McDonald's, IBM and Pepsi Cola.

Growth has gone hand in hand with the growth in multi-national corporations. Despite this, evidence suggests that the international diffusion of brands remains limited. Research in the United States (Rosen *et al.* 1989) into the internationalization of US brands concludes that the 'Cola Colonization of the World' is the result of a few brands rather than the wide distribution of many brands. Hence, while many international brands are known in many regions of the world, there are very few truly global brands.

However, there is an important point of definition which needs to be made. In this chapter we define international brands as those that are available internationally either in a number of regions in the world or globally. This is a broad definition as it not only embraces global brands such as those already listed but it also includes more regionally focused brands which, while international, are not truly global. The process of international branding is a continuum moving from a brand only available locally to a brand available globally. International branding is thus an incremental process that can be embarked upon, while global branding may or may not be the final objective.

*These ratings are based upon a study of over 6000 companies and brands involving more than 10 000 consumers across 11 countries. The results are based on consumers' familiarity with, and esteem for, each brand.

Global branding as a distinct issue was made prominent following the publication of Theodore Levitt's article on the globalization of markets (Levitt 1983). He argues that there is a growing convergence in markets across the world resulting from improved communications, international travel and the emergence of demographically similar segments in different regions. As a consequence, he argues that firms should take advantage of this by standardizing their products globally. Since the publication of this article, a fierce debate has ensued among academics and marketing practitioners as to the relative advantages and disadvantages of global branding. It is worth exploring this debate in order to determine whether there are any fundamental principles that can be used when evolving a strategy for entering major international markets.

The advantages of international branding

Many of the advantages of having a brand recognized internationally are associated with the cost savings resulting from economies of scale of one sort or another. Clearly, an item produced for mass consumption across major international regions can lead to significant reductions in unit costs of manufacturing, purchasing, inventories and finance. The more standardized the functional attributes of the brand, the greater are the cost advantages. Similarly, the more standardized the methods of production, the easier it is to set up production in any part of the world. It was largely these factors that gave rise to the first wave of American international brands and the growth in the multi-national corporation during the 1950s and 1960s.

This expansion was made possible by the growth in disposable incomes in countries outside the USA, and associated growth in demand for consumer products. In these early stages of international market development companies such as Hoover, Ford and Gillette pursued a relatively undifferentiated marketing strategy offering brands to mass markets across national boundaries. However, as disposable income has grown, consumers have become more discerning in their product choices, which has led to the increased segmentation of markets. As a consequence, companies have sought opportunities to exploit common market segments across national boundaries as an alternative means of deriving the economies of scale previously limited to mass marketing. More recent international brands such as Benetton, Dunhill and Gucci have targeted specific international market segments that have developed with the convergence in habits, life-styles and culture among consumers across the world (Winram 1984). Thus, international branding has provided opportunities for economies of scale not fully permitted by the limited size of local market segments.

However, it is important to distinguish between technical efficiency factors (which affect research and development and production) and marketing efficiency factors (which affect advertising, distribution costs, etc.). There can be no doubt that product development and manufacturing innovations spread very rapidly across the world, making it difficult to sustain a competitive advantage in this way. There is also no doubt that the production of many products tends to concentrate in the low-cost areas of the world, e.g. microcomputers in Malaysia, television sets in South Korea, etc. However, these factors argue only for international marketing of a standardized product. If the full marketing benefits of international branding are to be gained, it is necessary to establish a common international brand proposition which includes consistent symbolic values as well as functional attributes and positioning. Only when this has been achieved can the benefits of, for example, family branding and brand stretching be achieved. In this case, it has been suggested that savings are made as a result of 'economies of scope' rather than economies of scale (Teece 1980). There are similar savings to be made from internationally recognized brands when opening up new markets. The opening of McDonald's in Moscow was a cheaper and more effective product launch as a result of the existing reputation, among Muscovites, of McDonald's as an American institution representative of the free-market values to which they were aspiring.

Economic benefits can also derive from such factors as common packaging design and advertising campaigns. In particular, developments in satellite and cable television are rapidly expanding public access to a wide variety of international channels. As long ago as 1983, for example, British Airways ran the same commercial in four different countries and in six languages.

Levitt argues that these economies of scale from production, marketing and distribution have enabled multi-national corporations to use price successfully to establish their dominant positions in world markets and points to the expansion of American and Japanese companies as examples. However, experience suggests that while price may enable companies to gain a short-term lead in a marketplace, it rarely leads to a sustainable competitive advantage as the proliferation of small microcomputer manufacturers have found to their cost. In contrast IBM established its position in the microcomputer market largely on the strength of its brand name and certainly not on the basis of its price competitiveness.

Similarly, the success of the Japanese manufacturer, Sony, has largely been the result of its ability to develop, regularly, innovatory products such as the pocket transistor radio and the Walkman, which have enabled it to establish a strong international personality built around the core symbolic values of technological know-how, innovation and reliability with demonstrable functional attributes.

Therefore, it is argued that the full advantages of international branding can only be obtained through the development of a brand proposition that is common across countries or geographic regions.

The disadvantages of international branding

While Theodore Levitt and such advertising agencies as Saatchi and Saatchi argue that the key to success is the development of standardized international brands, others, notably Philip Kotler, believe that standardization on an international scale goes against the marketing concept of developing products to meet consumer needs (Kotler 1984). In contrast, he maintains that more success will be obtained through the adaptation of products and marketing strategies to the characteristics of individual markets. The argument centres around the practicability of standardization.

Barriers to standardization can take many forms. For example, many countries have their own regulations governing product design and standards: there have been more stringent regulations in the US affecting cars than in the UK. Other countries limit imports of key materials and components. The marketing infrastructure may also vary significantly; for example, approximately 75 per cent of retail sales in Portugal and Spain are through small retailers, not multiples. Competitive structure may also differ; for example, in Italy the price of drugs and pharmaceutical products is significantly below other European countries.

There may also be significant cultural differences between countries, which prevent total international standardization. The obvious examples are food and drink where tastes and traditions may necessitate quite significant changes both in flavour (functional attributes) and presentation (symbolic values). Even one of the world's most familiar brands, Pepsi Cola varies its flavour according to the country into which it is sold.

As a consequence, Kotler argues that the policy of global branding denies consumers the opportunity to purchase brands that meet their needs more specifically, and prevents companies from earning enhanced profits through more targeted branding strategies.

The international branding spectrum

The decision to develop, or not to develop, brands internationally is very complex. In reality, the alternative policy choices are not dichotomous but fall along a spectrum from the completely global brand, of which Cola-Cola is the most well-known example, to specific brands for specific markets or regions, which we call multi-domestic branding.

Many companies have chosen multi-domestic branding as a more feasible alternative method of achieving international growth. The UK company HJ Heinz provides one example of this approach. Despite the fact that the Heinz brand is internationally recognized, 65 per cent of its annual sales come from products that do not carry the Heinz label. For example, in Italy their baby food retails under the Plasmon brand. To some extent this reflects a policy of acquiring and building up local brands in order to take into account local traditions and tastes. Nestlé, the food and confectionery manufacturer, and McVitie's have pursued similar policies. Nestlé acquired Rowntrees in the UK, while McVitie's acquired Keebler, the snacks and cookies company, in the US. Neither company has attempted to impose a standard global brand name on its newly acquired local brands. A multi-domestic marketing strategy pursues competition with other multi-nationals and local brands on a market-by-market basis.

Most organizations with international coverage not only own a collection of brands—some purely local and others spread across a number of countries—but they also have a corporate identity which varies both in perceptions and strength in different countries. Their past growth has usually been uncoordinated and, unlike some of the global brands identified in the Landor survey, there is no single clearly identified brand proposition around which to centre international development. Even brands that are evidently successful globally do not employ identical strategies across all markets.

Most global branding strategies allow for minor adjustments to elements in the marketing mix in order to achieve the same brand proposition. Furthermore, strategies inevitably vary in their success region by region. Table 8.1 shows the top 10 brands from the Landor survey for Europe, the United States and Japan. As can be seen, even Cola-Cola does not consistently occupy the number one spot in each region, while the other nine places show even less consistency. There is, as might be expected, an increase in the representation of local brands in each region.

Table 8.1   Top 10 brands by region 1990

Rank	World	Europe	US	Japan
1	Cola-Cola	Coca-Cola	Coca-Cola	Sony
2	Sony	Sony	Campbell's	National
3	Mercedes-Benz	Mercedes-Benz	Disney	Mercedes-Benz
4	Kodak	BMW	Pepsi Cola	Toyota
5	Disney	Philips	Kodak	Takashimaya
6	Nestlé	Volkswagen	NBC	Rolls-Royce
7	Toyota	Adidas	Black & Decker	Seiko
8	McDonald's	Kodak	Kellogg's	Matsushita
9	IBM	Nivea	McDonald's	Hitachi
10	Pepsi Cola	Porsche	Hershey's	Suntory

This highlights a key strategic question that has to be considered in international branding strategy: Does the strength of a local brand make it too expensive to establish a new brand in pursuit of a global marketing strategy?

Factors favouring successful global brands

In practice, very few companies have been successful in developing truly global brands. Most have chosen, or found it necessary by virtue of their historical development, to adopt multi-domestic branding strategies. There has been little research into the factors determining the success of global branding, but a framework for the analysis of new markets has been suggested by Dahringer and Cundiff (1986). They list factors under five headings: the environment, market characteristics, the product, the cost of financial factors and the corporate environment. Table 8.2 shows the full set of factors under each heading. One test of this framework is, of course, the extent to which it would predict the success of the world's top 10 brands!

It is, indeed, difficult to evaluate the top 10 world brands against the Dahringer and Cundiff checklist. Clearly, some brands have defied some of these criteria—for example, many of Sony's products are technically complex in design (see III.3) yet they have achieved global rather than local status. However, the one key factor to emerge from this checklist is the necessity for would-be global brands to focus to a greater extent on the symbolic values of its brand personality rather than on its functional attributes—in other words, to use universal symbolism to override cultural, climatic, governmental or legal restrictions.

Table 8.2 Factors influencing the success of a global marketing strategy

	Favouring global strategy	Location of factors on a continuum	Favouring individualized strategy
		1 2 3 4 5 6 7	
The environment			
1 Unique cultural factors affecting consumption	Not present	1 2 3 4 5 6 7	Present
2 Legal environment	Similar	1 2 3 4 5 6 7	Different
3 Geographic factors	Similar	1 2 3 4 5 6 7	Different
4 Government involvement in business	*Laissez-faire*	1 2 3 4 5 6 7	Controlled
5 Attitude towards change	Flexible	1 2 3 4 5 6 7	Inflexible
Market characteristics			
1 Character of resident population			
(a) Degree of urbanization	Largely urban	1 2 3 4 5 6 7	Largely rural
(b) Size of total population	Similar	1 2 3 4 5 6 7	Small
2 Market infrastructure	Similar	1 2 3 4 5 6 7	Different
3 Sophistication of marketing institutions	Sophisticated	1 2 3 4 5 6 7	Primitive
The product			
1 Stage in the product life cycle	Same	1 2 3 4 5 6 7	Different
2 Breadth of market appeal	Narrow	1 2 3 4 5 6 7	Broad
3 Technical complexity of product	Simple	1 2 3 4 5 6 7	Technical
Cost of financial factors			
1 Level of R&D costs	High	1 2 3 4 5 6 7	Low
2 Importance of price	Important	1 2 3 4 5 6 7	Unimportant
3 Availability of investment capital	High	1 2 3 4 5 6 7	Low
Corporate environment			
Level of management flexibility and acceptance of change	Low	1 2 3 4 5 6 7	High

Source: Dahringer and Cundiff (1986).

In this context, it is easy to understand the success of Coca-Cola, which represents youth, fun and sociability. The importance of cultural similarities in determining common branding regions is supported by research among US brand managers (Shalofsky 1987) who indicated a preference for targeting culturally similar markets. However, even though a brand may have identical advertising and promotion in each country or region, market share may differ depending upon the size and relative share of specific market segments in individual countries and the competitive environment.

It is frequently argued by the opponents of global branding that attempts to create standard advertising across regions leads to boring and bland presentation which misses the subtle nuances of individual markets. However, it is difficult to argue this in the case of Coke and Pepsi advertising, two brands with relevant personalities in all geographical segments of the market. In these cases, as with other brands, the expression of the proposition works in each individual market. It is even possible to vary the execution of that expression in order to cater for different market nuances, provided that the essentials of the proposition are promoted and maintained. An example of such tailoring can be found in the car market. Audi's advertising in the UK emphasizes among other factors the Germanness of the brand via its strapline 'Vorsprung durch Tecnik'. This approach is not used in Audi's home market.

Thus, global branding does not necessarily mean global advertising. Reference is often made to the alcoholic beverages market as one of the best examples of differences between cultures and attitudes and one which, therefore, is not amenable to global advertising. Nonetheless, drink brands such as Bacardi, which is the largest-selling spirit brand in the world, has built a global brand name by tailoring the advertising message to local markets. In Europe it has been associated with sun, sea and sand, whereas in the United States the focus of advertising has been upon health awareness and diet consciousness.

National characteristics on brand attributes

It has been pointed out (Shalofsky 1987) that a further characteristic of the small number of highly successful global brands is their essentially national personality. Coca-cola is an *American* soft drink, Marlboro is an *American* cigarette, Chanel No. 5 is a *French* perfume, and Buitoni is an *Italian* pasta. It would seem that a plausible national base or home market appears to be an important characteristic of successful global brands. Global brands succeeding on this platform need to be 'culturally plausible'. Hence, it is argued, that perfume is French, pasta is Italian, jeans are American and whisky is Scottish. Thus, if you aspire to have a global brand in these markets you neglect your cultural origins at your peril. However, these are generic categories of product in which globalization has been possible for certain brands. When marketing cars, however, which is not a nationally based generic product category, it is less easy to use national characteristics or heritage to advantage. So, for example, Mercedes-Benz and Toyota, which are in the top 10 world brands, have not used their national origins as part of their personality development. In contrast, Audi and Jaguar, which have included their national origins as part of their personality, rank only 25 and 16 respectively in Europe. Thus, national heritage when applied to brands from a non-nationally rooted, generic product category is not necessarily a successful brand strategy.

The use of national heritage as a symbolic value in a brand personality requires careful consideration prior to implementation. Research clearly demonstrates that firm national stereotypes exist, and that these perceptions can vary from one region of the world to another. Such variations should act as a warning signal to the brand builder considering using national heritage as a core symbolic value. A recent example is provided by Rover Cars. In the early 1980s, Rover Group carried out market research among car buyers in Europe and the United States. In Europe, Britain was found to be regarded as strike-ridden and in economic decline with only a weak association with technology, advanced industry and future potential; whereas in the United States car buyers perceived Britain to be in the process of change for the better. As a consequence, the branding of Austin and Rover in Europe studiously avoided associations with Britishness, while in the United States the Rover Group chose to launch its new top-of-the-range model using the name Sterling and evoking images of traditional Britishness. The strategy in the United States failed to bring results, but probably more as a result of using a totally unknown brand name, Sterling, rather than the use of Britishness as a symbolic value. Tentative conclusions from these examples are that national heritage is best exploited, first, when the perceptions are consistent globally and, secondly, when they have been associated with a product category (e.g. fast food in the US) or brand for a long period of time.

An interesting special case of the national heritage problem relates to national airlines such as British Airways, who, by virtue of their chosen brand name, cannot avoid association with national stereotypes. The answer is to capitalize on those aspects of national character that can be positively used to support the brand and to exclude the negative characteristics from the brand personality (see the case study in Chapter 5).

Summary

In this chapter we have considered the relative advantages and disadvantages of global branding and examined the debate that is continuing regarding its desirability and practicability. On the positive side, global brands provide cost savings through scale economies in manufacturing, purchasing, inventories, research and development and finance. Global brands also provide opportunities for economies of scale in advertising, package design and distribution, particularly as satellite broadcasting and international media coverage expands. The convergence of cultures, purchasing patterns and habits internationally has allowed these economies to be obtained by a small number of national brands able to exploit transnational market segments, such as business travellers and markets for luxury goods. Similarly, global reputations offer economies of scope and can make it easier for brands to penetrate new national markets. On the negative side, many academics and practitioners regard global branding as a backward step and as contrary to the marketing concept, providing standard products supported by bland advertising which ignores differences in individual national and regional markets. However, global branding does not require complete standardization of marketing across national frontiers, and product differences can also be tolerated while still permitting many of the advantages associated with the handful of standardized global brands such as Coca-Cola, Sony and McDonald's. Variations in product features and the marketing mix can also be tolerated, provided that the final brand proposition developed and maintained remains consistent and relevant across national boundaries. In practice, this can probably only be achieved by a limited number of brands. Successful global branding is more likely in product categories not affected by cultural differences and strongly associated with positive national characteristics. Examples of potentially poor global products include food and alcoholic drink, while products with high potential include luxury items and consumer durables associated with growing consumer affluence.

CASE STUDY: Gordon's Gin

Gordon's is United Distiller's primary gin brand, sold throughout the world. Within the growing white spirits market, gin as a category has been in decline and Gordon's volume had been falling as a result. Nevertheless, it remains the best-selling gin in the world, outselling its nearest rival by over 2 million cases. Sales are concentrated in four key markets, the UK, USA, Spain and South Africa, which, between them, account for around 90 per cent of volume sales. In each of these markets Gordon's is produced domestically.

In the late 1980s the brand was in a strong position insofar as market share was either increasing or being maintained. In the UK, which accounted for around 30 per cent of Gordon's total volume, the brand was consolidating its dominant share of the declining market. In the US, Gordon's maintained its position as the number two domestic gin brand after Seagram's. In Spain, Gordon's was facing increasingly fierce competition in a flat market, from its main domestic competitor Larios. The latter had started life as a Gordon's me-too product, but now represented a serious threat in the standard gin market. In South Africa, the brand was outperforming the market and gaining volume from the key competitor, Mainstay.

Outside these key markets, Gordon's had strengthened its position as the clear brand leader where gin was a small but growing sector, notably in France, Germany and Italy. In addition, volumes in the duty-free markets were increasing, with the UK, Germany and the USA accounting for almost half of total brand sales.

As a brand name, Gordon's had a global reputation with a long-established heritage which gave it credibility with consumers and the distribution trade. However, its market positioning varied across countries depending upon culture, the stage in gin's development in the life cycle, and the local competition. In two of the key markets, the USA and Spain, Gordon's positioning was low image and price sensitive. This contrasted with the position in the UK where Gordon's was regarded as the best gin available in a mature market and therefore able to command a premium price.

In 1988, Gordon's commissioned a motivational research study across six markets, the UK, the USA, Spain, France, Germany and Italy, as the basis for the development of a global strategy.

The international market for gin

The research showed that the gin market could be divided into two basic categories: the mature, large markets notably the UK, the USA and Spain, and the 'up-coming', small markets such as Germany, France and Italy.

A summary of the research findings across the six markets is set out in Table 8.3, which shows the image profile of gin in each of the markets.

In the USA, where premium white spirits had grown at the expense of cheaper brands, the prestige/display value, high-quality brands were proving resilient to competition within their sectors. Highly social, quality brands were Tanqueray, Stolichnaya, Absolut and, to a lesser extent, Beefeater. Ordinary and everyday brands were being squeezed by a number of important trends:

- the search for prestige/display brands by young adults
- the trend to 'lighter … easy to take' spirits
- greater health consciousness … also 'drink–drive'
- the greater fashionability of vodka, Tequila and to a lesser extent white rum (Bacardi)
- the greater use of wine/champagne in drink situations which previously involved the use of spirit-based drinks
- the slow decline of the martini.

Table 8.3　The image profile of gin in the six markets

H+ = Very high　H = High　M = Medium　L = Low　NR = Not relevant
NA = Data not available　( ) = Not a firm conclusion

Dimension	USA	France	Spain	UK	Germany	Italy
Mixed drink usual	H/M	H	H	H+	H	H
Neat or Martini	(M/H)	(L)	(L/M)		L	(M/L)
English imagery	H (selected brands)	M (varies)	H (selected brands)	NR	H	H+
Purity/clarity	M	H	H	(M)	NA	H
Taste distinctive	H+	H	H	H	M/H	H
Sophistication	M (H for selected brands)	H	H (selected brands)	H	H	H+
Fresh/refreshing	H	H	H	H+	H	H
Romantic/sexy	H	H	M	(M/L)	NA	H
Sociability	H	H	H	H	(M/H)	H
Social display/ prestige value	M (H for selected brands)	H	H (selected brands)	M	H	H+
Sociability/sharing	H+	H	H	H	H	H
Informal/relaxed	H L (Martini)	H	(M/H)	H	H	M/H
Social gathering/ parties	H+	H++	H	H	H	H
Fun/frivolity/festive	H	H+	H	(M/L)	(M/L)	H
Intimacy/quiet	M H (Martini)	M	H (neat)	M	H	H (neat)

Table 8.3 – *continued*

Dimension	USA	France	Spain	UK	Germany	Italy
Contemplative	L M (Martini)	L	H (neat)	L	M	H (neat)
Versatility	M/L	H	(H)	L	NA	H
Part of 'another' drink/mixer	H (Gimlet G&T)	H+	H	H	H	H
Easy to make... simple drink	H	H	H	H	H	H
Exotic	L (brand variation)	H	M (brand variation)	L	L	H
Growing, getting more popular	L (excludes selected brands)	H	H	L	M/H (potential+)	H
Knowledge of making	L	L	L	L	L	L
Mystique 'ageing', etc.	L	L	L	L	L	L
Traditional values (English)	H (varies)	(L/M)	H (varies)	H	M/H	H
Restorative/fresh start	H	(M)	M/L	H	N/A	L
Urbane/'in'/ fashionable	L (except for selected brands)	H	H (varies by brand)	M	H	H
Assertive/ individual	L (excludes selected brands)	H	H	(M)	H	H
Neat or Martini	(M/H)	L	(M/L)	L	L	M
Androgynous	M	H	H	H	M	M
Modern/youthful/ contemporary	L (except for selected brands)	H	H (neat older)	L/M	H	H
At home	H	M	M/H	H	NA	L
At club/restaurant	H+ (Martini) H (mixer)	H	H+	H	NA	H/M

Table 8.3 – *continued*

Dimension	USA	France	Spain	UK	Germany	Italy
Conservative/ mature people	M (higher for martini)	L	H (neat) L (mixer)	H/M	L	H (neat) L (mixer)
Summertime/ warm weather	H (all year)	H	H	M	NA	H
Smooth/mellow	Varies by brand	H	H (variation by brand)	M (variation by brand)	NA	H

Furthermore, in the USA, where usage also included neat or 'martini' consumption, perceived quality, strength and mellowness were important variables for brand acceptance. It was uncommon for Gordon's to be seen as an appropriate base for martini. In general, such use favoured the premium brands. In contrast, an important characteristic of a white spirit was its perceived versatility. In the USA, medium-priced gins such as Gordon's tended to be used as a base for mixed drinks.

In Spain, the research identified the key market factors as being:

- the perception of gin as high status, fashionable plus youth and fun
- usage of gin as both a neat and mixed drink, with the latter having a youthful, fun, sociable image, and the former a masculine, older, quiet, contemplative and relaxed image
- a decline in non-mixable spirits
- an association of high alcohol proof spirits with status
- a susceptibility of consumers to brand status-images as a means of expressing 'self image'
- the association of 'English imported' with high status.

Vodka was not a serious competitor.

In Germany, contrastingly, gin was not an established spirit. There was little knowledge or familiarity with gins.

Nevertheless, where gin was known and consumed, it had positive images in terms of its status expressed in phrases like:

'it is yuppie'

'it is luxury'

'it is stylish man'

'it is modern'

etc.

It was also associated with the British élite, masculine types and independently minded people, as well as being fun/joyful, sociable/friendly, sexy and frivolous. However, in contrast to other countries, men usually determined the purchase of spirits in Germany and their approval was often necessary before women were interested in using the brand. Spirit drinking was also very much a social activity.

In France, gin appeared reasonably well understood and used, but was almost exclusively used in mixed form, although with a wider range of mixers, particularly compared to the UK.

As a refreshing drink in mixed form, gin was more frequently associated with warm weather usage. Gin-based drinks were regarded as easy to prepare and therefore readily usable either at home or in bars and were associated with relaxation, frivolity, fun, sexuality and sophistication. In France, the physical attributes of the product appeared to be particularly important in relation to:

- appetite appeal/refreshingness
- clarity of liquid
- freshness
- coolness
- bubbliness (with tonic).

While British/Englishness was regarded as a reinforcing element, it was not regarded as such an important factor in France compared to other countries.

In Italy, gin was seen as an imported spirit which gave it a relatively high status value where it was known. As in France and Spain, the image of gin was relatively versatile, being mixed with a wide range of other liquids. Gin was also associated with festivity and liveliness, particularly in mixed form. In Italy, gin penetration was relatively low and not a well-established product category. Consequently, there was a degree of confusion about what it was all about. Nevertheless, among gin users, it was associated with relaxation and contemplation, as well as liveliness, joyfulness and frivolity. Gin was also associated with mature, distinguished men such as English Lords, and to some extent it derived its high status from this. However, evidence indicated that both women and young people were also gin drinkers. The mature male adult was, however, more closely associated with gin in neat or martini form. There was also evidence that gin was regarded as a trendy drink.

These images contrasted with the UK where research identified gin as a classic spirit with restricted perceived versatility used largely for the G&T. It was middle class and 'establishment' in character, yet also aspirational associated with the executive classes and to some extent with 'yuppies'. Gin represented a 'coming to terms with parental values', maturity and seriousness, yet it was also perceived as sociable, friendly, an escape for executives with work-related stress. Gin was definitely not regarded as 'kid's stuff'! It represented a 'passage to adult status'. Frivolity, romance and excitement were less likely to be associated with gin in the UK compared to other countries.

Overall, the research concluded that, despite the variations between countries, all markets displayed, to a greater or lesser extent, certain basic emotional gratifications which were associated with gin in its mixed form. These were:

- sharing/friendship/sociability—useful in all markets
- joy/frivolity— less so in the UK
- sexuality/romance— less so in Germany or the UK
- intimacy— appropriate to Spain

Outdoors, home or club usage was not uncommon in warmer weather, especially in California, Italy, Spain and France – usually in small gatherings. Indoor usage at home and at restaurants/clubs was common in most markets, although somewhat less in Italy.

Table 8.4 Gordon's standing in six markets on the dimension

Dimension	Importance for gin	UK	Italy	USA	Germany	France	Spain
Social status	++	++	++	——	++	++	+
Prestige display	++	++	++	——	–	++	+
Trendiness	0	——	+	——	*	*	+
Belonging to the group	+	+	+	+	0	+	+
Fashionability	++	(*)	++	–	+	+	+
Masculine	(=)	(=)	+	(=)	+	=	=
Feminine	(=)	=	=	(=)	–	=	=
Independence	0	*	*	+	++	0	0
Connoisseurship	+	++	++	——	+	+	+
Youthfulness	+	——	+	0	(*)	+	+
Older	–	+	(*)	(*)	0	–	–
Sophistication	++	++	++	——	+	++	+
Maturity	++	++	++	+	+	*	+

Key:
++ Very high rating
+ High rating
0 irrelevant
– Low rating
—— Very low rating
= Equally applicable (i.e. both masculine and feminine)
( ) Not a firm conclusion
* Not a strong parameter

Gordon's image

Table 8.4 shows Gordon's standing in the six markets on 13 emotional values, which the brand expresses to varying degrees in each of the markets. In contrast to the values associated with the gin category as a whole, which showed a degree of commonality across markets, Gordon's specific values showed considerable variation.

In the United States Gordon's was regarded as a mass market brand. Among non-Gordon's drinkers, the brand had a distinctive downmarket, blue-collar, pedestrian image. In some cases it was also associated with 'ordinary' white-collar jobs or lower executive levels.

For users of the brand, particularly those who also used a premium brand, the product was associated with adequate quality, a perfectly acceptable brand to be used for everyday occasions. Since people tended to feel that a gin, when it is mixed, loses its distinctive character, the qualities of Gordon's were quite acceptable for mixer drink situations; particularly, more informal occasions.

However, very few people were willing to mix Gordon's with a martini. Here the properties of the gin needed to be high quality, and consequently Gordon's was not used since it was not perceived as being of the highest quality. High quality was associated with Beefeaters, Tanqueray and Bombay.

The term most frequently used for Gordon's was 'bottom of the shelf', 'a frequently used bar brand'. It was thought to be the kind of brand that you get if you order a gin and tonic in a bar and do not specify the brand. Essentially Gordon's was a functional, practical, everyday gin, representing fairly good value for money. In the American market Gordon's was thought of as a domestic brand, and few people appreciated its English origins.

For many people in Spain, Gordon's had a high-quality image, although it was seen as the worst of the premium brands and the best of the middle-market brands. Its high quality derived from being an authentic London gin with British and international credentials. However, not all respondents appreciated this particular aspect. Without doubt Gordon's was regarded as the best brand for mixing with other liquids. However, despite its upmarket status as a mellow and smooth product, it was not regarded as being as high quality as brands like Tanqueray and Beefeater. The need in the Spanish market was to differentiate Gordon's from Larios. Various dimensions were under discussion, including authenticity and originality, as discriminating characteristics.

In Germany, Gordon's Gin did not have a long history, but it was regarded as the best gin available. 'Gordon's was gin and gin was Gordon's.' Thus, the brand set the standard for gin in that market. In Germany, it was associated with high-class, macho Englishmen having a quality of quiet, intimate dignity. It was seen as being consumed by high-status individuals, in suitable, mature, social situations.

In France, Gordon's Gin was top of the range, the best-quality gin available. It was known and respected and it dominated the gin market (albeit a small market). A significant minority of people seemed to appreciate that it was an authentic, original London gin, which contributed to its status.

Though regarded as a traditional London gin it was nevertheless seen as a contemporary brand. It was 'yuppie' and aspirational, the best-tasting gin and a refined product. The brand thus had high-status value and was associated with successful, affluent, contemporary life-styles.

In Italy, Gordon's was also regarded as the best-quality gin. It had pronounced prestige display value and very high social status as an international brand which was a genuine, authentic, British, London gin. However, it was still seen as a modern, contemporary brand, appealing to the connoisseurs who know about gin and to people who needed reassurance and wanted to know that they were buying the best gin. If any gin brand was established in the Italian market, it was Gordon's.

In the United Kingdom, Gordon's Gin was seen as prestigious and aspirational, a mature and sophisticated gin associated with business success and upward mobility. Gordon's Gin gave confidence to the user and gained status gratification from usage of the brand. The brand had some 'yuppie' qualities, but concurrently had a very clubby, upmarket more conservative set of imagery associated with it and there was a need to move the brand 'from Hanson to Branson', i.e. from a conservative, high-status, dignified establishment character to one which was youthful, achievement oriented, successful, but with a modern context. The brand also had a kind of coldness and superiority but it also lacked human warmth.

Target consumer groups

Across the six markets there appeared to be three distinct groups of gin consumers.

1 Young adults in their mid-20s, both male and female, slightly upmarket and emerging from experimentation with alcohol. This group was seeking sophistication but also fun from a white spirit. They were infrequent users of gin and enjoyed a diverse repertoire of alcoholic drinks.
2 Ginophiles and regular gin drinkers who regarded themselves as discriminating gin drinkers seeking value for money and quality in an everyday brand. This group were not particularly brand loyal. They were both male and female, 21–29 years old, middle income and conservative. They primarily mixed their gin with tonic or as a cocktail and regarded themselves as unpretentious, strongly rejecting the 'yuppie style' image.
3 Gordon's loyalists, both young and old, who regarded Gordon's as *the* standard in gin and felt comfortable with the brand's associated values of prestige, status and style. They conformed to the rules and rituals of their life-styles. The younger element were seen as aspiring,

upwardly mobile, concerned with status symbols and 'doing the right thing'. They appreciated quality, heritage, well-known status and reputation. They almost always mixed gin with tonic, responding to gin's imagery of style, discernment and sophistication, while highlighting their understanding of society's norms of tradition and status.

The strategy options

The results of this research presented United Distiller's with what appeared to be at least three strategies for Gordon's Gin. The most convenient strategy was to exploit each market with different campaigns tailored to its needs. Alternatively, there was the possibility of an integrated campaign, although it was accepted that, by so doing, each market's needs might remain unsatisfied to a limited extent. A third option was to develop a common strategy over all markets, which allowed a degree of focus varying by market.

There appeared to be core values that cut across all markets, but some of these 'gratifications' could also be identified with other beverages such as vodka, Tequila and Bacardi which were also associated with sociability, friendship and fun. However, there were some aspects of gin that were unique to gin as far as white spirit was concerned, such as maturity/responsibility, sophistication and success while not being 'showy'. By integrating these features and linking them with Gordon's there was a possibility of a common strategy across all six markets but with variation specific to individual market needs.

In any promotional strategy, it was regarded as important to differentiate Gordon's from vodka, while at the same time capitalizing on the similarities in values which provided access to the young adult market that was shown to be a key segment for the brand, particularly outside the UK. This differentiation could be achieved using the following market delimiters:

- Target age 25–34—mature sophistication
- A serious liquor which was not overly 'hard'
- Relaxation/stress reduction/gathering oneself together
- High-class English traditions and focus
- Somewhat more independence of mind.

Factors which Gordon's should promote in common with vodka were:

- appealing to both sexes
- whiteness
- fashionableness and style
- sociability and fun.

The research also made it clear that, in the UK, Gordon's, while having extremely high status, was seen as conservative and therefore needed to become more youthful, contemporary and stylish in line with the consumer perceptions that already existed to some extent in other countries.

References

Dahringer, L.D. and Cundiff, E. 'To globalise or not—a managerial decision framework', *Journal of Marketing Management*, **2** (2), 1986.

Kotler, P., 'Globalization standardization—courting danger', Panel discussion, *23rd American Marketing Association Conference on Advertising*, Washington DC, vol. 3(1), 1984, pp 17–26.

Landor Associates, *Image Power Survey*, 1990.

Levitt, T., 'The globalization of markets', *Harvard Business Review*, May/June 1983.

Rosen, B., Boddewyn, J. and Lewis, E., 'US brands abroad: an empirical study of global branding', *International Marketing Review*, **6** (1), 1989.

Shalofsky, I., 'Research for global brands', *European Research*, May 1987.

Teece, D., 'Economies of scope and the scope of the enterprise', *Journal of Economic Behaviour and Organization*, 1, 1980.

Winram, S., 'The opportunity for world brands', *International Journal of Advertising*, **3** (1), 1984, 17–26.

9

Brand strategies and competitive advantage

The building of strong brands is one of the ways in which a company can develop and sustain an advantage over its competitors, and thereby maintain or increase its sales or market share. The development of competitive advantage through branding is particularly crucial in mature, low-tech stationery markets. Thus, while brands such as Sony and IBM have sought to sustain their competitive position through product innovation, technological leadership and the development of new market sectors, in many product sectors this is more difficult. In fast-moving consumer goods, for example — which, in general, tend to be static and low-tech markets — the development of competitive advantage through building the brand proposition is vital. In the food and drink industries, in particular, it is difficult to identify companies who have sought to maintain their competitive position through the regular introduction of truly new products. Improvements have tended to be through packaging (e.g. easy-to-open drinks cans) or added convenience (e.g. frozen or chilled foods). However, because these developments are low-tech they are very soon copied by competitors and the advantage is lost.

In such markets the building of a strong brand proposition helps to establish a clear long-term competitive advantage. This is not to say that in growing or hi-tech markets the building of strong brands is not important, but in these markets it may not be the main source of competitive advantage, especially in the early stages of the life cycle. It will, nevertheless, aid the introduction of product innovations and brand extensions as we have seen. However, in mature markets in which competitors can easily imitate product developments or packaging improvements, branding provides consumers with a basis for choice and companies with an opportunity for sustained competitive advantage.

Even in markets that have shown growth in recent years, such as the service sector of the economy, it has been difficult for companies to sustain a long-term lead through product development. The availability of technology is now such that competitors are able to leapfrog each other in the provision of new and improved products, and non-patentable services. The banking sector, where non-patentable technology has transformed the services offered, provides a clear example of an industry that is now using branding to establish competitive advantage. Thus, Midland Bank presents its personality as the 'listening bank'. Onvist and Shaw (1989) have in fact argued that branding is more critical for service marketing than for product marketing.

Brand strategy and competitive structure

According to Michael Porter (1980), 'the essence of competitive strategy for a company is to find a position in its industry where it can best cope with competitive forces or can influence them in its favour'.

Porter considers that the competitive state of, and hence profitability of, an industry depends upon five basic forces:

- rivalry among existing firms
- the bargaining power of suppliers
- the bargaining power of buyers
- the threat of substitute products
- the threat of new entrants.

Any one or combination of these forces, if prominent, will tend to drive down long-run profitability, even in companies with a strong market position. Having diagnosed the underlying forces of competition in its industry, the company should analyse its strengths and weaknesses *vis-à-vis* these forces and take action to improve its relative position.

Porter suggests that the strategic response by an organization to its competitive environment should fall into one of three categories:

- Cost-leadership strategy
- Differentiation strategy
- Focus strategy.

Cost-leadership strategy

By adopting a cost-leadership strategy, an organization aims to increase its market share and restrict the competition by keeping its costs down and selling at lower prices than its competitors—a strategy adopted by many Japanese companies. However, this strategy is not always successful on its own, and can often lead to price wars which drive down margins to totally unrealistic levels. Such strategies have been adopted in the electronics and computer industries, but, in order to succeed, companies have also had to maintain the elusive technological edge. In recessionary periods firms that rely solely on a cost-leadership strategy are often the first to be affected. It is necessary for survival to combine a cost-leadership strategy with either a differentiation or focus strategy.

Differentiation strategy

If a firm adopts a differentiation strategy then it will attempt to identify a key benefit or combination of benefits which both appeal to consumers and distinguish its performance from its competitors. This, of course, is the essence of branding. In pursuing this strategy an organization is attempting to position itself as a monopoly supplier of its own unique combination of product benefits, both functional and symbolic, thereby enabling it to charge a higher price and attract a higher margin. The quasi-monopoly status of the brand works in two ways: first, it increases the company's bargaining power with the trade or end-users, depending upon its point in the supply chain; secondly, a strong brand personality can make it difficult for substitute products to challenge its position in the market. However, the higher margins may increase the threat from new entrants and lead to a proliferation of me-too brands which can erode market share and profitability.

Ries and Trout (1986) argue that, to be successful in pursuit of a differentiation strategy, it is important to be first into the market. This notion is supported by the finding that pioneering brands, who establish themselves in the marketplace with no established competition, earn on average more than one-third higher returns on investment than late entrants (Clifford and Cavanagh 1985). The corollary of this, of course, is that many me-too products fail. Nevertheless, it is possible to attack a market leader which occupies a quasi-monopoly position by establishing an alternative position in the market. Thus, Avis car rentals in the USA successfully established a point of differentiation and hence alternative market positioning with the strapline 'We're no. 2 and so try harder!'. This example is the exception which proves the rule that it is important to establish a clear brand proposition, including market positioning, from the outset and to be first in claiming that position.

Focus strategy

Organizations pursuing a focus strategy begin by identifying one or more market segments and distinguish their brands, either through cost leadership and/or product differentiation to meet the needs of those segments. Such 'niche' marketing strategies are highly attractive to middle-sized and small companies who do not have the resources to sell to the whole market. The 1980s saw considerable growth in the use of focus strategies, particularly in the UK retail industry, with the emergence of highly targeted clothing businesses such as Next, Sock Shop and Tie Rack. In parallel with this, larger companies began to separate out their business units and, where appropriate, focus them on specific market segments. In some cases, for example Jaguar cars, these business units were sold off. In other cases, particularly in the service sector, individual market segments were catered for by the creation of separate business units with separate brands. Thus, the Royal Mail separated out their parcels business and branded it ParcelForce, giving it a clear identity and enabling it to compete more effectively with its private sector competitors such as TNT. Royal Mail International was separated for similar reasons. Similar, focused marketing strategies have been used by firms in the financial services sector. Take, for example, the British bank National Westminster (NatWest). Like other European banks, their domestic services have been broken down according to identifiable product segments, such as:

- Mortgage services
- Stockbroking
- Personal financial planning
- Insurance.

These business units trade under the corporate brand of NatWest 'the action bank', but tailor their individual brand to meet the needs of specific segments.

However, while it can be argued that large organizations have benefited from focus strategies, many small organizations have not. The smaller organizations, while successfully establishing their businesses on the basis of focus strategies, provoked an equal and opposite reaction from their larger, more broadly based competitors, resulting in the emergence of more targeted business units within the larger organizations. As a consequence, the 1990s have seen the disappearance of many small niche marketers or their absorption into larger organizations. However, in many cases—e.g. Jaguar cars and Ruddles beer—the brands survived.

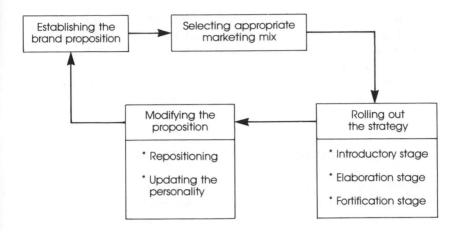

Figure 9.1 Stages in brand strategy development

Brand strategy development

It is often the case that the management of the brand eventually loses sight of, or neglects, the original proposition either through the need to prune budgets and prices in recessionary periods or through the organizational structure which, in many companies, gives brand management responsibility to relatively junior personnel whose life expectation in the post is short. As a consequence, brand planning becomes tactical rather than strategic, and continuity of the brand proposition is threatened. Successful brands with a clear competitive advantage require integrated strategies with long-term coherence. A brand strategy can usefully be divided into stages, as illustrated in Figure 9.1—viz. establishing the brand proposition, selecting the appropriate marketing mix, rolling out the strategy and, finally, modifying the proposition.

Establishing the brand proposition

The concept of the brand proposition has been discussed in Chapter 1. In essence, the first stage in the development of a brand strategy is the preparation of a clear statement which sets out clearly the positioning of the brand relative to its perceived competition, the functional attributes and the symbolic values that make up the distinctive brand personality.

As an example, take the Mars Bar and its familiar UK strapline 'a Mars a day helps you work, rest and play'. This suggests, first, that its personality is functionally rather than symbolically oriented in the sense that it helps in three aspects of people's lives. Secondly, by implication, omission of any reference to enjoyment suggests a rejection of anything symbolic or superficial. Thirdly, the absence of any product descriptor such as confectionery or chocolate suggests a unique positioning, avoiding as it does reference to any competing products or product category, e.g. savoury snacks and crisps.

Selecting the appropriate marketing mix

The marketing mix is usually summarized as the four Ps: product, promotion, price and place (Kotler 1991). An effective brand strategy requires a combination of these four elements, which will communicate the brand proposition to the target audience and thereby create a competitive advantage that can be built up and sustained over time.

The building of successful brands is often thought to be related to the amount of advertising and promotion supporting them. This is a fallacy. While it is true that advertising and promotion can help communicate the personality and positioning of a brand more rapidly than word-of-mouth, it is the ability of the product or service to meet or surpass expectations consistently that ultimately builds the success of a brand. For example, the leading retailer brands in the UK—such as Marks & Spencer, Sainsbury or Boots—established their leadership with virtually no advertising at all.

Consumers' expectations are not only influenced by advertising and promotion, they are also affected by price and distribution. Higher prices relative to competition will not only potentially limit sales volume but they will also lead the consumer to expect more from the brand in terms of functional or symbolic benefits. Both the product and its brand personality must match up to this premium price positioning. Conversely, a low price relative to the competition would be inconsistent with a premium product. It might nevertheless increase market penetration, provided that it was widely available. Limiting distribution of a brand such as Gucci to expensive outlets such as Harrods at relatively low prices would, however, lead to low sales at low margins. This is of course, an extreme example intended to illustrate the need for consistency in the marketing if a sustainable competitive advantage is to be established. Inconsistencies can leave positioning gaps in the market, which can be exploited by a competitor.

As Chapter 3 illustrates, the communication mix is vital in today's competitive environment. It is the means of accelerating the communication process and building the personality and positioning of the brand; but this is only possible if these characteristics are also supported by the other three elements in the marketing mix.

Rolling out the strategy

The roll-out of a strategy over the life of a brand has been broken down by Whan Park *et al.* (1986) into three stages:

- Introductory stage
- Elaboration stage
- Fortification stage

Introductory stage

The primary task of the marketing mix in the introductory stage, when there is no established competitive brand, is to build market share. This involves two broad areas of activity. The first relates to the removal of barriers to sales such as inadequate distribution cover and stocks, concerns about value for money and too little product information. The second area of activity relates to the build-up of the brand personality and positioning in a manner consistent with the brand proposition. These two elements of the strategy are, of course, interactive. For example, the communication of a strong brand personality may increase consumers' determination to overcome some of the 'transaction' barriers. The purpose of the strategy at this stage may also be to prepare the foundation for brand extensions if these are envisaged. The marketing mix appropriate to achieve the market share objectives at this stage will clearly be dependent upon the competitive situation facing the firm.

Elaboration stage

During the elaboration stage the strategy should seek to emphasize the brand's perceived superiority over its competitors, enhancing the brand's perceived value as the entry of 'me-too' products makes it increasingly difficult for consumers to distinguish between brands. Similarly, greater product knowledge amongst consumers may require a sharper focused communication of the original brand proposition (both personality and positioning). To this end, the above and below the line strategies, discussed in Chapter 3, can play an important role in reinforcing the communication of the brand's functional attributes and symbolic values in its competitive set.

Fortification stage

The fortification stage requires a broadening of the brand proposition to allow for brand stretching to other product areas. It has to be acknowledged, however, that movement to this stage is a policy decision. A company may well decide not to dilute the original brand proposition in this way and therefore the brand will remain in the elaboration stage. We have, of course, dealt with this issue more fully in Chapter 4. It should nevertheless be noted that whereas the objective of the introductory and elaboration stages are achieved through the manipulation of the marketing mix, the aims of the fortification stage require changes in the product mix also. A recent example has been the extension of the Mars Bar brand into new product categories such as ice-cream and flavoured milk. The multi-product basis of the brand may then serve to reinforce the original brand proposition rather than dilute it.

Modifying the proposition

Brands, like most things, age! At some stage a company faces the decision of whether to milk it, kill it or revive it. In some cases, such as Lucozade, it may be a question of repositioning and revitalizing a perfectly acceptable product, but in others, such as Beecham's Brylcream, the brand may be very closely associated with an unfashionable product (men's hair cream), making the revival of the brand more difficult.

There is also a particular problem caused by ageing consumers! Although they grew up with a brand and still buy it as adults, the brand may fail to attract young consumers. Retargeting the brand at a younger segment and changing its personality appropriately has proved a successful revitalization strategy for several declining brands and demonstrates the long-run competitive advantage of branding.

For example, in 1986, research carried out by Ever Ready Batteries in the UK showed that their Gold Seal brand, which had been launched to compete with the successful Duracell 'long-lasting battery', was suffering from a personality problem. The research also showed that, although batteries were perceived as being fairly dull, the equipment they powered was associated with fun and excitement. Furthermore, much of this equipment was bought primarily by young people, recognized by adults as being experts in new technology.

Consequently, the Gold Seal brand was retargeted at young consumers focusing the personality of the batteries as being 'the heart of the machine' and appearing 'streetwise'. The result was a doubling in brand share within three months and, in the longer term, the ability to maintain share against the growth in own-label products.

Summary

Branding is a source of sustainable competitive advantage. Successful brand-building strategies create a distinctive market position for a company, protecting it against the five basic competitive forces defined by Porter (1980). Successful branding not only reduces rivalry between existing firms, it increases the company's bargaining power (particularly with the trade) and protects it against substitutes and new entrants to the market. This is evidenced by the fact that strong brands are able to charge higher prices (or offer lower trade discounts), have higher margins and have higher returns on investment than weaker brands. Success in the marketplace is more likely to come from successful differentiation and focus-led strategies than from cost-leadership strategies on their own. Increasingly, organizations are building competitive advantage through focus strategies, creating separate business units with separate brands to meet specific market segment requirements.

Brand strategies need to adapt to changing market conditions as the brand becomes established. However, this should be a gradual process, in keeping with the original brand proposition. There are four stages in brand strategy development: establishing the brand proposition, selecting the appropriate marketing mix, rolling out the strategy and, finally, modifying the proposition to meet changes in the market and competitive environment.

Case Study: Competitive sparkle — Champagne's strategic response

Champagne is a luxury, highly priced product whose supply is constrained by geographical limits, and by the demands of farming— yields per hectare, inputs versus outputs, seasonal growing, and other such factors. Champagne is a niche market, whose brands and brand owners shy away from classical marketing 'engineering', religiously continuing the traditions of its inventor Dom Perignon, cellar master of the Abbey of Hautviliers, in the seventeenth century. The people who sell champagne are known to the world over as 'Champagne Charlies'. Yet it is actually a market in which clever and sophisticated strategic innovation is alive and thriving. The developments in this market during the 1980s and early 1990s can be seen as an example of strategic competitive response to a changing market and product innovation.

It began centuries ago when the region of Champagne in France was the only place in the world where a sparkling wine was fermented in the bottle, not in tanks—a method which produced natural rather than man-made bubbles—and gained a reputation of being the best. Even in more recent times when the *methode champenoise* production technique was copied in other countries, it was recognized that for geophysical reasons—climate and soil in particular—the Champagne region of France produced a wine of that type with untouchable quality.

For Champagne, both geography and production expertise were the real competitive discriminators. And yet they could have become the downfall of the companies and brands in its market.

Like all products dependent upon the weather, the Champagne market is always volatile. The economic problems of the 1970s and early 1980s, brought about by the oil crisis, had a limiting effect on the market's ability to grow. As a luxury product, demand was under pressure, exacerbated by a number of poor harvests forcing prices to move sharply upwards.

Then in the early to mid-1980s the supply side was boosted by a number of consistently good summers with consequent increases in harvest. The economic climate also improved significantly, and the yuppie era was born. As one of the badges of the yuppie was champagne, this in turn boosted the demand side. By 1987 there was still an excessive supply, even for the growing demand. In addition, the cooperatives and own-label producers began flooding markets with lower priced, lower quality product. It was the time of the Big Bang, and a Big Bang happened not just in the financial markets, but also in the Champagne market.

In 1987 came the price war. The major Champagne brands fought back; by 1989 volumes had soared to the point where the major brands had to purchase from other producers. Their own supply was proving insufficient. Whereas Champagne was always allowed a minimum of four years to mature in bottle, there was considerable strength of opinion that many were being sold at a lesser age.

But by 1990 the trap was sprung. Journalists and wine experts began to criticize the quality of the product; the recession was taking its toll on demand; and the major brands began to feel the financial squeeze as there had been no price increase for five years. Therefore, prices had to rise.

At the same time, more consumers had developed a taste for the product, and the technology had begun to improve to provide an alternative to Champagne's competitive advantages—geography and production expertise. The new world producers began to be seen by consumers as real alternatives. Countries like Australia, New Zealand, and the US region of California, where reputation for quality wines had grown significantly, were producing sparkling wines of a quality that compared favourably with lesser quality Champagnes— and at lower prices.

The Champagne companies and brands, who had grown richer in the 1980s boom, had apparently become fat and complacent, and it seemed that their apparent lack of strategic substance had finally been revealed. During the boom years of the 1980s a number of the major brands had realized that the long-term competitive environment was changing. They recognized that 'local' (new world) product quality was improving, and that world demand for high-quality sparkling wines would continue to grow. They also recognized that they needed to ensure the long-term protection of the Champagne industry in France, and, in particular, its image. Strategically they moved to protect their core business and to take maximum advantage of the opportunities in the new market for 'local' sparkling wines.

Thus, in the mid-1980s, the French Champagne companies began investing in production in California, Australia and New Zealand. Their competitive advantage against local producers was the ability to bring to this investment their expertise in the *methode champenoise* production technique, adapting to the new technology, taking maximum advantage of what one might describe as the deregulation opportunities. In the Champagne region many restrictions are imposed on the growing of the crop, as well as the production of the wine, which do not exist in the new world. Freedom from these restrictions could be exploited. Their goal was to produce the best products in those countries.

Having established product advantage, they also set about establishing brand and image advantage through brand stretching. While much debate has taken place in many markets, particularly with regard to its usage in luxury goods markets, the Champagne brands decided not to shy from using their names in marketing these new products.

Their rationale was that technology would never finally undermine the values of real Champagne. If they remained at the forefront of production technique (i.e. from growing to making the wine), and if they could control their image as the top brands in both market sectors (i.e. Champagne and 'local' sparkling wine), then they would not suffer adversely by using their brand names in both sectors. In fact it could, it was argued, help them to maximize shares in both markets.

To date this strategy has led to the development of Moët and Chandon's Domaine Chandon in California and Australia; Charles Heidsieck's Heidsieck in Australia; Mumm's Cuvec Napa in California; Louis Roederer's Roederer Estate in California; Deutz's California Deutz, and New Zealand Deutz; and Bollinger's Croser in Australia.

Many of these brands are already proving their success internationally, not just in the local markets. Yet, the question must be asked, are they achieving that success at the expense of their core brands—either in terms of volume, or image?

Certainly, there may be a volume advantage in the short term. As the sparkling wine market continues to show dramatic worldwide growth, Champagne market volume has reduced in the recession. But the Champagne brands adopted their strategy recognizing that the boom of the 1980s was unrealistic in terms of pricing, supply and demand. Continued growth in volume could not be expected.

The Champagne companies' strategic response of attacking the new 'local' (low price) sparkling wine market, was accompanied by a move to achieve strategic protection for their original core business. Prices of traditional Champagne rose significantly to establish realistic margins, consistent with a product with a high-quality image and high costs of production, ensuring that demand was matched to the supply of product. Product quality was already starting to return to the levels that were jealously guarded until the mid-1980s.

Changes in the legal environment also helped the recovery. New laws in Europe ensured that the descriptor 'methode champenoise' could no longer be used for any product other than Champagne. New laws also forbade the use of the word 'Champagne' as a descriptor for anything other than the real product—to the extent that no longer could a Champagne Bar describe itself in this way.

By 1992 the Champagne companies had moved from being quite traditional marketers of Champagne to aggressively developing new product opportunities in the 'new world', while strengthening and protecting their core business.

References

Clifford, D. and Cavanagh, R., *The Winning Performance: How America's High Growth Midsize Companies Succeed*, Sidgwick & Jackson, 1985.

Kotler, P., *Marketing Management Analysis, Planning, Implementation and Control*, 7th edition, Prentice-Hall International, 1991.

Onvist, S. and Shaw, J., 'Service marketing: image, branding and competition', *Business Horizons*, January/February 1989.

Porter, M., *Competitive Strategy: Techniques for Analysing Industries and Competitors*, The Free Press, 1980.

Ries, A. and Trout, J., *Positioning: The Battle for the Mind*, 1st edition revised, McGraw-Hill, 1986.

Whan Park, C., Jaworski, B. and Macinnis, D., 'Strategic brand concept—image management', *Journal of Marketing*, **50**, October 1986.

10

Research methodologies for branding

Qualitative versus quantitative

Research into branding employs both qualitative and quantitative methodologies, each using a variety of techniques designed to reveal the essential 'truth' about a brand's personality and positioning. Qualitative research is exploratory; it seeks to identify a brand's functional attributes and symbolic values. Quantitative research is evaluative; it seeks to measure those attributes and values.

Qualitative research uses small samples of consumers, open-ended questioning and an information base that involves not only the spoken word but verbal omissions, pauses and body language. It asks the 'how and why' of the consumer–brand relationship. Qualitative research focuses on understanding: understanding how consumers perceive a brand, how they experience a brand and, importantly, why they choose some brands and reject others. This research approach has been found particularly instructive when exploring the differentiation between a consumer's rational and emotional beliefs about a brand (Gordon and Langmaid 1988). It is all the more important in markets where there is product parity at a rational level but brand distinction at an emotional level. Qualitative research also plays a vital role in understanding how consumers speak about a brand and the vocabulary they use to describe its personality. The identification and naming of a brand's functional attributes and symbolic values are key concerns of the qualitative approach.

Quantitative research, on the other hand, is statistically based. It employs highly systematic procedures for sample design, data collection, questionnaire design and data analysis. It asks the questions 'how much?' and 'how many?'. It therefore provides hard data. In branding research, quantitative methodologies may be used to measure the incidence of previously exposed brand attributes and values or, in other words, how many consumers ascribe such attributes and values to a brand.

Quantitative research employs large samples, typically 200 to 1000 in commercial research. Samples may be drawn on a random basis in which there is a known chance of being selected in the sample, which enables a researcher to quantify results and, more important, their level of accuracy. Alternatively, and more typical of commercial research, quota samples may be used in which quotas are set by age, income group, and gender, for example, in order to mirror relevant characteristics in the population. Quantitative studies may be conducted face-to-face, in homes, in shopping precincts and town halls or they may be carried out over the telephone or by mail. The questionnaires are structured to allow for standardized responses to standardized questions in order to facilitate quantification.

Quantitative methodologies, therefore, are about numbers. They provide the statistical evaluation of the qualitative information which often precedes it. Thus, quantitative research quantifies in an objective way what qualitative research seeks to reveal in a subjective way. Below we describe four qualitative and four quantitative research techniques designed to access the brand's perceived personality and positioning. Some of these techniques are proprietary services that the authors consider useful and interesting in the context of branding research. This is by no means a complete coverage of the research methods available. There are many excellent texts on basic market research methods and applications e.g., Birn *et al.* (1990).

Qualitative research methods

Group discussions

One of the most frequently applied qualitative methodologies is the group discussion. Here, seven or eight consumers, all of whom share certain common characteristics like age, income and gender, are invited to exchange their views, perceptions and experiences of, say, a series of brands within a particular product sector under the leadership of a trained moderator.

A number of groups may be conducted, typically four to eight, to allow representation of a cross-section of views from different but relevant types of consumer. If, for instance, the product area under discussion were 'crisps and savoury snacks', then a typical group structure might include children aged 8–10 and 11–12, teenagers aged

13–15 (all of whom would be crisp/savoury snack consumers) plus a group of mother-purchasers. Replicating this four-group structure in the North as well as the South to allow for geographic differences would require an eight-group sample structure.

The key benefit of group discussions is the interaction that occurs between group members, with one member sparking off ideas in another until there is a veritable roller-coaster of views, perceptions and ideas being expressed about their experiences with brands.

The style of interviewing is characterized by being 'unstructured' and 'open-ended', with questions like:

- 'What does this brand mean to you?'
- 'How would you describe it?'
- 'What sort of people buy this brand?'

This allows the consumers free rein to express their views in whatever way they wish, uninhibited by the potential constraints of a structured questionnaire with a set format of wording for both the questions and the answers. The group discussion, as a dynamic process provides unconstrained insights into the 'inner world' of the brand.

Stimulus material plays an important role in the group discussion. This can be 'real' stimulus material as in existing brand packs, advertising or promotional material such as leaflets and in-store posters. Alternatively, the stimulus material may be 'rough' as in mock-up packs or advertising animatics. In the case of the latter, however, there is a distinct danger that the consumer take-out may be different to that intended. It has been suggested by Rose and Heath (1984) that:

> Consumers evaluate all research stimuli as (real) advertisements. Most find it difficult to deal with (rough) concepts and ideas and need to evaluate these within a known (real) framework.

As a result, many group discussion moderators have abandoned 'roughs' in favour of 'indirect' stimulus material, the nature of which is discussed in the next section on Extended Creative Groups. In general, stimulus material should aid the communication process rather than hinder it. As a general guideline, the closer it is to the real thing, the better the communication.

An example of how group discussions may be used in branding is provided by some research concerning Ross Young's fish products. Here brand differentiation was low and the possibility of own-label encroachment was high. In response, Young's felt a need to extend their fish portfolio, and establish a more distinctive personality for the range by developing a 'brand charter' that could be translated into packaging, advertising and new product development.

A series of group discussions were convened with housewife-purchasers of fish products including purchasers of Young's brands, own-label and other competitors, such as Bird's Eye and Blue Crest. After an informal warm-up covering what respondents bought, for whom and for what occasions, they were asked to explore usage scenarios for different brands. These ranged from fairly formal, adult dinner parties to young kids in front of the television. Thereafter, group respondents were encouraged to explore the boundaries of Young's brand in order to establish how far it could be stretched before losing its caché. Concept boards featuring different product statements ranging from lobster thermadore through ethnic variants to plain fish fingers were shown to respondents to communicate these various product ideas.

It was also important to explore with consumers the 'tonal quality' of different pack design options. Concept boards were again used to communicate different 'tonal' positionings like 'health', 'premium', 'light and contemporary', 'Masters of the Sea'.

Brand personality was explored in a variety of ways, one of which incorporated the *personification technique*. This involved inviting group respondents to imagine different brands of fish products as people and to describe the sorts of hobbies they would have, the clothes they would wear, the cars they would drive, and so on. It helped access the symbolic values of the brand which, in a market situation of performance parity, may be all that differentiates one brand from another.

The intensity and interactive dimension of group discussions thus enables not only the researcher to gain a thorough understanding of the brand dynamics but also the pack designer, the advertising planner, and the brand manager, who is ultimately responsible for the brand's success.

Extended Creativity Groups®

The Extended Creativity Group,* or ECG, was developed in the 1970s as a forum for using a series of projective techniques designed specifically to explore the 'deeper' side of experience. Such techniques are not always confined to ECGs but may also be used in standard one and a half hour group discussions. However, with ECGs typically

*Registered name, CRAM International, 1978.

lasting 3–4 hours, there is more opportunity to use a greater range and variety of these techniques.

Projective techniques allow the respondent to project feelings onto something or someone else — a pile of paper, a ball of clay or through a role-play. Many of the techniques have evolved from clinical psychology. Psychoanalysts have described projection as a defence mechanism to safeguard or protect the ego from anxiety.

In market research, however, projective tests may be seen as a means of disarming those defence mechanisms in order to reveal unconscious desires, feelings and emotions about a brand or the consumers' relationship with that brand. Instead of asking consumers direct questions about why they buy one brand and reject another, they may be asked to imagine themselves as that brand and to externalize their feelings and emotions into a story or role-play.

This dissociation of the private self from the public self, the inner world from the outer world, results from a sympathetic interview situation where 'permission' is granted for complete freedom of expression without fear of censorship. What is also crucial is that the consumers be allowed to interpret their *own* response material. Otherwise, the researcher may be guilty of misinterpretation.

Stimulus material for use with projective techniques is almost always 'indirect' or 'ambiguous'. It may be a 'mood' board on which there is a pastiche of colours, shapes, objects and people. Respondents may then be asked to identify which stimuli they associate with which brands. Alternatively, it may be a blank piece of paper on which respondents are asked to draw a theme or the type of advertisement they would expect to see for different brands. Children are particularly adept at this kind of task. Drawing competence is not nearly as important as the attitudes, feelings and perceptions that are projected onto the blank piece of paper.

Projective techniques are many and varied. Described below, are some which many researchers have found instructive in the context of branding.

Word association   This is one of the oldest projective techniques. Here respondents are asked to 'write down the first three things that come to mind when you think about brand X'. For a brand like Ford, a Ford loyalist might say 'reliable', 'value for money', 'sporty'. A Ford rejecter, on the other hand, might say 'common', 'boring', 'cheap'. However, as has been mentioned above, it is vital that respondents be allowed to explain what they mean. Thus, the Ford loyalist might go on to explain:

> They're reliable because I've had a Ford for ten years and rarely had any trouble with it. They're value for money because they're competitively priced and also because they're British and there are a lot of dealers around so it's easy to get parts and servicing done cheaply. They're sporty because that's the image they put over in advertising.

The Ford rejecter, however, who said it was 'common', 'boring' and 'cheap' might give the following explanation:

> Common because everyone has a Ford, you see them all the time. I want something with a bit more individuality. They strike me as boring because of their shape, and I always think of Ford as cheap because of their downmarket image.

Metaphor and analogy   These form a projective technique which accesses the brand personality in a different way. The respondent might, for instance, be asked to 'imagine that BMW is a type of animal, what would it be?'. The respondent might reply

> A cheetah ... because it is fast, sleek and a little mysterious.

Again, the interpretation by the respondent is as important as the metaphor itself in explaining the symbolic values he or she associates with the brand (BMW).

Collage   This is another projective technique. Here respondents are invited to select those pictures from a pile of magazines that they associate with a particular brand or aspect of a brand. When teenagers, for instance, were asked to compile a collage of visuals associated with 'healthy' brands and 'unhealthy' brands (Cowking 1988), the results were as shown in Figure 10.1. Active, vital images were associated with 'healthy' brands while dull, tired, images were associated with 'unhealthy' brands.

Bubble cartoons   These are also instructive in accessing the brand personality. The drawing might show a family at the dinner table with mother bringing in a plateful of Bird's Eye Fishfingers. Respondents might be asked to complete the quotation bubble according to how each family member perceives the situation. The results might be as set out in Figure 10.2. Repeat bubble cartoons might also be used with competitive brand names to demonstrate perceptional differences in brand personality.

Projective techniques, therefore, allow access to the inner world of the brand, particularly as regards the symbolic values of the brand. For a more comprehensive list of different projective techniques, see Cooper (1987) and Gordon and Langmaid (1988).

Figure 10.1 Collage of visuals associated with healthy and unhealthy brands

Figure 10.2 Bubble cartoon of how family members might perceive Bird's Eye Fishfingers

Synectics®

The name (Synectics) is the name of an international consulting organization who specialize in innovation and the management of change. It aims to provide a creative problem-solving process, which seeks to stimulate creative thought in areas like management training and team building as well as new product development, advertising, brand mapping, customer services and quality programmes. The name is derived from the Greek words 'syn' meaning 'together' and 'ectics' meaning 'diverse elements'.

Synectics was originated in the 1960s by William Gordon who, through a process of applied analogy, personal, direct, symbolic and fantasy, broke through rational analytic but restrictive modes of thinking (often associated with the brain's left hemisphere) and replaced these with more innovative, divergent modes of thinking (right hemisphere).

George Prince subsequently applied Gordon's theory to the area of business meetings to make them more productive, more solution-oriented and more cost-effective. By encouraging an atmosphere in which it was acceptable to take verbal risks, to draw comparisons from apparently unrelated fields, to make the strange familiar and the familiar strange, he was able to generate quite novel solutions. One such example concerns an ammunitions factory in the United States (Stein 1975). The problem concerned a conveyor belt on which guns kept falling out of the holding hole. In the subsequent Synectics series, an analogy from nature was expressed in the form of a question. 'What lives in a hole and cannot easily be pulled out?' The answer that emerged was an earthworm, because it is covered in tiny brush-like spines which provide an inverse grip on the hole. This provided the springboard for four devices that were eventually considered as feasible solutions to the problem. All were based on the inverse grip principle:

- Expanding rubber
- Fish barbs
- Rifle brush
- Gravity-activated hook.

Synectics recommend working with groups of 6–8 people from *different* backgrounds to bring differing perspectives to the problems. This aspect of the Synectics process could not be more opposed to qualitative group discussions where homogeneity is the norm. Each member of the Synectics group is, therefore, an expert in something — a design expert, a packaging expert, a housewife/family expert, a managing director. The downside to heterogeneity, however, is that some participants may feel their particular expertise is more important than others and, as a result, 'challenging' other people's ideas or asking 'loaded' questions may be ill-disguised put-downs.

To help overcome these problems, Synectics provide the following 10-step 'blueprint' to facilitate the creative process.

1   SPEAK FOR EASY LISTENING
    Headline thoughts with 'I want …' to express commitment or 'How to …' to encourage solutions or 'I wish …' to encourage speculation. This also invites single sentence concepts rather than paragraphs of explanation.
2   ASSOCIATIVE LISTENING
    When a thought or view expressed in the group triggers the mind of another participator, he or she leaves the discussion temporarily, jots the thought down on a notepad and uses it in subsequent discussions.
3   MAKE STATEMENTS RATHER THAN ASK QUESTIONS
    Participants are invited to produce ideas through statements rather than test other's ideas through 'loaded' questions.

4 UNDERSTAND BEFORE EVALUATING
Participants may be asked to separate their understanding of
ideas before evaluating them by paraphrasing the concept first.

5 FIND VALUE IN IDEAS
Look for positives; build on each other's ideas.

6 USE NEGATIVES FOR DIRECTIONS
Use negatives to point the way forward rather than presenting
them as blocks. For example 'How to reduce the number of
components' instead of 'It's too complicated'.

7 DON'T MAKE A DECISION ON AN IDEA UNTIL YOU HAVE TO
Defer quick and immediate solutions until you arrive at the best.
Initially, at least, quantity is more important than quality.

8 MIND YOUR OWN BUSINESS
Distinguish between second opinion and consequential problems.
We need to deal with consequential problems in an ordered and
thoughtful way.

9 HEAR IN THE BEST WAY
Assume constructive content. Misunderstanding can frequently
occur by accident.

10 SPEAK FOR YOURSELF
And let others do the same.

Synectics have developed what they describe as a common-sense
approach to setting people to work on problems together. This may be
schematized as follows:

- Outline the problem

- Springboard ideas (100+)   e.g. 'I want to ...'
                                          'How to ...'
                                          'I wish ...'

- Excursions/flights of fantasy   e.g. Word association
                                          Role playing
  To take a mental trip, i.e. like   Story telling
  sleeping on a problem   Walk outside

- Select front-runners, 3–4

- Evaluate   ⟶   List plusses
                                     Acknowledge concerns
                                     Get new/refined ideas
                                          to overcome concerns

- Next steps   ⟶   Action
                                     Managing director
                                          involvement
                                     Legal searches, etc.

In the context of brand name generation, springboard ideas might include

- 'I want a fun-sounding name.'
- 'I want it to reflect symbolic values like family caring and tradition.'
- 'How to make a name onomatopoeic but not childish.'

Flights of fantasy might involve participants making personal analogies of how they would feel being called 'Stein', 'Silver Eagle' or 'Kessler'—all contenders for a brand of no-alcohol lager which eventually became Kaliber!

The 'next steps', an important feature of the Synectics process, might include trade mark registration, the production of logo alternatives for the proposed brand name and a creative brief for a new advertising campaign majoring on the name.

The Synectics approach therefore, contains ways of generating new ideas; ways of stimulating people to think creatively. It is applicable to many areas of management including the management of change, but it can also play an important role in such areas as brand name development and brand building.

Repertory grid

The repertory grid technique can be used as a method of accessing the brand personality and the relevant consumer language used to describe that personality. As a technique, its particular benefit is in teasing out brand attributes and values which discriminate between brands in markets where brand differentiation is poor.

The technique derives from Kelly's personal construct theory, a theory which explores the 'dimensions of appraisal' Evansella and Bannister 1977) that people use to handle their environment. Kelly defines a construct as 'a way in which two or more things are alike and thereby different from a third' (Kelly 1969). Constructs are therefore bi-polar. By affirming one thing, the opposite is denied. If, for instance, a soft drinks brand A is 'fizzy', it cannot be 'still'. Furthermore, if brand A is similar to brand B, but dissimilar to brand C, then brands A and B are 'fizzy' and brand C is 'still'.

In repertory grid research, the respondent is given sets of three stimuli. The stimuli may be in the form of brand names on cards, brand packs or photographs of brands. The respondent is asked to say in which way two of the three brands are similar and in which way they differ from the third. The consumer language for the discrimination is noted. The remaining brands are then sorted into two groups according to their conformity or otherwise to the dimension. The whole process is then repeated until the respondent cannot think of any other discriminating dimensions. The collection of dimensions may then be used to form bi-polar scales for subsequent quantitative research using questionnaires.

An example is provided by reference to the use of the technique on business studies students. The product area was hair shampoo and the brands were as follows: Timotei (T), Silvikrin Two in One (S), Head and Shoulders (H&S), Revlon Flex (F), Boots Frequent Wash (B), Vidal Sasoon Wash & Go (W&G).

Each brand name was communicated on a card. In addition, a set of the six brand packs was displayed as a prompt for recall and reference. Twelve pairs of students sorted 12 different combinations of three brand names. Each brand name featured six times across the 12 combinations.

The technique, as described above, elicited 39 dimensions into which all the brands were sorted according to conformity or otherwise to the dimension. Six of the 39 dimensions are presented in Table 10.1.

Table 10.1 Dimensions associated with hair shampoo using Kelly's grid

Dimension	Brands sharing dimension	Brands *not* sharing dimension
Gentle product formula	T, B, S	W&G, F, H&S
Natural ingredients	T, B	F, H&S W&G S
Flip-top cap	T, W&G, F, S, B	H&S
Busy life-style	W&G	H&S, F, T, S, B
Cheaper	B	H&S, F, T, S, W&G
For older people	H&S, S, F, B	W&G, T

Each of these dimensions, linguistically so described by student consumers, were then translated into a series of bi-polar dimensions for quantitative use, for example:

- gentle product formula v strong product formula
- natural ingredients v artificial ingredients
- flip-top cap v screw-top cap
- busy life-style v relaxed life-style
- cheaper v more expensive
- for older people v for younger people

Arriving at the appropriate opposite for the bi-polar dimension may sometimes be consumer-led (as when the technique itself reveals both ends of the spectrum) *or* it may be subjectively derived by the researcher—a task not always as easy as might be supposed. From our example, the opposing dimension to 'natural' might be 'chemical' or 'medicated' rather than 'artificial'; the opposite of 'more expensive' might be 'value for money' rather than 'cheaper'. Nevertheless Kelly's repertory grid provides a productive technique for the elicitation of both the consumer perception and the vocabulary used to describe that perception. It undoubtedly helps in questionnaire construction where the vocabulary used is sometimes more marketing-led than consumer-focused.

Quantitative research methods

Brand mapping

We have discussed in earlier chapters the need for clear 'positioning' of a brand in the marketplace. Positioning a brand successfully is, first, to provide the consumer with the answer to the question: 'What is this brand?' Thus, the answer to the question 'What is this brand of yogurt?' could be:

- 'It's a health food.'
- 'It's a dessert for children.'

Both of these separate responses or perceived positionings places the yogurt brand in close competition with a different set of brands. If it is a health food then it could be competing with other health products— muesli or dried fruit. In some cases it could in fact be bought as a complement to these products. If so, this might have implications for the distribution of the yogurt or its location within the store. On the other hand, if the yogurt is a children's dessert then the competitive set could include brands of jelly, ice-cream or even rice pudding!

Although the ideal positioning is always to differentiate the brand from its competitors, the outcome of the process, whether successful or not, is often the alignment of the brand with the competition which has similar positioning. In terms of the consumers' perceptions, the brand will be closer to some competitors and further from others. The object of brand mapping is to measure their perceptual similarities and represent them graphically. There are in fact several mapping techniques, including principal components analysis, principal coordinates analysis and multi-dimensional scaling, which have been developed by mathematicians and can be used to produce such brand maps (or perceptual maps as they are sometimes referred to). In all these techniques the similarities between brands are measured across a large collection of relevant dimensions (or variables), which in the

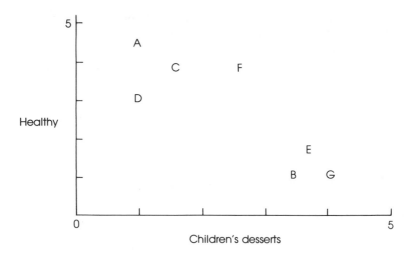

Figure 10.3 Simple two-dimensional brand map for yogurt

case of our yogurt example would include measures of its perceived popularity as a health food and as a children's dessert, perhaps in the form of attitude statements.

In its simplest form a brand map can be constructed from two rating scales which measure the product on two relevant dimensions. For example, we could ask a sample of consumers to rate a selection of leading brands of yogurt on the dimensions, 'healthy' and 'a children's dessert'. Average scores on, say, a five-point scale could be presented graphically, as in Figure 10.3.

The map shows two clear segments for yogurt. A, C and D are regarded as health foods while E, B and G are seen essentially as children's desserts. F, however, has an identity crisis! Consumers are not sure what it stands for; a signal to the brand manager that a more clearly defined positioning may be required.

The more complex mapping techniques listed above are simply analytical devices for reducing multi-dimensional rating of brands to two (or sometimes three) summary dimensions. Each technique has its advantages and disadvantages.

Factor analysis and principal components analysis typically produce a three-dimensional matrix of consumer ratings of brands from a variety of dimensions both subjective and objective. The disadvantage, however, is that the dimensions obtained are actually a function of the collected data. If one dimension, for example, is repeatedly measured, albeit in different forms, it will inevitably appear as a summary dimension. One example given is the factor or summary dimension 'fuel efficiency', which could be generated if consumers are asked to rate cars on miles per gallon, acceleration, power, economy of running a car, etc. In this case the emerging summary dimension is a function of the dimensions investigated rather than of the dimensions regarded as important by consumers.

Discriminant analysis uses similar data inputs to factor analysis, but it determines the 'factors' on the basis of which dimensions best differentiate the brands. They are, however, still a function of the attributes being discussed and often tend to be difficult to convert into marketing action as they do not directly describe brands but rather acccentuate differences between them.

Multi-dimensional scaling (MDS) is another technique frequently applied to brand mapping. Unlike the dimension-based techniques summarized above, where the resulting dimensions reflect the input dimensions, MDS is based upon consumers' preferences for brands. No dimension, either subjective or objective, is specified. The resulting dimensions are postulated on the basis of the consumers' evaluations of the brands in a product category. These evaluations are usually summarized on a spatial map together with consumers' ideal points for particular clusters (closely related brands). These ideal points are positioned in such a way that a brand's proximity to an individual's ideal point best preserves the rank order preferences of that individual. However, the dimensions produced by conventional MDS maps are often difficult to interpret without a detailed understanding of the brands under analysis. More recent developments of this technique, such as trinodal mapping routines (Kear 1983), combine two map constructs to obtain a single three-node map which allows an assessment of both brands and advertisements in relation to a consumer's ideal point. Among other things, this development enables the brand manager to assess the relative position of a new advertising campaign in relation to a brand's current and desired positionings.

Brand Personality Inventory®

The Brand Personality Inventory* (BPI) is a technique for measuring the personality characteristics of brands. It consists of a 41-item questionnaire in which 40 of the items relate to personality attributes and values like 'homely', ' cheeky', 'determined' and 'mean' and the 41st item measures a relational component, 'the kind of person I'd like to have as a friend'.

Respondents are asked to rate each brand on each of the items using a

*This technique was developed by Creative Research Limited.

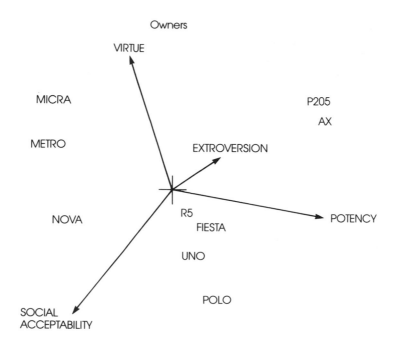

Figure 10.4 Similarity across small car brands with the four dimensions superimposed

7-point agree–disagree scale to indicate the extent to which they feel the attributes and values are true of the brand's personality. The brand is, therefore, described in terms of these individual scores. In addition, it aggregates scores according to four key dimensions that were identified in the development of this technique, such as extroversion, potency, virtue and social acceptability (Alt and Griggs 1988).

Extroversion, for example, might consist of such personality characteristics as 'cheeky' and 'fun loving', while potency might include 'determined' and 'strong'. Virtue might include 'homely' and 'gentle' while social acceptability (actually social unacceptability, but its scores are reversed to produce a positive dimension) might include 'mean' and 'superficial'.

These characteristics, once converted to scores on the BPI, may then be mapped in the way described earlier (brand mapping). The example in Figure 10.4 shows a number of different marques or brands of small car according to how they were perceived by owners.

Dimensions that are at 180° to the car marques discriminate in a negative sense, i.e. the dimension is less relevant. The further a dimension is from the origin, the more it discriminates, e.g. extroversion is a less important discriminator than virtue or potency. Also, the further a brand is from the origin, the more clearly discriminated is the brand personality. Hence our example in Figure 10.4 shows that:

- the Peugeot 205 and Citroen AX are more extrovert but less socially acceptable;
- the Metro and Micra are more virtuous but less potent;
- the Polo is more socially acceptable but less virtuous than the Micra;
- the Fiesta and Renault 5 are both close to the origin and, as such, are not discriminated by any dimension; this could mean they lack a clear personality.

If we then take one particular marque, the Ford Fiesta, and express the scores of both owners and non-owners in terms of a bar chart, we can demonstrate differences in brand personality perceptions according to two market segments (owners v non-owners) (see Figure 10.5). Owners, for example, perceive the Fiesta as more extrovert, more potent, and more virtuous than non-owners and, predictably, want the Fiesta 'as a

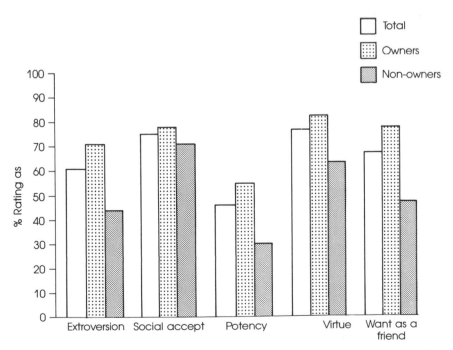

Figure 10.5 Brand personality perceptions of Ford Fiesta by owners and non-owners

friend'. In terms of social acceptability, however, there are no marked differences of perceptions between owners and non-owners.

The graph, therefore, implies that stressing the Fiesta's social acceptability is unlikely to win it any new friends, whereas, if more people could be convinced of its extroversion, potency and/or virtue, it would attract more 'friends'. The relationship between personality and 'want as a friend' can be explored further by developing regression models in which changes in the number of people wanting a brand for a 'friend' can be related to changes in each of the personality dimensions. In this way, brand owners can investigate which dimensions of a brand's personality should be enhanced/ exploited to enable it to win more friends.

The BPI, therefore, is a method of measuring brand personality using a common set of attributes and values across all brands. As a result it may be used to:

- map markets to determine where brands are positioned relative to the product sector;

- segment markets according to either the brands themselves or consumers (e.g. owners v non-owners);

- track brands over time to monitor perceptual shifts in brand personality.

Tracking studies

Tracking studies provide a continuous measure over time of factors like brand awareness, trial, usage and brand personality. They are often carried out in the context of advertising effectiveness but also in the context of sponsorship and significant promotional campaigns like the Pepsi Challenge (referred to in Chapter 3).

In most instances, at least 100 interviews are carried out per week, say 20 each working day, with a cumulative sample of 400, on a rolling basis, as shown in Figure 10.6.

Alternatively, data may be aggregated for longer periods of time by looking at rolling three-monthly samples of 1200 for example, or a yearly sample of 5000.

Data may be plotted against the precise timing and weight of the advertising input in order to determine whether brand personality or brand awareness shifts are a result of advertising or another marketing variable.

The socio-demographic profile of the sample will reflect in some way that of the target user. So, for example, tracking studies of alcoholic

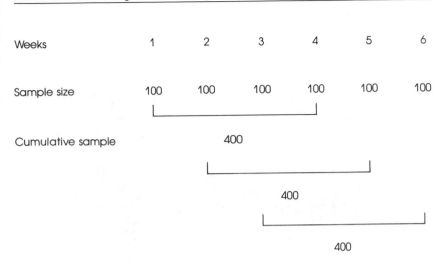

Weeks	1	2	3	4	5	6
Sample size	100	100	100	100	100	100
Cumulative sample		400				
				400		
					400	

Figure 10.6 Tracking study sample data

drinks will take a sample of adults aged 18+ who consume alcohol. If the study focuses on one particular type of drink, say whisky, then quotas may also be set on whisky drinkers.

One major benefit of tracking studies is the quick and effective monitoring of new brand launches in terms of

- growth of awareness
- growth of trial
- growth in the number of consumers considering themselves regular purchasers.

For established brands, prompted awareness may be more static and usership relatively stable, but levels of *spontaneous* awareness may be more susceptible to an advertising burst.

On brand personality a typical question might be:

'Which of these brands of coffee do you think of as:

– good quality
– expensive
– strong in flavour?'

Generally speaking, tracking studies show that advertising can affect a brand's personality for the duration of the campaign but that the effect declines after the end of the burst. Tracking studies can, therefore, identify when the decline occurs, or how long the positive shift lasts.

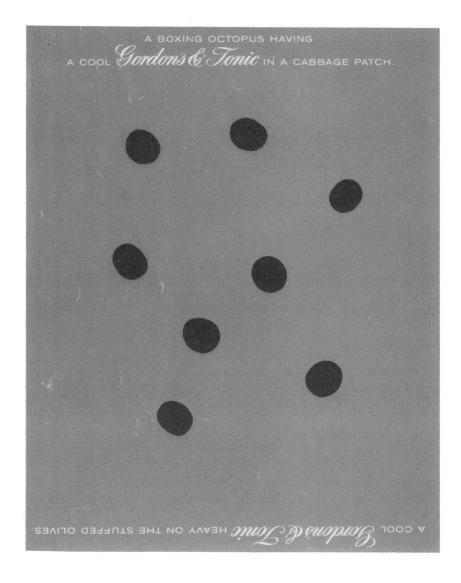

Figure 10.7 Press advertisement for Gordon's 'green' campaign

Tracking study data, for example, provided by United Distillers UK, show the effect of the Gordon's 'green' and 'mixer' campaigns on awareness of gin advertising and brand awareness, The 'green' campaign featured unusual and witty creative executions of a frog or other creatures consuming Gordon's gin (Figure 10.7). The 'mixer' campaign featured a series of product shots against an impressive scenic backdrop, e.g. Jaffa (Israel).

The data are derived from 2000 interviews per 8-weekly period (250 per week). Figure 10.8 clearly demonstrates pre-Christmas peaks in awareness of gin advertising corresponding to high spend levels (£1.8 million in November/December 1989 and £1.7 million in 1988). The chart also demonstrates superior awareness of gin advertising for the 'green' campaign compared to the 'mixer' campaign.

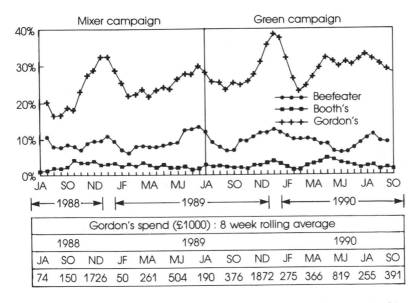

Figure 10.8 Total awareness of gin advertising. Total G.B. base: Gin drinkers

Figure 10.9 (see page 206) tracks spontaneous awareness of Gordon's, Beefeater and Booth's and clearly demonstrates that awareness of Gordon's is considerably higher than two of its competitors, Beefeater and Booth's.

Tracking studies, therefore, monitor brands over time, and thereby allow brand managers to chart the changing fortunes of their brands.

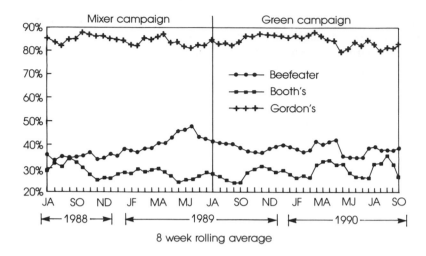

Figure 10.9 Spontaneous awareness of gin brands. Total G.B. base: Gin drinkers

BrandWorks®*

Qualitative research would seem best placed to tease out consumer perceptions of brands with its flexible, unstructured methods of questioning which, as noted earlier, allow respondents the freedom to express 'in their own words' how they perceive, relate to and experience brands. Yet, in the final analysis, these 'teased out' perceptions are based on sometimes no more than 30 or 40 people whose statistical representation of the population at large counts for next to nothing. Quantitative research, on the other hand, can provide that statistical validity, based, as it is, on large samples and batteries of attitude statements which provide some scope for measured evaluation of the consumer–brand response.

Yet in this search for objective, 'hard' data there are several problems. First, it is a big assumption to expect consumers to translate emotions, perceptions and feelings into numbers or points on a rating scale. Sometimes more than 100 or even 200 to 300 quantitative answers may be required if six or seven brands are being rated across, say, 20 or 30 attitude statements. Secondly, some questions are clearly more marketing-driven than consumer relevant. 'Intention to purchase' scales can become quite meaningless as consumers are often unaware, at a conscious level at least, of why they accept one brand but reject another. Thirdly, there is the issue of 'fat' words—words which mean different things to different people. Gordon (1990) quotes an example of Dulux and Crown, who scored identically on the attitude statement

*A technique developed and practised by The Research Business.

'has a good range of colours'. Further questioning, however, showed that whereas Dulux was associated with pastel colours, Crown was associated with bright colours. The perceptual difference was lost within the straitjacket of the conventional questionnaire.

These sorts of concerns gave rise to the development of BrandWorks, a proprietary quantitative research methodology which uses qualitative disciplines. It is based on some fundamental principles of Neuro Linguistic Programming—a conceptual model which explores the relationship between neurological functioning (i.e. thought) and learned patterns of response (i.e. language). It is a model which seeks to understand the communication process between the consumer and the brand. BrandWorks aims to access that process, quantitatively, using five qualitative measures described as user image, occasion image, product image, brand personality and saliency.

User image is understood by asking what sort of people buy brand X—young or old, male or female, 'green' or 'yuppy'? Such questions can be asked directly using prompted answer options or accessed through a visual collage board featuring a range of different types of user (a qualitative technique). The important factor here is the extent to which the target user identifies with the perceived user.

Occasion image explores the times or occasions on which the brand is eaten, drunk or experienced. Again direct questions or collage boards may be used to access this information.

Product image arises out of beliefs or perceptions about the functional performance of the brand, which may or may not be consistent with its actual performance. Blind testing often reveals such inconsistencies. For example, in personality-led markets such as alcoholic drinks, brand A may be perceived as better tasting and therefore preferred to brand B, but when stripped of its advertising, packaging and brand name, may be experienced as an equally preferred or even less preferred brand to brand B.

Brand personality refers to the personification of the brand and the consumer response to it. An example using different brands of newspaper is set out in Table 10.2.

Finally, brand saliency refers to the 'closeness' of the consumer to the brand. If anything, it is this dimension that ultimately 'describes' the consumer–brand relationship.

Methodologically, consumers are invited to create a spatial map around themselves of all the relevant brands (Figure 10.10).

Table 10.2 Personality of selected newspapers

Newspaper	Personality	Consumer response	
		Positive	**Negative**
The Times	Likes to win Follows rules A leader	Safe	Overshadowed
The Guardian	Good listener Thoughtful Peaceful		Irritated
The Independent	Friendly Happy Likes a challenge	Not defensive	

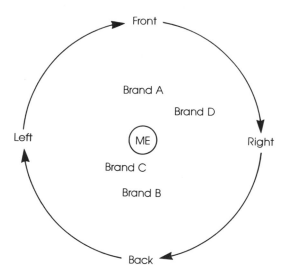

Figure 10.10 Spatial map

Brands to the front are perceived positively, i.e. warmer or closer; brands the consumer likes. Brands to the back are perceived negatively, which can indicate rejection or simply unfamiliarity, as with a new brand which has yet to establish itself within the consumer's experience. Brands to the side may be falling either into or out of favour. An example of brand saliency using high street shops is summarized in Table 10.3. It illustrates how the saliency of Marks & Spencer contrasts in this example with the recessiveness of C&A.

In conclusion, BrandWorks aims to provide quantitative measures of

Table 10.3 Example of brand saliency

Emotion	M&S (%)	BHS (%)	C&A (%)
Close	47	22	22
Distant	2	38	51

qualitative perceptions. The challenge it addresses is not so much one of delivering the techniques (most are in fairly common use in qualitative research) but of delivering the technique over large samples of consumers.

Summary

This chapter has explored a number of research met.   ılogies, both qualitative and quantitative, which seek to reveal and/or measure the brand's personality and positioning. Qualitative methodologies include *group discussions* which involve seven or eight consumers who are invited to exchange their views, perceptions and experience of several brands within a product category; *Extended Creative Groups*, which build on this process using a variety of projective techniques like word association, collage and bubble cartoons; *Synectics*, which focuses on creative problem-solving including brand name development; and the *repertory grid* technique, which uses card sorting to elicit brand attributes and values and the consumer language used to describe them.

Four quantitative methodologies have been described. First, *brand mapping*, which measures a brand's similarity to others and thereafter represents them graphically using a variety of statistical techniques; *Brand Personality Inventory*, which uses a 41-item questionnaire to measure the brand personality of any brand across four key dimensions—extroversion, potency, virtue and social acceptability; *tracking studies*, which provide a continuous measure over time of such responses as brand awareness, trial, usage and brand personality in order to chart the changing fortunes of a brand; and, finally, *BrandWorks*, which aims to access the brand quantitatively using the five qualitative measures of user image, occasion image, product image, brand personality and salience—a research technique illustrated in the case study that follows.

CASE STUDY: The Toshiba brand personality

Introduction

Toshiba is the seventh largest computer and electronics company in the world, and the third largest in Japan. In the UK Toshiba is best known for consumer products, notably televisions, and latterly lap-top and personal computers. The consumer products division began trading in the UK in 1973 and currently markets a full range of audio-visual equipment in addition to being a major player in the microwave oven market.

At the beginning of 1984 the Toshiba brand had just a 3 per cent share of the colour television market, with four brands significantly ahead in terms of brand awareness and image—Philips, Ferguson, Hitachi and Sony. By 1988, however, largely due to the hugely successful 'Blueprint' campaign 'Hello Tosh...', consumer awareness of Toshiba had risen from a low base in 1984 to an impressive 89 per cent. At the start of 1989, there was a feeling within the company that 'Blueprint' had run its course. The marketplace had become increasingly sophisticated and there was a need to establish Toshiba as a quality brand. The 'On my New Toshiba' advertising campaign was developed and, though it was quite successful against the competition, Toshiba was still perceived as a 'nice to have' rather than a 'need to have' brand.

At the beginning of 1990, Toshiba sought a method of determining which brand image and personality values were most influential in terms of brand choice and how Toshiba performed against these.

The Research approach

Toshiba approached The Research Business, a London-based market research agency, and commissioned them to carry out research that would provide an audit of how the brand was perceived in the UK; to understand the image of Toshiba, particularly compared to Sony, Panasonic and Hitachi; and to identify the relationship that consumers had with the brand. This was done using The Research Business's 'BrandWorks' approach.

A total of 431 personal interviews were conducted in-home among a national sample of adults (see Table 10.4), all of whom were current owners of at least two brown goods items and who were considering buying additional or replacement brown goods items within the next two years.

Propensity to purchase plus four key facets of the brand—user image, product image, brand personality and saliency—were accessed using different techniques as follows.

- *Propensity to purchase* was accessed by giving respondents a bubble cartoon (see Figure 10.11 on page 212) and asking them to choose which 'thought' summed up their feelings about buying the brand in question. Importantly, these scores were not averaged but were interpreted linguistically—that is, as expressions of commitment to the brand.

- *User image* was accessed by using a visual collage board (see Figure 10.12 on page 213) of stereotypical users, the interpretative

Table 10.4   Characteristics of research for Toshiba based on 431
at-home personal interviews

	Interviews: %	431 No.
Male	58	249
Female	42	182
Age 25–39	50	216
Age 40–54	50	215
Brands covered in questionnaire		
Toshiba/Panasonic/Sony	35	149
Sony/Toshiba/Hitachi	33	142
Panasonic/Hitachi/Toshiba	32	140
Toshiba owner	32	136
Toshiba non-owner	68	295

emphasis being on the reasons given by the respondent, why
certain types of people were associated with each brand.

- *Product image* was measured conventionally using a series of six-
  point, bi-polar scales, such as:
  very reliable   –   not very reliable
  good quality –   poor quality
  innovative   –   not innovative

- *Brand personality* was elicited through a personification technique, a
  prompted personality checklist and a further adjectival checklist on
  the consumer's relationship with the brand.

- *Saliency* or emotional closeness/distance to each brand was
  accessed through a spatial mapping technique (see Figure 10.13 on
  page 214) in which consumers were invited to place brands around
  themselves according to how emotionally 'close' or otherwise they
  felt towards those brands. Hence, brands to the front were
  perceived positively or 'close', those to the back were perceived
  negatively, and those to the sides were moving in or out of favour.

The Results

Propensity to purchase

There was very little evidence of brand loyalty in the market,
demonstrated by the propensity to purchase results. Table 10.5 on
page 214 shows the statement used on the stimulus card and, in
brackets—not shown to respondents—the linguistic interpretation of its

Figure 10.11 Propensity to purchase bubble cartoons

meaning. The table demonstrates how few consumers expressed purchase propensity in terms of loyalty (necessity/compulsion) and also, how few expressed strong rejection (impossibility). All four brands achieved a high 'possibility' potential, indicating the degree of likely competition at point of sale.

Where Toshiba was noticeably differentiated from its competitors was in the emotional values the brand evoked—particularly brand personality, emotional salience and user image.

User Image

The most frequently given reasons for associating certain of the visual images with Toshiba rather than with other brands, were to do with youth (in the sense of chronological age as well as a younger outlook), modernity and being forward thinking. This contrasted with the user image profiles of Sony and Panasonic particularly, which were associated with maturity, affluence and a need to buy the best-quality goods.

Product image

The results from the six-point rating scales on brand-based product dimensions such as reliability, simple to use, good quality, and

Figure 10.12 An example of a visual collage board

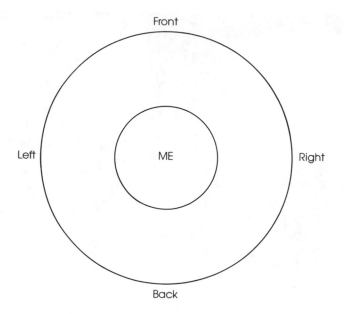

Figure 10.13 Spatial map

Table 10.5   Propensity to purchase

	Toshiba 431 (%)	Sony 291 (%)	Panasonic 289 (%)	Hitachi 282 (%)
Base:				
Would never buy (impossibility)	8	10	9	13
Could buy (possibility)	60	54	56	60
Wish I could buy (desirability)	13	14	14	10
Ought to buy (necessity)	11	13	13	9
Must buy (compulsion)	7	8	8	6

appearance showed that consumers viewed these four brands very similarly. This lack of differentiation between the brands is highlighted in Table 10.6.

These results suggested that brand-based product characteristics could be ruled out as determinants of brand choice; so too could price and availability in different outlets.

Brand personality

Toshiba achieved the most distinctive brand personality, clearly demonstrating the heavy influence of the Blueprint advertising campaign. The brand personality was extremely well formed and came across as sociable, extroverted and energetic. Tonally, the

Table 10.6 Product image–brand attributes (mean score)

Base:	Toshiba 431 (%)	Sony 291 (%)	Panasonic 289 (%)	Hitachi 282 (%)
Reliability	4.83	5.00	4.78	4.93
Simple to use	4.69	4.85	4.61	4.65
Looks good	4.84	4.88	4.73	4.72
Known world wide	5.11	5.47	5.10	5.19
Value for money	4.61	4.61	4.58	4.55
Available high street/multiple	4.56	4.47	4.45	4.52

personality was experienced as warm to hot, pacey and magnetic. This personality profile was particularly pronounced among younger and C2 respondents. Highlights from the brand personality results are shown in Tables 10.7–10.11.

In response to a prompted list of personality traits, the clusters which differentiated Toshiba from all three competitive brands (particularly Sony), were sociability, restlessness and compliance as shown in Table 10.8.

A comparison between the five most frequently mentioned traits of Toshiba and Sony clearly showed the difference between the two. Toshiba's personality was more extroverted than Sony's, as can be seen in Table 10.9.

One of the unique questions within the questionnaire was used to evaluate the tone of the brand personality in terms of pace and temperature (Table 10.10). For example 'confidence' as a personality trait in relation to cosmetic brands can either be cool and measured in pace, like Chanel, or warm and energetic, like Charlie. So too with

Table 10.7 Most important aspect of personality (spontaneous)

Base:	Toshiba 431 (%)	Sony 291 (%)	Panasonic 289 (%)	Hitachi 282 (%)
Happy, friendly, outgoing, warm, amusing	30	23	19	19
Lively, energetic, fast, go-getter, busy	14	7	7	9
Reliable, steady, laid back	8	14	18	12

Table 10.8   Personality trait clusters

Base:	Toshiba 431 (%)	Sony 291 (%)	Panasonic 289 (%)	Hitachi 282 (%)
Sociability	59	50	46	41
Restlessness	43	31	31	37
Compliance	34	50	43	43

Table 10.9   Personality traits—top five

Base:	Toshiba 431 (%)		Sony 291 (%)
Likes to be noticed	34	Reliable	32
Energetic	30	Cares about details	27
Entertaining	30	Likes to be noticed	27
Good talker	29	Friendly	25
Friendly	26	A leader	22

Table 10.10   Tonal qualities

Base:	Toshiba 431 (%)	Sony 291 (%)	Panasonic 289 (%)	Hitachi 282 (%)
Temperature				
Icy-cool	26	30	32	28
Lukewarm	16	20	22	22
Warm-hot	56	49	44	48
Pace				
Fast	45	33	31	38
Moderate	41	52	49	43

Toshiba. Its extroverted personality was experienced as warm and pacey, compared to the cooler, more moderately paced competitors.

The responses to the four brand personalities ('how the personality makes me feel') are shown in Table 10.11, for the AB socio-economic segment of the sample.

Among upmarket (and older) consumers the Toshiba brand personality lacked authority. It made people feel lighthearted, but not as proud, safe, intelligent and interesting as did Sony. This was *not* the case with

Table 10.11   Response to the brand personalities

Base:	Toshiba 192 (%)	Sony 129 (%)	Panasonic 123 (%)	Hitachi 132 (%)
Intelligent	15	24	16	14
Interesting	18	24	20	14
Lighthearted	20	6	8	9
Proud	8	19	15	6
Safe	14	24	20	17
Irritated	13	2	8	8
Wary	15	5	7	13

Table 10.12   Brand saliency

Total samples 431	Ferguson (%)	Hitachi (%)	Panasonic (%)	Philips (%)	Sony (%)	Toshiba (%)
Very close	10	12	13	10	17	16
Close (total)	39	51	51	44	54	56
Distant (total)	29	15	13	16	16	13

C1C2 consumers and younger people, among whom the brand also elicited feelings of enthusiasm and creativity.

Saliency

Table 10.12 shows the emotional closeness or distance of the sample's relationship to the four major Japanese brands, as well as to Ferguson and Philips.

C1C2, younger consumers and Toshiba owners demonstrated a greater closeness to the brand than their counterparts: importantly, however, older and AB consumers showed no significant alienation from the brand.

It was apparent, that in a market within which brand image measurement had been fairly difficult, Toshiba could boast a clear and powerful emotional brand image differentiation. The diamond shown in Figure 10.14 sums up the Toshiba image.

Next steps

The research raised a number of issues, both tactical and strategic for Toshiba.

- *Positioning*
  What was the desired positioning and how might it be achieved?

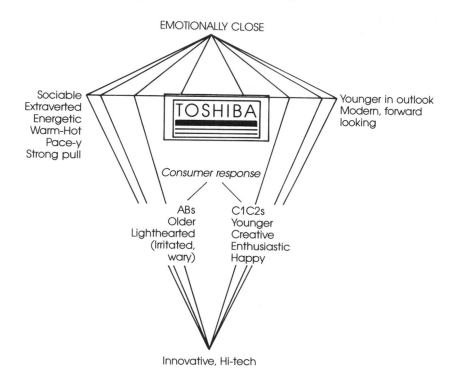

Figure 10.14 The Toshiba Image

- *Above-the-line advertising*
  What should be the media objectives? What creative avenues might be suitable?

- *Below-the-line communication*
  How should they promote to (a) the consumer and (b) the trade? What objectives should be set and how could they get greater brand commitment?

- *Brand building*
  How could the brand personality be strengthened in line with the marketing objectives? What elements in the mix might benefit from (a) change, (b) fine tuning and (c) maintenance?

References

Alt, M. and Griggs, S., 'Can a brand be cheeky?', MRS Conference
  Paper, 1988.
Birn, R., Hague, P. and Vangelder, P., *A Handbook of Market Research
  Techniques*, Kogan Page, 1990.
Cooper, P., *The New Qualitative Technology*, Esomar Market Research
  Monograph Series, Vol. 2, 1987.
Cowking, P., 'Consumers of tomorrow', PHD Research, Weybridge,
  1988.
Evansella, A. and Bannister, D., *A Manual for Repertory Grid Technique*,
  Academic Press, 1977.
Gordon, W., 'The ... space ... between ... words', MRS Conference
  Paper, 1990.
Gordon, W. and Langmaid, R., *Qualitative Market Research*, Gower,
  1988.
Kear, J., 'Product positioning: trinodal mapping of brand images,
  advertising images and consumer preference', *Journal of Marketing
  Research*, 20, November 1983.
Kelly, G., 'Clinical psychology and personality' *in Selected papers of
  George Kelly* (ed. B.A. Maker), Wiley, 1969.
Rose, J. and Heath, S., 'Stimulus material: a dual viewpoint', MRS
  Conference Paper, 1984.
Stein, M., *Stimulating Creativity*, Vol. 2. Group Procedures, 1975.

Glossary

A brand   A product or service made distinctive by its positioning and personality.

Brand equity   The value of a brand, both operationally and strategically, ideally expressed as a capitalized value of expected net earnings.

Brand franchise   The product categories and market segments in which the brand name is established.

Brand name   A trigger to the brand proposition offered by the brand.

Brand personality   A unique combination of functional attributes and symbolic values which characterize the brand.

Brand positioning   A brand's point of reference with respect to the competition.

Brand proposition   A set of statements which summarize the positioning and personality of the brand.

Brand stretching   The process of extending the brand franchise to product variants, other product categories and markets.

Corporate branding   Use of the company name either as a product brand or to endorse other product brands.

Corporate identity   The visual and verbal communication of an organization in terms of what it does and what it stands for.

Endorsed brand   A brand which uses the company name as support for its own name.

Family brands   A fairly homogeneous group of products using a common brand name.

Line extension   Using a brand name to introduce product variants into the same market segment.

Own-label   Distributor as opposed to manufacturers' brands, which include retailer as well as wholesaler brands.

Stand-alone brands   A single brand name for a single product.

Strapline   A short punchy slogan encapsulating the brand proposition.

Index